ADOBE® PHOTOSHOP® CS3

CLASSROOM IN A BOOK®

The official training workbook from Adobe Systems

www.adobepress.com

Adobe

Adobe Systems Incorporated, 345 Park Avenue, San Jose, California 95110, USA

Adobe Press books are published by Peachpit, Berkeley, CA. To report errors, please send a note to errata@peachpit.com.

Printed in the U.S.A.

ISBN-13: 978-0-321-49202-9
ISBN-10:   0-321-49202-1

9 8 7 6 5 4 3 2 1

Writer: Judy Walthers von Alten
Design Director: Andrew Faulkner, afstudio design
Designers: Annie Tsou, Heather Landry, Rachel Lightfoot
Production: Dawn Dombrow-Thompson, dtstudio

We offer our sincere thanks to the following people for their support and help with this project: Russell Brown, Tyler Munson, Laurel Katz, Jill Merlin, Steve Muller, Arne Hurty, John Nack, Lee Unkrich, and Christine Yarrow. We couldn't have done it without you.

Working with Selections   page 103

Vector Drawing   page 281

Layer Basics   page 139

Advanced Layers   page 313

Digital Photography   page 211

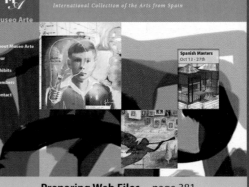

Preparing Web Files   page 381

From the Authors

Welcome to Adobe® Photoshop® CS3 Classroom in a Book. Whether you just purchased your first digital camera and want to learn the basics of the world's leading imaging software application, or you're a graphic designer who spends six hours a day in Photoshop and you need to maximize your productivity, this book is for you.

In 14 lessons, you will learn everything from compositing images into artistic montages, to processing camera raw digital photographs, to producing web animations. We've consolidated content from the previous edition, offering a streamlined, hands-on training course that will teach you Photoshop essentials as well as how to use many of the exciting new features in Photoshop CS3, in concise, colorful, comprehensive exercises.

Plus, we've included some fun stuff—for example, Photoshop guru Russell Brown will show you how to experiment with the new Clone Source feature as he spray-paints a clone of himself in his entertaining QuickTime movies. (Be sure to check out his QuickTime movies on the book's CD.) In addition, Photoshop evangelist Julieanne Kost shares some of her best power-user tips. We've also included some "extra-credit" assignments for students who want to challenge themselves further. (For details on what's new in this edition of the book, see page 2.)

Good luck and have fun!

Andrew Faulkner and Judy Walthers von Alten

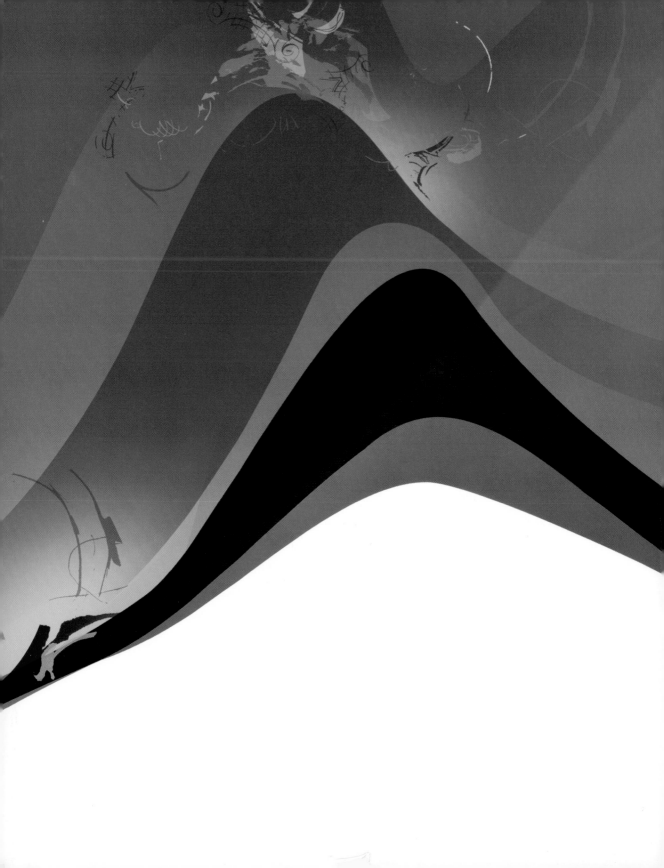

Contents

Getting Started

1 Getting to Know the Work Area

5 Layer Basics

6 Masks and Channels

7 **Correcting and Enhancing Digital Photographs**

8 **Typographic Design**

9 **Vector Drawing Techniques**

10   **Advanced Layering**

11   **Advanced Compositing**

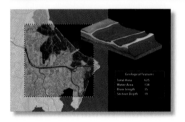

John Nack
Photoshop Product Manager
Adobe Systems, Inc.

Hello Photoshop fans:

Thank you for purchasing Adobe Photoshop CS3 Classroom in a Book, the official training workbook for the world's best image-editing program. I am especially excited about this edition because it showcases many of the groundbreaking features new to Photoshop CS3. For example, Lesson 5 shows how to align separate layers and composite the best of them in a few quick steps. In Lesson 11, you'll try out the new, nondestructive Smart Filters. Other lessons walk you through the new Zoomify feature, for panning and tiling large files in your web browser; the robust Adobe Bridge browser and Camera Raw dialog box; and the revolutionary Vanishing Point feature to design and transform objects in perspective. Photoshop CS3 has lots of great new features, and this Classroom in a Book will get you up to speed using them.

Good luck with your learning, and thanks,

John Nack
Adobe Photoshop Product Manager

Getting Started

Adobe® Photoshop® CS3, the benchmark for digital imaging excellence, delivers a new level of power, precision, and control, as well as exciting new features and next-generation enhancements. Included with Photoshop CS3 is Adobe Bridge® CS3, the visual file browser that provides both workaday productivity as well as creative inspiration. Photoshop CS3 pushes the boundaries of digital image editing and helps you turn your dreams into designs more easily than ever before.

About Classroom in a Book

Adobe Photoshop CS3 Classroom in a Book® is part of the official training series for Adobe graphics and publishing software developed by experts at Adobe Systems. The lessons are designed to let you learn at your own pace. If you're new to Adobe Photoshop, you'll learn the fundamental concepts and features you'll need to master the program. And, if you've been using Adobe Photoshop for a while, you'll find that Classroom in a Book teaches many advanced features, including tips and techniques for using the latest version of the application and for preparing images for the web.

Although each lesson provides step-by-step instructions for creating a specific project, there's room for exploration and experimentation. You can follow the book from start to finish, or do only the lessons that match your interests and needs. Each lesson concludes with a review section summarizing what you've covered.

What's new in this edition

This edition covers many new features in Adobe Photoshop CS3, such as Smart Filters that let you edit filter effects at any time; Zoomify for zooming in and panning large, high-resolution images; and the Align Content feature for one-step alignment of several similar layers. In addition, these lessons step you through the new Quick Selection tool that makes complicated selections with a single click of the mouse button; the new interface common to the Creative Suite 3 family of products; and enhancements to the Camera Raw format, the Vanishing Point filter, and Adobe Bridge.

New lessons cover:

- How to use masks and channels to get the best selections and make sophisticated composite images.
- New layer techniques including enhancements to the Layer Comps feature.
- Advanced compositing techniques for precisely compositing images, repairing them, and matching color schemes.
- Preparing files for the web, including creating slices, rollovers, and GIF animations.
- Working with scientific images—measuring and enhancing image data, analyzing images, and sharing them.

This edition is also chock-full of extra information on Photoshop features and how best to work with this robust application. You'll learn about Adobe® Lightroom™—a new toolbox for professional photographers that helps them manage, adjust, and present large volumes of digital photos. You'll also learn best practices for organizing, managing, and showcasing your photos, as well as how to optimize images for the web. And throughout this edition, look for tips and techniques from two of Adobe's own experts, Photoshop evangelist Julieanne Kost and senior creative director Russell Brown.

Watch the movies

Be sure to watch the movies included on the *Adobe Photoshop CS3 Classroom in a Book* CD in the Movies folder. Almost a dozen movies showcase new features in Photoshop CS3—from the new interface in Photoshop, to quick selections, Smart Filters, and the ins and outs of the Vanishing Point feature. You can even learn how to clone and animate yourself with the new Clone Source tool, under the impeccable direction of Adobe's Russell Brown. Look for this icon 目 in the lessons to indicate related movies. Enjoy!

What's on the CD*

* Here is an overview of the contents of the Classroom in a Book CD

Lesson files . . . and so much more

The *Adobe Photoshop CS3 Classroom in a Book* CD includes the lesson files that you'll need to complete the exercises in this book, as well as other content to help you learn more about Adobe Photoshop and use it with greater efficiency and ease. The diagram below represents the contents of the CD, which should help you locate the files you need.

Lessons
Each lesson has its own folder inside the Lessons folder. You will need to copy these lesson folders to your hard drive before you can begin each lesson.

Movies
Tutorial movies** by Adobe senior creative director Russell Brown, Adobe product manager John Nack, Total Training, and other Photoshop experts, are in the Movies folder.

Fonts
The fonts required for some lessons in this book are located in the Fonts folder.

Adobe Garamond
Myriad
Minion italic

Stock Photos

This CD contains stock photos from Amana, Comstock and Zefa.

Adobe Press
Find information about other Adobe Press titles, covering the full spectrum of Adobe products, in the Adobe Press folder.

Adobe Certified
Information about how to become an Adobe Certified Expert is in the Adobe Certified folder.

Adobe Design Center
Find a wealth of information in Adobe Design Center, from quick tips and tutorials to in-depth backgrounders and other valuable resources.

** The latest version of Apple QuickTime can be downloaded from www.apple.com/quicktime/download.

What's in Photoshop Extended

This edition of Adobe Photoshop CS3 Classroom in a Book touches on some of the features in Adobe Photoshop CS3 Extended—a version with additional functions for professional, technical, and scientific users, intended for those creating special effects in video; or in architectural, scientific, or engineering images.

Just some of the Photoshop Extended features include:

• The ability to import three-dimensional images and video, and edit individual frames or image sequence files by painting, cloning, retouching them, or transforming them.

• Measurement and counting tools to measure any area, including an irregular area, defined with the Ruler tool or a selection tool. You can also compute the height, width, area, and perimeter, or track measurements of one or many images. See Lesson 13, "Working with Scientific Images," for more on how to use these features.

• Image stacks, stored as Smart Objects, that let you combine a group of images with a similar frame of reference, and then process the multiple images to produce a composite view, for example, to eliminate unwanted content or noise.

• Animation features that show the frame duration and animation properties for document layers in Timeline mode, and that let you navigate through frames, edit them, and adjust the frame duration for layers.

• Support for specialized file formats, such as DICOM—the most common standard for receiving medical scans; MATLAB, a high-level technical computing language and interactive environment for developing algorithms, visualizing and analyzing data, and computing numbers; and 32-bit high-resolution images, including a special HDR Color Picker and the capability to paint and layer these 32-bit HDR images.

• Support for three-dimensional (3D) files including the U3D, 3DS, OBJ, KMZ, and Collada file formats, created by programs like Adobe Acrobat 3D® Version 8, 3D Studio Max, Alias, Maya, and Google Earth. With 3D models placed on separate layers, you can use the Photoshop 3D tools to move or scale a 3D model, change the lighting, or change render modes—for example, from solid to wireframe mode.

Prerequisites

Before you begin to use *Adobe Photoshop CS3 Classroom in a Book*, you should have a working knowledge of your computer and its operating system. Make sure that you know how to use the mouse and standard menus and commands, and also how to open, save, and close files. If you need to review these techniques, see the documentation included with your Microsoft® Windows® or Apple® Mac® OS X documentation.

Installing Adobe Photoshop

Before you begin using *Adobe Photoshop CS3 Classroom in a Book*, make sure that your system is set up correctly and that you've installed the required software and hardware. You must purchase the Adobe Photoshop CS3 software separately. For system requirements and complete instructions on installing the software, see the Adobe Photoshop CS3 Read Me file on the application DVD or on the web at www.adobe.com/support/.

Photoshop and Bridge use the same installer. You must install these applications from the Adobe Photoshop CS3 application DVD onto your hard disk; you cannot run the programs from the CD. Follow the on-screen instructions.

Make sure that your serial number is accessible before installing the application.

Starting Adobe Photoshop

You start Photoshop just as you do most software applications.

To start Adobe Photoshop in Windows:

1   Choose Start > All Programs > Adobe Photoshop CS3.

2   In the Welcome Screen, click Close.

To start Adobe Photoshop in Mac OS:

1   Open the Applications/Adobe Photoshop CS3 folder, and double-click the Adobe Photoshop program icon.

2   In the Welcome Screen, click Close.

Installing the Classroom in a Book fonts

To ensure that the lesson files appear on your system with the correct fonts, you may need to install the Classroom in a Book font files. The fonts are in the Fonts folder on the *Adobe Photoshop CS3 Classroom in a Book* CD. If you already have these on your system, you do not need to install them.

Use the following procedure to install the fonts on your hard drive.

1 Insert the *Adobe Photoshop CS3 Classroom in a Book* CD into your CD-ROM drive.

2 Install the font files using the procedure for the version of your operating system:

• Windows: Drag the fonts from ...\Adobe\Fonts. For more information on installing fonts in Windows, see the Read Me file in the Fonts folder of the CD.

• Mac OS: Open the Fonts folder on the CD. Select all of the fonts in the Fonts folder and drag them into the Library/Fonts folder on your hard disk. You can select and drag multiple fonts to install them, but you cannot drag the entire folder to install the fonts.

Copying the Classroom in a Book files

The *Adobe Photoshop CS3 Classroom in a Book* CD includes folders containing all the electronic files for the lessons in the book. Each lesson has its own folder; you must copy the folders to your hard disk to complete the lessons. To save room on your disk, you can install only the folder necessary for each lesson as you need it, and remove it when you're done.

To install the Classroom in a Book lesson files, do the following:

1 Insert the *Adobe Photoshop CS3 Classroom in a Book* CD into your CD-ROM drive.

2 Browse the contents and locate the Lessons folder.

3 Do one of the following:

• To copy all the lesson files, drag the Lessons folder from the CD onto your hard disk.

• To copy only individual lesson files, first create a new folder on your hard disk and name it **Lessons**. Then, drag the lesson folder or folders that you want to copy from the CD into the Lessons folder on your hard disk.

If you are installing the files in Windows 2000, you may need to unlock the lesson files before you can use them. If you use Windows 2000 and encounter locked files, proceed to Step 4.

Note: *As you complete each lesson, you will preserve the start files. In case you overwrite them, you can restore the original files by recopying the corresponding Lesson folder from the Adobe Photoshop CS3 Classroom in a Book CD to the Lessons folder on your hard drive.*

Restoring default preferences

The preferences files store palette and command settings information. Each time you quit Adobe Photoshop, the positions of the palettes and certain command settings are recorded in the respective preferences file. Any selections you make in the Preferences dialog box are also part of this type of application file.

At the beginning of each lesson in this book, you will be told to reset the default preferences, using a three-key combination. This deletes any options you may have selected in the Preferences dialog box.

You can ignore the instructions to reset your preferences. If you do so, be aware that the tools, palettes, and other settings in your Photoshop CS3 application may not match those described in this book, so you may have to be slightly more resourceful in finding things. With that in mind, you should be able to do the lesson without other difficulties.

Saving your monitor-calibration settings is a simple procedure that you should perform before you start work on this book; the procedure is described in the following section. If you have not custom-calibrated your color monitor, this procedure is unnecessary.

Saving the options you may have selected in the Preferences dialog box is beyond the scope of this book. If you are not sure how to do this yourself, get help from your network administrator. Otherwise, you can simply keep a record of preferences that you've customized, and then restore them manually after you finish these lessons.

To save your current color settings:

1 Start Adobe Photoshop.

2 Choose Edit > Color Settings.

3 In the Color Settings dialog box, examine the Settings menu.

• If the Settings menu is Custom, go on to Step 4 of this procedure.

• If the Settings option is anything other than Custom, click OK to close the dialog box. You do not need to do anything else.

4 Click the Save button. (Be careful to click Save, *not* OK.)

The Save dialog box opens. The default location is the Settings folder, which is where you want to save your file. The default file extension is .csf (color settings file).

5 In the File Name field (Windows) or Save As field (Mac OS), type a descriptive name for your color settings, preserving the .csf file extension. Then click Save.

6 In the Color Settings Comment dialog box, type any descriptive text that will help you identify the color settings later, such as the date, specific settings, or your workgroup.

7 Click OK to close the Color Settings Comment dialog box, and again to close the Color Settings dialog box.

To restore your color settings:

1 Start Adobe Photoshop.

2 Choose Edit > Color Settings.

3 In the Settings menu in the Color Settings dialog box, select the color-settings file you defined in the previous procedure.

4 Click OK.

Additional resources

Adobe Photoshop CS3 Classroom in a Book is not meant to replace documentation that comes with the program or to be a comprehensive reference for every feature in Photoshop CS3. Only the commands and options used in the lessons are explained in this book. For comprehensive information about program features, refer to any of these resources:

• Adobe Photoshop CS3 Help, which you can view by choosing Help > Photoshop Help.

• Printed copies of Adobe Photoshop CS3 documentation (a subset of Help) are available for purchase from www.adobe.com/go/buy_books.

• Adobe Design Center provides you with hundreds of tutorials from experts and authors in the community, as well as thoughtful articles about design and technology. Go to www.adobe.com/designcenter/.

- Adobe CS3 Video Workshop DVD, included in the product box, provides you with 250 instructional movies on Photoshop CS3 and other products across the Adobe Creative Suite 3 lineup.

Also check out these useful links:

- The Photoshop CS3 product home page at www.adobe.com/products/photoshop/.

- Photoshop user forums at www.adobe.com/support/forums/ for peer-to-peer discussions of Adobe products.

- Photoshop Exchange at www.adobe.com/cfusion/exchange/ for extensions, functions, code, and more.

- Photoshop plugins at www.adobe.com/products/plugins/photoshop/.

- Photoshop training resources at www.adobe.com/products/photoshop/training.html.

Adobe certification

The Adobe Certification program is designed to help Adobe customers and trainers improve and promote their product-proficiency skills. There are three levels of certification:

- Adobe Certified Expert (ACE)

- Adobe Certified Instructor (ACI)

- Adobe Authorized Training Center (AATC)

The Adobe Certified Expert program is a way for expert users to upgrade their credentials. You can use Adobe certification as a catalyst for getting a raise, finding a job, or promoting your expertise.

If you are an ACE-level instructor, the Adobe Certified Instructor program takes your skills to the next level and gives you access to a wide range of Adobe resources.

Adobe Authorized Training Centers offer instructor-led courses and training on Adobe products, employing only Adobe Certified Instructors. A directory of AATCs is available at http://partners.adobe.com.

For information on the Adobe Certified program, visit www.adobe.com/support/certification/main.html.

As you work with Adobe Photoshop, you'll discover that you can often accomplish the same task several ways. To make the best use of the extensive editing capabilities in Photoshop, you must first learn to navigate the work area.

1 Getting to Know the Work Area

Lesson overview

In this lesson, you'll learn how to do the following:

- Open Adobe Photoshop files.

- Select and use some of the tools in the toolbox.

- Set options for a selected tool using the tool options bar.

- Use various methods of zooming in and out on an image.

- Select, rearrange, and use palettes.

- Choose commands in palette and context menus.

- Open and use a palette docked in the palette well.

- Undo actions to correct mistakes or to make different choices.

- Customize the workspace.

- Find topics in Photoshop Help.

This lesson will take about 90 minutes to complete. Before starting Adobe Photoshop, locate the Lesson01 folder on the *Adobe Photoshop CS3 Classroom in a Book* CD, and copy the folder into the Lessons folder that you created on your hard disk for these projects (or create it now). As you work on this lesson, you'll preserve the start files. If you need to restore the start files, copy them again from the *Adobe Photoshop CS3 Classroom in a Book* CD.

Starting to work in Adobe Photoshop

The Adobe Photoshop work area includes the command menus at the top of your screen and a variety of tools and palettes for editing and adding elements to your image. You can also add commands and filters to the menus by installing third-party software known as *plug-in modules*.

Photoshop works with bitmapped, digitized images (that is, continuous-tone images that have been converted into a series of small squares, or picture elements, called *pixels*). You can also work with vector graphics, which are drawings made of smooth lines that retain their crispness when scaled. You can create original artwork in Photoshop, or you can import images into the program from many sources, such as:

- Photographs from a digital camera.

- Commercial CDs of digital images.

- Scans of photographs, transparencies, negatives, graphics, or other documents.

- Captured video images.

- Artwork created in drawing programs.

For information on the kinds of files you can use with Adobe Photoshop CS3, see "About file formats" in Photoshop Help.

Starting Photoshop and opening a file

To begin, you'll start Adobe Photoshop and reset the default preferences.

Note: Usually, you won't reset the defaults when you're on your own. However, while you're working in this book, you'll reset them each time so that what you see on-screen matches the descriptions in the lessons. See "Restoring default preferences" on page 6.

1 On the desktop, double-click the Adobe Photoshop icon to start Adobe Photoshop and then immediately hold down Ctrl+Alt+Shift (Windows) or Command+Option+Shift (Mac OS) to reset the default settings.

If you don't see the Photoshop icon on your desktop, choose Start > All Programs > Adobe Photoshop CS3 (Windows) or look in either the Applications folder or the Dock (Mac OS).

2 When prompted, click Yes to confirm that you want to delete the Adobe Photoshop Settings File, and then click Close to close the Welcome Screen.

The Photoshop work area appears as shown in the following illustration.

Note: The following illustration shows the Windows version of Photoshop. On Mac OS, the arrangement is the same, but operating system styles may vary.

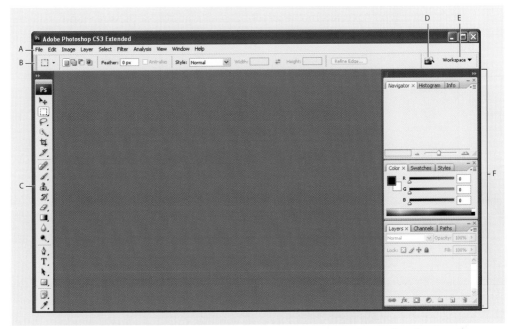

A. Menu bar B. Tool options bar C. Toolbox D. Adobe Bridge button E. Palette well F. Floating palettes

The default work area in Photoshop consists of a menu bar at the top of the screen, a tool options bar below the menu bar, a floating toolbox on the left, floating palettes (also called panels), and one or more image windows, which are opened separately. This interface is the same one you'll see in Adobe Illustrator®, Adobe InDesign®, and Flash®— so learning how to use the tools and palettes in one application means that you'll know how to use them in the others.

Watch the New UI QuickTime movie to get a quick overview of the new CS3 interface. The movie is located on the Adobe Photoshop CS3 Classroom in a Book *CD in Movies/New UI.mov. Double-click the movie file to open it; then click the Play button.*

3 Choose File > Open, and navigate to the Lessons/Lesson01 folder that you copied to your hard drive from the *Adobe Photoshop CS3 Classroom in a Book* CD.

4 Select the 01A_End.psd file and click Open.

The 01A_End.psd file opens in its own window, called the *image window*. The end files in this book show you what you are creating in the different projects. In this end file, a collage of old currency and coins has been enhanced so that one coin appears spotlighted while the rest of the picture appears to be in shadow.

5 Choose File > Close, or click the close button on the title bar of the window in which the photograph appears. (Do not close Photoshop.)

Opening a file with Adobe Bridge

In this book, you'll work with different start files in each lesson. You may make copies of these files and save them under different names or locations, or you may work from the original start files and then copy them from the CD again if you want a fresh start. This lesson has three start files.

In the previous exercise, you used the classic method of opening a file. Now you'll open another file using the Adobe Bridge visual file browser, which helps take the guesswork out of finding the image file that you need.

1   Click the Go To Bridge button (⬛) in the tool options bar.

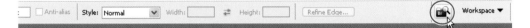

Watch the Bridge Intro QuickTime movie to get a quick overview of Adobe Bridge. The movie is located on the Adobe Photoshop CS3 Classroom in a Book *CD in Movies/ Bridge Intro.mov. Double-click the movie file to open it; then click the Play button.*

Adobe Bridge opens, displaying a collection of panels, menus, buttons, and panes.

Note: *You can also open Adobe Bridge by choosing File > Browse.*

2   From the Favorites panel in the upper left of Bridge, browse to the Lessons folder you copied from the CD onto your hard disk. The Lessons folder appears in the Content panel.

3   Drag the Lessons folder to the Favorite panel in the upper left corner of Bridge to add the folder to the list of favorites. (You can also select the folder and then choose File > Add To Favorites.) Adding files, folders, application icons, and other assets that you use often to the Favorites panel lets you quickly access the items.

4   In the Favorites panel, double-click the Lessons folder to open it; then double-click the Lesson01 folder.

Thumbnail previews of the folder contents appear in the center pane of Bridge.

5 Select the 01A_Start.psd file in the Contents pane and open the file by double-clicking its thumbnail, or use the Bridge menu bar and choose File > Open.

The 01A_Start.psd image opens in Photoshop.

Adobe Bridge is much more than a convenient visual interface for opening files. You'll have the chance to learn more about the many features and functions of Adobe Bridge in Lesson 13, "Working with Scientific Images."

Note: Leave Bridge open for the moment; you may use it to locate and open files later in this lesson.

Using the tools

Photoshop provides an integrated set of tools for producing sophisticated graphics for print, Web, and mobile viewing. We could easily fill an entire book with details on the wealth of Photoshop tools and tool configurations. While that would certainly be a useful reference, it's not the goal of this book. Instead, you'll start gaining experience by configuring and using a few tools on a sample project. Every lesson will introduce you to more tools and ways to use them. By the time you finish all the lessons in this book, you'll have a solid foundation for further explorations of the Photoshop tool set.

Selecting and using a tool from the toolbox

The toolbox—the long, narrow palette on the far left side of the work area—contains selection tools, painting and editing tools, foreground- and background-color selection boxes, and viewing tools.

Let's start by using the Zoom tool, which appears in many other Adobe applications, including Illustrator, InDesign, and Acrobat.

Note: For a complete list of the tools in the toolbox, see the toolbox overview on page 50.

1 Notice the toolbar that appears to the left of the image window as a single column. Click the double-arrow button just above the toolbox to toggle to a double-column view. Click the arrow again to return to a single-column toolbox and use your screen space more efficiently.

2 Examine the status bar at the bottom of the image window and notice the percentage listed on the far left end. This represents the current enlargement view of the image, or zoom level.

A. *Zoom level* **B.** *Status bar*

Note: In Windows, the status bar may appear across the bottom of the work area.

3 Move the pointer over the toolbox and hover it over the magnifying-glass icon until a tooltip appears, identifying the tool by name and providing its keyboard shortcut.

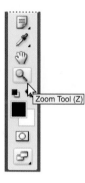

4 Select the Zoom tool by either clicking the Zoom tool button ($\mathcal{Q}$) in the toolbox or by pressing Z, the keyboard shortcut for the Zoom tool.

5 Move the pointer over the image window. Notice that it now looks like a tiny magnifying glass with a plus sign (+) in the center of the glass.

6 Click anywhere in the image window.

The image enlarges to a preset percentage level, which replaces the previous value in the status bar. The location you clicked when you used the Zoom tool becomes the center of the enlarged view. If you click again, the zoom advances to the next preset level, up to a maximum of 3200% on Windows and 1600% on the Macintosh.

7 Hold down the Alt key (Windows) or Option key (Mac OS) so that the Zoom tool pointer appears with a minus sign (–) in the center of the magnifying glass, and then click anywhere in the image. Then release the Alt or Option key.

Now the view zooms out to a lower preset magnification. Examine the photograph and the coins in the center.

Note: You can zoom out other ways. For example, you can select the Zoom In ($\mathcal{Q}$) or Zoom Out ($\mathcal{Q}$) mode on the Zoom tool options bar. You can choose View > Zoom In or View > Zoom Out. Or, you can type a lower percentage in the status bar and press Enter or Return.

8 Using the Zoom tool, drag a rectangle to enclose the area of the image that includes the French coin that you will spotlight.

The image enlarges so that the area you enclosed in your rectangle now fills the entire image window.

You have now tried three ways of using the Zoom tool to change the magnification in the image window: clicking, holding down a keyboard modifier while clicking, and dragging to define a magnification area. Many of the other tools in the toolbox can be used with keyboard combinations. You'll have opportunities to use these techniques in various lessons in this book.

Selecting and using a hidden tool

Photoshop has many tools you can use to edit image files, but you will probably work with only a few of them at a time. The toolbox arranges some of the tools in groups, with only one tool shown for each group. The other tools in the group are hidden behind that tool.

A small triangle in the lower right corner of a button is your clue that other tools are available but hidden under that tool.

1 Position the pointer over second tool from the top in the toolbox column until the tooltip appears, identifying it as the Rectangular Marquee tool (⬚) with the keyboard shortcut M. Then select that tool.

2 Select the Elliptical Marquee tool (○), which is hidden behind the Rectangular Marquee tool, using one of the following methods:

• Press and hold the mouse button over the Rectangular Marquee tool to open the pop-up list of hidden tools, and select the Elliptical Marquee tool.

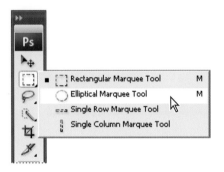

• Alt-click (Windows) or Option-click (Mac OS) the tool button in the toolbox to cycle through the hidden marquee tools until the Elliptical Marquee tool is selected.

• Press Shift+M, which switches between the Rectangular and Elliptical Marquee tools.

3 Move the pointer over the image window so that it appears as cross hairs (-¦-) and move it to the upper left side of the French coin.

4 Drag the pointer down and to the right to draw an ellipse around the coin and then release the mouse button.

An animated dashed line indicates that the area inside it is *selected*. When you select an area, it becomes the only editable area of the image. The area outside the selection is protected.

5 Move the pointer inside your elliptical selection so that the pointer appears as an arrow with a small rectangle (▸▫).

6 Drag the selection so that it is accurately centered over the French coin.

When you drag the selection, only the selection border moves, not pixels in the image. When you want to move the pixels in the image, you'll need to use a different technique, which you'll learn a little later. There's more about making different kinds of selections and moving the selection contents in Lesson 4, "Working with Selections."

Using keyboard combinations with tool actions

Many tools can operate under certain constraints. You usually activate these modes by holding down specific keyboard keys as you move the tool with the mouse. Some tools have modes that you choose in the tool options bar.

The next task is to make a fresh start at selecting the French coin. This time, you'll use a keyboard combination that constrains the elliptical selection to a circle that you'll draw from the center outward instead of from the outside inward.

1 Make sure that the Elliptical Marquee tool (◯) is still selected in the toolbox, and deactivate the current selection by doing one of the following:

- In the image window, click anywhere outside the selected area.
- Choose Select > Deselect.
- Use the keyboard shortcut Ctrl+D (Windows) or Command+D (Mac OS).

2 Position the pointer in the center of the French coin.

3 Press Alt+Shift (Windows) or Option+Shift (Mac OS) and drag outward from the center of the coin until the circle completely encloses the coin.

4 Carefully release first the mouse button and then the keyboard keys.

If you are not satisfied with the selection circle, you can move it: Place the pointer inside the circle and drag, or click outside the selection circle to deselect it and then try again.

Note: If you accidentally release one or both of the keys prematurely, the tool reverts to its normal behavior (unconstrained and drawing from the edge). If, however, you haven't yet released the mouse button, you can just press the keys down again, and the selection changes back. If you have released the mouse button, simply start again at Step 1.

5 In the toolbox, double-click the Zoom tool (🔍) to return to 100% view. If the entire image doesn't fit in the image window, then click the Fit Screen button in the tool options bar.

Notice that the selection remains active, even after you use the Zoom tool.

Applying a change to a selected area

In order to spotlight the selected coin, you'll want to darken the rest of the image, not the area inside the current selection. Normally, you change the area within the selection. To protect that area, you'll invert the selection, making the rest of the image active and preventing the change from affecting the one center coin.

1 Choose Select > Inverse.

Although the animated selection border around the French coin looks the same, notice that a similar border appears all around the edges of the image. Now the rest of the image is selected and can be edited, while the area within the circle is not selected and cannot be changed while the selection is active.

A. Selected (editable) area B. Unselected (protected) area

2 Choose Image > Adjustments > Curves.

The keyboard shortcut for this command, Ctrl+M (Windows) or Command+M (Mac OS) appears by the command name in the Adjustments submenu. In the future, you can just press that keyboard combination to open the Curves dialog box.

3 In the Curves dialog box, make sure that the Preview option is selected. If necessary, drag the dialog box to one side so that you can see most of the image window.

The Preview option shows the effect of your selections in the image window, so the picture changes as you adjust settings. This saves you from having to repeatedly open and close dialog boxes as you experiment with different options.

4 Drag the control point in the upper right corner of the graph straight down until the value shown in the Output option is approximately 150. (The Input value should remain unchanged.)

As you drag, the highlights are reduced in the selected area of the image.

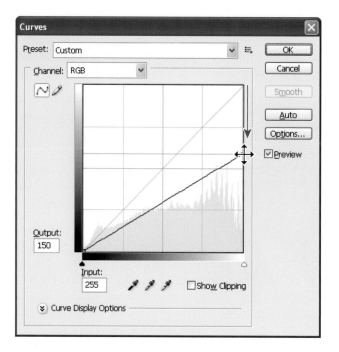

5 Examine the results in the image window and then adjust the Output value up or down until you are satisfied with the results.

6 Click OK to close the Curves dialog box.

7 Choose Select > Deselect to deselect your selection. The marquee disappears.

8 Do one of the following:

• If you want to save your changes, choose File > Save and then choose File > Close.

• If you want to revert to the unaltered version of the file, choose File > Close and click No when you are asked if you want to save your changes.

• If you want to do both of the above, choose File > Save As, and then either rename the file or save it to a different folder on your computer, and click OK. Then choose File > Close.

You don't have to deselect, because closing the file cancels the selection.

Congratulations! You've just finished your first Photoshop project. Although the Curves dialog box is actually one of the more sophisticated methods of altering an image, it isn't difficult to use, as you have seen. You will learn more about making adjustments to images in many other lessons in this book. Lessons 2, 3, and 7, in particular, address techniques like those used in classic darkroom work, such as adjusting for exposure, retouching, and correcting colors.

Zooming and scrolling with the Navigator palette

The Navigator palette is another speedy way to make large changes in the zoom level, especially when the exact percentage of magnification is unimportant. It's also a great way to scroll around in an image, because the thumbnail shows you exactly what part of the image appears in the image window.

The slider under the image thumbnail in the Navigator palette enlarges the image when you drag it to the right (toward the large mountain icon) and reduces it when you drag to the left.

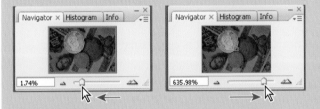

The red rectangular outline represents the area of the image that appears in the image window. When you zoom in far enough that the image window shows only part of the image, you can drag the red outline around the thumbnail area to see other areas of the image. This also is an excellent way to verify which part of an image you're working on when you work at very high zoom levels.

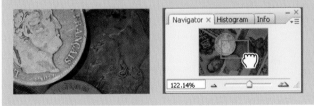

Using the tool options bar and other palettes

You've already had some experience with the tool options bar. In the previous project, you saw that there are options in the tool options bar for the Zoom tool that change the view of the current image window. Now you will learn more about setting tool properties in the tool options bar, as well as using palettes and palette menus.

Previewing and opening another file

The next project involves a promotional postcard for a community project. First, let's preview the end file to see what we're aiming to do.

1 Click the Go To Bridge button () in the tool options bar.

2 In the Bridge Favorites pane, open the Lessons/Lesson1 folder.

3 Select the 01B_End.psd file in the thumbnail preview area so that it appears in the Content panel.

4 Examine the image and notice the text that is set against the sandy area across the lower part of the image.

Beach photo: Amana Stock Photography

5 Select the thumbnail for the 01B_Start.psd file and double-click to open it in Photoshop.

Setting tool properties in the tool options bar

With the 01B_Start.psd file open in Photoshop, you're ready to select the characteristics for the text and then to type your message.

1 In the toolbox, select the Horizontal Type tool (T).

The buttons and menu in the tool options bar now relate to the Type tool.

2 In the tool options bar, select a font you like from the first pop-up menu. (We used Adobe Garamond, but you can use another font if you prefer.)

3 Specify 38 pt as the font size.

You can specify 38 points by typing directly in the font-size text box and pressing Enter or Return, or by scrubbing the font-size menu label. You can also choose a standard font size from the font-size pop-up menu.

You can place the pointer over the labels of most numeric settings in the tool options bar, in palettes, and in dialog boxes in Photoshop, to display a "scrubby slider." Dragging the pointing-finger slider to the right increases the value; dragging to the left decreases the value. Alt-dragging (Windows) or Option-dragging (Mac OS) changes the values in smaller increments; Shift-dragging changes them in larger increments.

4 Click once anywhere on the left side of the image and type **Monday is Beach Cleanup Day.**

The text appears with the font and font-size formatting that you selected.

5 In the toolbox, select the Move tool (⊕) at the top of the column on the right.

Note: *Don't select the Move tool using the V keyboard shortcut, because you're in text-entry mode. Typing V will add the letter to your text in the image window.*

6 Position the Move tool pointer over the text you typed and drag the text into the misty white rectangle near the bottom of the image, centering the text inside it.

Using palettes and palette menus

The text color in your image is the same as the Foreground Color swatch in the toolbox, which is black by default. The text in the end-file example was a dark blue that coordinates nicely with the rest of the image. You'll color the text by selecting it and then choosing another color.

1 In the toolbox, select the Horizontal Type tool (T).

2 Drag the Horizontal Type tool across the text to select all the words.

3 In the Color palette group, click the Swatches tab to bring that palette forward.

4 Select any swatch. The color you select appears in three places: as the Foreground Color in the toolbox, in the text color swatch in the tool options bar, and in the text you typed in the image window. (Select any other tool in the toolbox to deselect the text so that you can see the color applied to it.)

Note: When you move the pointer over the swatches, it temporarily changes into an eyedropper. Set the tip of the eyedropper on the swatch you want, and click to select it.

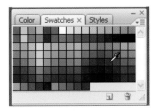

That's how easy it is to select a color, although there are other methods in Photoshop. However, you'll use a specific color for this project, and it's easier to find it if you change the Swatches palette display.

5 Select another tool in the toolbox, such as the Move tool (⤢) to deselect the Horizontal Type tool. Then, click the arrow (⊙) on the Swatches palette to open the palette menu, and choose the Small List command.

6 Select the Type tool and reselect the text, as you did in Steps 1 and 2.

7 In the Swatches palette, scroll down to near the bottom of the list to find the Light Violet Magenta swatch, and then select it.

Now the text appears in the lighter violet color.

8 Select the Hand tool (🖐) to deselect the text. Then click the Default Foreground And Background Colors button (▣) in the toolbox to make Black the foreground color.

Resetting the default colors does not change the color of the text, because the text is no longer selected.

9 You've finished the task, so close the file. You can either save it, close it without saving, or save it under a different name or location.

It's as simple as that—you've completed another project. Nice job!

Undoing actions in Photoshop

In a perfect world, you'd never make a mistake. You'd never click the wrong item. You'd always perfectly anticipate how specific actions would bring your design ideas to life exactly as you imagined them. In a perfect world, you'd never have to backtrack.

For the real world, Photoshop gives you the power to step back and undo actions so that you can try other options. Our next project provides you with an opportunity to experiment freely, knowing that you can reverse the process.

This project also introduces you to layering, which is one of the fundamental and most powerful features in Photoshop. Photoshop features many kinds of layers, some of which contain images, text, or solid colors, and others that simply interact with layers below them. The file for this next project has both kinds of layers. You don't have to understand layers to complete this project successfully, so don't worry about that right now. You'll learn more about layers in Lesson 5, "Layer Basics," and Lesson 10, "Advanced Layering."

Undoing a single action

Even beginning computer users quickly learn to use and appreciate the familiar Undo command. As we will do each time we start a new project, we'll begin by looking at the final result.

1   Click the Go To Bridge button (⬛) and navigate to the Lessons/Lesson01 folder.

2   Select the 01C_End.psd file so that you can see the results you'll achieve in this exercise. After you've studied it in the Preview panel, double-click the 01C_Start.psd file thumbnail to open it in Photoshop.

3   In the Layers palette select the Tie Designs layer.

Notice the listings in the Layers palette. The Tie Designs layer is a clipping mask. A clipping mask works somewhat like a selection in that it restricts the area of the image that can be altered. With the clipping mask in place, you can paint a design over the man's tie without worrying about any stray brush strokes disturbing the rest of the image. The Tie Designs layer is selected, because it's the layer you'll be editing now.

4 In the toolbox, select the Brush tool (✐), or press B to select it by its keyboard shortcut.

5 In the Brush tool options bar click the brush size to reveal the Brushes palette. Scroll down the list of brushes and select the Soft Round 65-pixel brush. (The name will appear as a tooltip if you hover the pointer over a brush.)

If you want to try a different brush, that's OK, but select a brush that's reasonably close to 65 pixels—preferably between 45 and 75 pixels.

6 Move the pointer over the image so that it appears as a circle with the diameter you selected in Step 5. Then draw a stripe anywhere in the orange tie. You don't have to worry about staying within the lines, because the brush won't paint anything outside the tie clipping mask.

Illustration: Pamela Hobbs

Oops! Your stripe may be very nice, but the design calls for dots, so you'll need to remove the painted stripe.

7 Choose Edit > Undo Brush Tool, or press Ctrl+Z (Windows) or Command+Z (Mac OS) to undo the Brush tool action.

The tie is again a solid orange color, with no stripe.

Note: You'll get more experience with clipping masks in Lesson 6, "Masks and Channels," Lesson 8, "Typographic Design," and in Lesson 10, "Advanced Layer Techniques."

Undoing multiple actions

The Undo command reverses only one step. This is a practicality because Photoshop files can be very large, and maintaining multiple Undo steps can tie up a lot of memory, which tends to degrade performance. However, you can still step back through multiple actions using the History palette.

1 Using the same Brush tool settings, click once over the (unstriped) orange tie to create a soft dot.

2 Click several more times in different areas on the tie to create a pattern of dots.

3 Click the History palette icon (🔂) alongside the palette dock on the right side of the window. This expands the palette so that you can see its contents. Then drag a corner of the History palette to resize it so that you can see more steps.

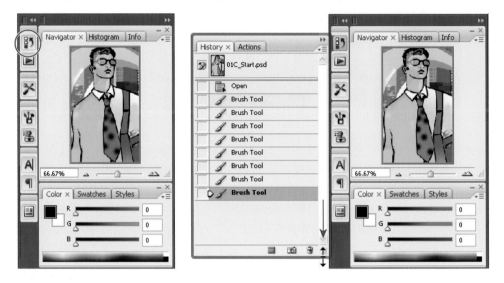

💡 *You can also expand the History palette by clicking the minimize/maximize button on the palette title bar. This resizes the palette so that all the current history states are in view.*

The History palette records the recent actions you've performed in the image. The current state is selected, at the bottom of the list.

4 Click one of the earlier actions in the History palette, and examine the changes this causes in the image window: Several previous actions are undone.

5 In the image window, create a new dot on the tie with the Brush tool.

Notice that the History palette has removed the dimmed actions that had been listed after the selected history state and has added a new one.

6 Choose Edit > Undo Brush Tool or press Ctrl+Z (Windows) or Command+Z (Mac OS) to undo the dot you created in Step 5.

Now the History palette restores the earlier listing of dimmed actions.

7 Select the state at the bottom of the History palette list.

The image is restored to the condition it was in when you finished Step 2 of this exercise.

By default, the Photoshop History palette retains only the last 20 actions. This is also a compromise, striking a balance between flexibility and performance. You can change the number of levels in the History palette by choosing Edit > Preferences > Performance (Windows) or Photoshop > Preferences > Performance (Mac OS) and typing a different number in the History States option.

You'll explore the History palette more in Lesson 3, "Retouching and Repairing."

Using a context menu

Context menus are short menus that are appropriate to specific elements in the work area. They are sometimes referred to as "right-click" or "shortcut" menus. Usually, the commands on a context menu are also available in some other area of the user interface, but using the context menu can save time.

1 If the Brush tool (✎) is not still selected in the toolbox, select it now.

2 In the image window, right-click (Windows) or Control-click (Mac OS) anywhere in the image to open the Brush tool context menu.

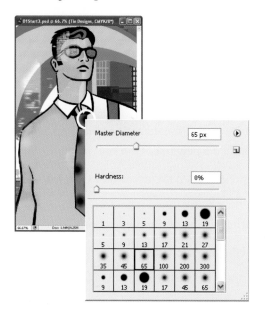

Context menus vary with their context, of course, so what appears can be a menu of commands or a palette-like set of options, which is what happens in this case.

3 Select a finer brush, such as the Hard Round 9-pixel brush. You may need to scroll up or down the list in the context menu to find the right brush.

4 In the image window, use the selected brush to create smaller dots on the tie.

Note: Clicking anywhere in the work area closes the context menu. If the tie area is hidden behind the Brush tool context menu, click another area or double-click your selection in the context menu to close it.

5 Place additional dots on the tie.

6 As it suits you, use the Undo command and the History palette to backtrack through your painting actions to correct mistakes or make different choices.

When you finish making changes to your tie design, give yourself a pat on the back because you've finished another project. You can choose File > Save if you want to save your results, or File > Save As if you want to save it in another location or with a different name, or you can close the file without saving.

More about palettes and palette locations

Photoshop palettes are powerful and varied. You rarely would have a project in which you needed to see all palettes simultaneously. That's why they're in palette groups and why the default configurations leave some palettes unopened.

The complete list of palettes appears in the Window menu, with check marks by the names of the palettes that are open at the front of their palette groups. You can open a closed palette or close an open one by selecting the palette name in the Window menu.

You can hide all palettes at once—including the tool options bar and toolbox—by pressing the Tab key. To reopen them, press Tab again.

Note: When palettes are hidden, a thin, semitransparent strip is visible at the edge of the document. Hovering the mouse pointer over the strip displays its contents.

You already used the palette well when you opened the Brushes palette for 01C_Start.psd. You can drag palettes to or from the palette well. This is convenient for bulky palettes or ones that you use only occasionally but want to keep handy.

Other actions that you can use to arrange palettes include the following:

• To move an entire palette group, drag the title bar to another location in the work area.

• To move a palette to another group, drag the palette tab into that palette group so that a black highlight appears inside the group, and then release the mouse button.

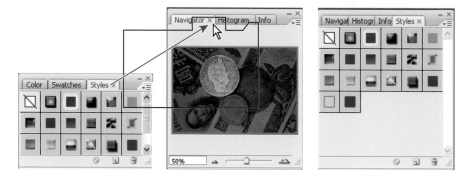

• To stack a palette in the palette well in the tool options bar, drag the palette tab into the palette well so that the palette well is highlighted.

Expanding and collapsing palettes

You can also resize palettes to use screen space more efficiently and to see fewer or more palette options, either by dragging or clicking to toggle between preset sizes:

• To collapse open palettes to icons, click the right double-headed arrows in the gray dock above the palette group. To expand the palette, click the icon or the double-headed arrow.

• To change the height of a palette, drag its lower right corner.

• To change the width of a palette or palette group, position the pointer in the left corner above the palette or palette group; when a double-headed arrow appears, drag either left or right to widen or narrow the palette, respectively.

• To expand a palette to show as much as possible of its contents, click the minimize/ maximize button. Click a second time to collapse the palette group.

• To collapse a palette group so that only the dock header bar and tabs are visible, double-click a palette tab or palette title bar. Double-click again to restore it to the expanded view. You can open the palette menu even when the palette is collapsed.

Notice that the tabs for the various palettes in the palette group and the button for the palette menu remain visible after you collapse a palette.

Note: You can collapse, but not resize, the Color, Character, and Paragraph palettes.

Special notes about the toolbox and tool options bar

The toolbox and the tool options bar share some characteristics with the other palettes:

• You can drag the toolbox by its title bar to a different location in the work area. You can move the tool options bar to another location by dragging the grab bar at the far left end of the palette.

• You can hide the toolbox and tool options bar.

However, some palette features are not available or do not apply to the toolbox or tool options bar:

• You cannot group the toolbox or tool options bar with other palettes.

• You cannot resize the toolbox or tool options bar.

• You cannot stack the toolbox in the palette well. (The same is true for the tool options bar, because the palette well appears in the tool options bar.)

• The toolbox and tool options bar do not have palette menus.

Customizing the workspace

It's great that Photoshop offers so many ways to control the display and location of the tool options bar and its many palettes, but it can be time-consuming to drag palettes around the screen so that you can see some palettes for certain projects and other palettes for other projects. Luckily, Photoshop lets you customize your workspace, controlling what palettes, tools, and menus are available at any time. In fact, it comes with a few preset workspaces suitable for different types of workflows—tone and color correction, painting and retouching, and so on. Let's experiment with them.

Note: If you closed 01C_Start.psd at the end of the previous exercise, open it—or open any other image file—to complete the following exercise.

1 Choose Window > Workspace > Color And Tonal Correction. If prompted, click Yes to apply the workspace.

If you've been experimenting with opening, closing, and moving palettes, you'll notice that Photoshop stacks the floating palettes along the right edge of the workspace. Otherwise, it may appear that nothing changes in the workspace. As you're about to see, however, Photoshop has colored many of the menu commands that are commonly used for color and tonal corrections.

2 Click the Window menu, and drag over the other menus to see that color and tonal-correction commands now appear orange.

3 Choose Window > Workspace > Web Design. If prompted, click Yes to apply the workspace.

4 Click the Window menu, and drag over the other menus to see that Web design–related commands now appear purple.

For times when presets don't suit your purposes, you can customize the workspace to your specific needs. Say, for example, that you do lots of web design, but no digital video work.

5 Click the Image menu and drag down to see the Pixel Aspect Ratio subcommands.

These subcommands include several DV formats that many print and web designers don't need to use.

6 Choose Window > Workspace > Keyboard Shortcuts And Menus.

The Keyboard Shortcuts And Menus dialog box lets you control availability of the application and palette menu commands, as well as create custom keyboard shortcuts for menus, palettes, and tools. For instance, you can hide commands that you use infrequently, or highlight commonly used commands to make them easier to see.

7 In the Menus tab of the Keyboard Shortcuts And Menus dialog box, choose Menu For: > Application Menus.

8 Toggle open the Image menu command by clicking its right-pointing triangle.

When it's open you will see the Image menu commands and subcommands, including Mode, Adjustments, and Duplicate.

9 Scroll down to Pixel Aspect Ratio and click the eye icon to turn off visibility for all of the DV and video formats—there are eight of them, beginning with D1/DV NTSC (0.9) through Anamorphic 2:1 (2).

10 Now scroll up to the Image > Mode > RGB Color command, and click None in the Color column. Choose Red from the pop-up menu.

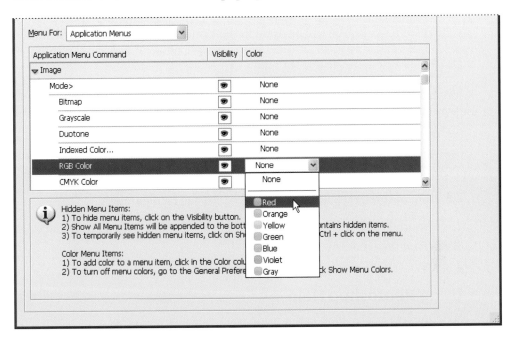

11 Click OK to close the Keyboard Shortcuts and Menus dialog box.

12 Click the Image menu command and scroll down: The Image > Mode > RGB Color command is now highlighted in red, and the DV and video formats are unavailable from the Pixel Aspect Ratio subcommand.

You can save this workspace by choosing Window > Workspace > Save Workspace. In the Save Workspace dialog box, give your workspace a name; make sure the Menus, Palette Locations, and Keyboard Shortcuts boxes are checked; and then click Save. Then, your custom workspace will be listed in the Window > Workspace submenu.

For now, however, return to the default workspace configuration.

13 Choose Window > Workspace > Default Workspace. When prompted, click Don't Save to not save changes to the menu file.

Using Photoshop Help

For complete information about using palettes, tools, and other application features, refer to Photoshop Help. Photoshop Help includes all the topics in the printed *Adobe Photoshop CS3 User Guide,* and more. It includes the complete list of keyboard shortcuts, how-to tips, tutorials, and explanations of Photoshop and Adobe Bridge concepts and feature descriptions.

Photoshop Help is easy to use, because you can look for topics in several ways:

- Scanning the table of contents.

- Searching for keywords.

- Using the index.

- Jumping to related topics using text links.

First, you'll try looking for a topic using the Contents palette.

1 Choose Help > Photoshop Help.

Note: *You can also open Photoshop Help by pressing F1 (Windows) or Command+/ (Mac OS).*

The Adobe Help Viewer opens. The topics for the Help content appear in the left pane of the floating window.

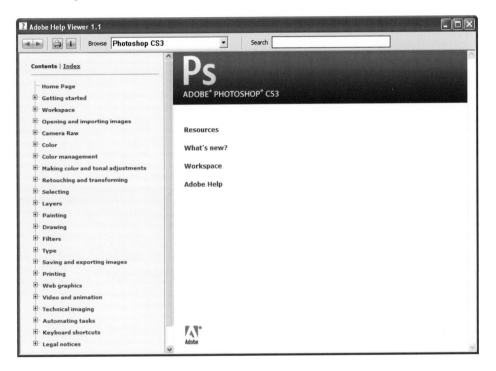

2 In the Contents section of the left pane of the Help window, scroll down to skim through the Help contents. They are organized in topics, like the chapters of a book.

3 Near the top of the list of topics, click the plus sign (+) to toggle open the topic Workspace, and then toggle open the Tools topic.

4 Click the entry "About Tools" to select and view that topic. Click the "View full size graphic" to display an illustration, with each tool called out by name.

Some Help Center entries include links to related topics. Links appear as blue, underlined text. When you position the mouse pointer over a link, the pointer changes to a pointing-finger icon (👆) and the text turns red. You can click any text link to jump to that related topic.

5 Scroll down (if necessary) to Related Information and click the Selection tools gallery text link.

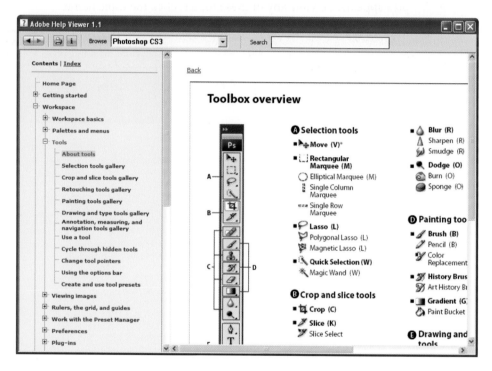

6 Click Next one or two more times to see information the rest of the tools.

Using Help Viewer keywords, links, and index

If you can't find the topic you're interested in by skimming the Contents page, you can try searching on a keyword.

1 At the top of the window, click Search.

2 Type a keyword in the search text box, such as **lasso**, and press Enter or Return. A list of topics appears. To view any of these topics, click the topic name.

You can also search for a topic using the index.

3 In the left pane, click the Index ("i") button to display the Index contents. An alphabetical list of letters appears in the left pane.

4 Click a letter, such as "T," to display index entries for that letter.

Index entries appear alphabetically by topic and subtopic, like the index of a book. You can scroll down the list to see all the entries that begin with the letter "T."

5 Click an entry to open the topic about that entry. If a topic has more than one entry, click the plus sign (⊞) to toggle open visibility for all of the entries, and then click the entry that you want to read.

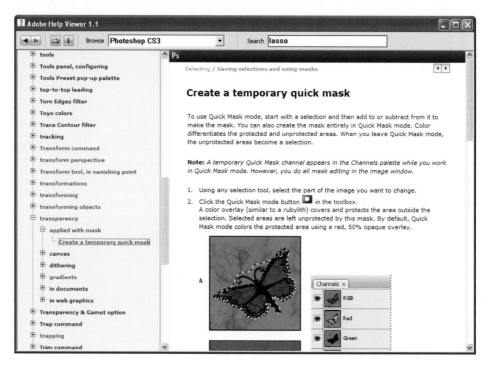

6 When you have finished browsing, click the close button at the top of the Adobe Help Viewer, or choose Adobe Help Viewer > Quit Adobe Help Center (Mac OS) to close Photoshop Help.

Using Adobe online services

Another way to get information about Adobe Photoshop and to stay abreast of updates is to use Adobe online services. If you have an Internet connection and a web browser installed on your system, you can access the Adobe Systems website (www.adobe.com) for information on Photoshop and other Adobe products. You can also be notified automatically when updates are available.

1 In Photoshop, choose Help > Photoshop Online.

Your default web browser launches and displays the Photoshop product page on the U.S. Adobe Systems website. You can explore the site and find such information as tips and techniques, galleries of artwork by Adobe designers and artists around the world, the latest product information, and troubleshooting and technical information. Or, you can learn about other Adobe products and news.

Now, you'll return to Photoshop and set it up so that you can automatically receive software updates.

2 Close your browser.

3 Return to Photoshop, and choose Help > Updates. In the Adobe Updater dialog box that appears, click the Preferences button.

4 In the Adobe Updater Preferences dialog box, select the option, "Automatically Check For Updates Every Month." Then, decide whether you want updates to be downloaded automatically, or whether you want to be alerted before updates are downloaded.

If you choose to not automatically check for updates every month, you can still manually go to the Adobe website (as in Step 1) and check for Photoshop updates.

5 Click OK to save your changes.

Congratulations again; you've finished Lesson 1.

Now that you're acquainted with the basics of the Photoshop work area, you can explore more about the Adobe Bridge visual file browser, or jump ahead and begin learning how to create and edit images. Once you know the basics, you can complete the *Adobe Photoshop CS3 Classroom in a Book* lessons either in sequential order, or according to the subject that most interests you.

Toolbox overview

The marquee tools *make rectangular, elliptical, single row, and single column selections.*

The Move tool *moves selections, layers, and guides.*

The lasso tools *make freehand, polygonal (straight-edged), and magnetic (snap-to) selections.*

The Quick Selection tool *lets you quickly "paint" a selection using an adjustable round brush tip.*

The Magic Wand tool *selects similarly colored areas*

The Crop tool *trims images.*

The Slice tool *creates slices.*

The Slice Select tool *selects slices.*

The Spot Healing Brush tool *quickly removes blemishes and imperfections from photographs with a uniform background.*

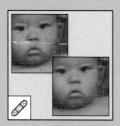

The Healing Brush tool *paints with a sample or pattern to repair imperfections in an image.*

The Patch tool *repairs imperfections in a selected area of an image using a sample or pattern.*

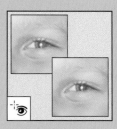

The Red Eye tool *removes red-eye in flash photos with one click.*

The Color Replacement tool *substitutes one color for another.*

The Brush tool *paints brush strokes.*

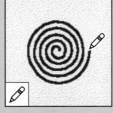

The Pencil tool *paints hard-edged strokes.*

The Clone Stamp tool *paints with a sample of an image.*

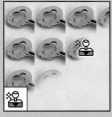

The Pattern Stamp tool *paints with a part of an image as a pattern.*

The History Brush tool *paints a copy of the selected state or snapshot into the current image window.*

The Art History Brush tool *paints stylized strokes that simulate the look of different paint styles, using a selected state or snapshot.*

The Eraser tool *erases pixels and restores parts of an image to a previously saved state.*

The Magic Eraser tool *erases solid-colored areas to transparency with a single click.*

The Background Eraser tool *erases areas to transparency by dragging.*

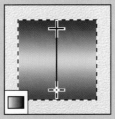

The Gradient tool *creates straight-line, radial, angle, reflected, and diamond blends between colors.*

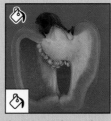

The Paint Bucket tool *fills similarly colored areas with the foreground color.*

Toolbox overview (continued)

The Blur tool *blurs hard edges in an image.*

The Sharpen tool *sharpens soft edges in an image.*

The Smudge tool *smudges data in an image.*

The Dodge tool *lightens areas in an image.*

The Burn tool *darkens areas in an image.*

The Sponge tool *changes the color saturation of an area.*

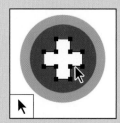

The path selection tools *make shape or segment selections showing anchor points, direction lines, and direction points.*

The type tools *create type on an image.*

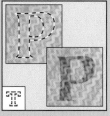

The type mask tools *create a selection in the shape of type.*

The pen tools *draw smooth-edged paths.*

The shape tools and Line tool *draw shapes and lines in a normal layer or shape layer.*

The Custom Shape tool *makes customized shapes selected from a custom shape list.*

The annotations tools *make notes and audio annotations that can be attached to an image.*

The Ruler tool *measures distances, locations, and angles.*

The Color Sampler tool *samples up to four areas of the image.*

The Eyedropper tool *samples colors in an image.*

The Hand tool *moves an image within its window.*

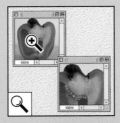

The Zoom tool *magnifies and reduces the view of an image.*

Photoshop CS3 Toolbar

— Move (V)

— Rectangular Marquee (M)

— Lasso (L)

— Magic Wand (W)

— Crop (C)

— Slice (K)

— Spot Healing Brush (J)

— Brush (B)

— Clone Stamp (S)

— History Brush (Y)

— Eraser (E)

— Gradient (G)

— Blur (R)

— Dodge (O)

— Pen (P)

— Horizontal Type (T)

— Path Selection (A)

— Rectangle (U)

— Notes (N)

— Ruler (I)

— Hand (H)

— Zoom (Z)

Review

▶ **Review questions**

1 Describe two types of images you can open in Photoshop.

2 How do you open image files using Adobe Bridge?

3 How do you select tools in Photoshop?

4 Describe two ways to change your view of an image.

5 What are two ways to get more information about Photoshop?

Review answers

1 You can scan a photograph, transparency, negative, or graphic into the program; capture a digital video image; or import artwork created in a drawing program. You can also import digital photos.

2 Click the Go To Bridge button in the Photoshop tool options bar to jump to Bridge; locate the image file you want to open, and double-click its thumbnail to open it in Photoshop.

3 Click a tool in the toolbox, or press the tool's keyboard shortcut. A selected tool remains active until you select a different tool. To select a hidden tool, use either a keyboard shortcut to toggle through the tools, or hold down the mouse button on the tool in the toolbox to open a pop-up menu of the hidden tools.

4 Choose commands from the View menu to zoom in or out of an image, or to fit it on-screen; or use the zoom tools and click or drag over an image to enlarge or reduce the view. You can also use keyboard shortcuts or the Navigator palette to control the display of an image.

5 The Photoshop Help system includes all the information in the *Adobe Photoshop CS3 User Guide* plus keyboard shortcuts, task-based topics, and illustrations. Photoshop also includes a link to the Adobe Systems Photoshop web page for additional information on services, products, and tips pertaining to Photoshop.

PARIS

aris is the home of the Rodin Museum. The beautiful surroundings attracted artists including Henri Matisse, and August Rodin rented several rooms in which to store his art. The rooms became his studio where he worked and entertained friends among the wild gardens. The mansion escaped the Reign of Terror unharmed, but during Napoleon's reign, it fell victim to the times. It was sold to the Dames du Sacre-Coeur, a religious group dedicated to the education of young women, who converted the hotel into a boarding school for girls of royal and aristocratic families.

The Church and State separated in 1905 and the school was forced to close. Plans were made to demolish the mansion and replace it by rental apartments. In the meantime, it was divided into several small lodgings. The beautiful surroundings attracted artists including Henri Matisse, and August Rodin rented several rooms in which to store his art. The rooms became his studio where he worked and entertained friends among the wild gardens. Ever since 1919, the sculptures of Auguste Rodin have been housed in a mansion known as the Biron Hotel. The mansion was built by a hairdresser named Abraham Peyrenc in the seventeenth century when Paris Left Bank was still uninhabited.

Adobe Photoshop includes a variety of tools and commands for improving the quality of a photographic image. This lesson steps you through the process of acquiring, resizing, and retouching a photo intended for a print layout. The same basic work-flow applies to web images.

2 | Basic Photo Corrections

Lesson overview

In this lesson, you'll learn how to do the following:

- Understand image resolution and size.

- Straighten and crop an image.

- Adjust the tonal range of an image.

- Remove a color cast from an image using Auto Color correction.

- Adjust the saturation and brightness of isolated areas of an image using the Sponge and Dodge tools.

- Apply the Unsharp Mask filter to finish the photo-retouching process.

- Save an image file for use in a page-layout program.

This lesson will take 45 minutes to an hour to complete. If needed, remove the previous lesson folder from your hard drive, and copy the Lesson02 folder onto it. If you need to restore the start files at any time, copy them from the *Adobe Photoshop CS3 Classroom in a Book* CD.

Strategy for retouching

Adobe Photoshop provides a comprehensive set of color-correction tools for adjusting the color and tone of individual images. You can, for example, correct problems in color quality and tonal range created during the original photography or during image scanning, and you can correct problems in composition and sharpen the overall focus of the image.

Organizing an efficient sequence of tasks

Most retouching follows these eight general steps:

• Duplicating the original image or scan. (Always work in a copy of the image file so that you can recover the original later if necessary.)

• Checking the scan quality and making sure that the resolution is appropriate for the way you will use the image.

• Cropping the image to final size and orientation.

• Repairing flaws in scans of damaged photographs (such as rips, dust, or stains).

• Adjusting the overall contrast or tonal range of the image.

• Removing any color casts.

• Adjusting the color and tone in specific parts of the image to bring out highlights, midtones, shadows, and desaturated colors.

• Sharpening the overall focus of the image.

Usually, you should complete these processes in the order listed. Otherwise, the results of one process may cause unintended changes to other aspects of the image, making it necessary for you to redo some of your work.

Note: Later in this book you'll use adjustment layers, which give you great flexibility to try out different correction settings without risking damage to the original image.

Adjusting your process for intended uses

The retouching techniques you apply to an image depend in part on how you will use the image. Whether an image is intended for black-and-white publication on newsprint or for full-color Internet distribution affects everything from the resolution of the initial scan to the type of tonal range and color correction that the image requires. Photoshop supports the CMYK color mode for preparing an image to be printed using process colors, as well as RGB and other color modes for web and mobile authoring.

To illustrate one application of retouching techniques, this lesson takes you through the steps of correcting a photograph intended for four-color print publication.

For more information about CMYK and RGB color modes, see Lesson 14, "Producing and Printing Consistent Color."

Resolution and image size

The first step in retouching a photograph in Photoshop is to make sure that the image is the correct resolution. The term *resolution* refers to the number of small squares known as *pixels* that describe an image and establish its detail. Resolution is determined by *pixel dimensions*, or the number of pixels along the width and height of an image.

Pixels in a photographic image

In computer graphics, there are different types of resolution:

The number of pixels per unit of length in an image is called the *image resolution*, usually measured in pixels per inch (ppi). An image with a high resolution has more pixels (and therefore a larger file size) than an image of the same dimensions with a low resolution. Images in Photoshop can vary from high resolution (300 ppi or higher) to low resolution (72 ppi or 96 ppi).

The number of pixels per unit of length on a monitor is the *monitor resolution*, also usually measured in pixels per inch (ppi). Image pixels are translated directly into monitor pixels. In Photoshop, if the image resolution is higher than the monitor resolution, the image appears larger on-screen than its specified print dimensions. For example, when you display a 1-x-1-inch, 144-ppi image on a 72-ppi monitor, the image fills a 2-x-2-inch area of the screen.

4 x 6 inches at 72 ppi; file size 364.5KB   *100% on-screen view*   *4 x 6 inches at 200 ppi; file size 2.75 MB*   *100% on-screen view*

Note: It is important to understand what "100% view" means when you work on-screen. At 100%, 1 image pixel = 1 monitor pixel. Unless the resolution of your image is exactly the same as the resolution of the monitor, the image size (in inches, for example) on-screen may be larger or smaller than the image size will be when printed.

The number of ink dots per inch (dpi) produced by a platesetter or laser printer is the *printer,* or *output, resolution.* Of course, higher-resolution printers combined with higher-resolution images generally produce the best quality. The appropriate resolution for a printed image is determined both by the printer resolution and by the *screen frequency,* or lines per inch (lpi), of the halftone screens used to reproduce images.

Keep in mind that the higher the image resolution, the larger the file size and the longer the file takes to download from the Web.

Note: To determine the image resolution for the photograph in this lesson, we followed the computer-graphics rule of thumb for color or grayscale images that are intended for print on large commercial printers: Scan at a resolution 1.5 to 2 times the screen frequency used by the printer. Because the magazine in which the image will be printed uses a screen frequency of 133 lpi, the image was scanned at 200 ppi (133 x 1.5).

For more information on resolution and image size, see Photoshop Help.

Getting started

The image you'll work on in this lesson is a scanned photograph. You'll prepare the image to be placed in an Adobe InDesign layout for a fictitious magazine. The final image size in the print layout will be 2 x 3 inches.

You'll start the lesson by comparing the original scan to the finished image.

1 Start Photoshop and then immediately hold down Ctrl+Alt+Shift (Windows) or Command+Option+Shift (Mac OS) to restore the default preferences. (See "Restoring default preferences" on page 6.)

2 When prompted, click Yes to confirm that you want to reset preferences, and Close to close the Welcome Screen.

3 Click the Go To Bridge button ( ) in the tool options bar to open Adobe Bridge.

4 In the Favorites panel in the upper left corner of Bridge, click the Lessons favorite, and then double-click the Lesson02 folder to see its contents in the preview area.

5 Make sure that your thumbnail previews are large enough for a good look at the images, and compare the 02Start.psd and 02End.psd files. To enlarge the preview, drag the Thumbnail slider at the bottom right of the Bridge window to the right.

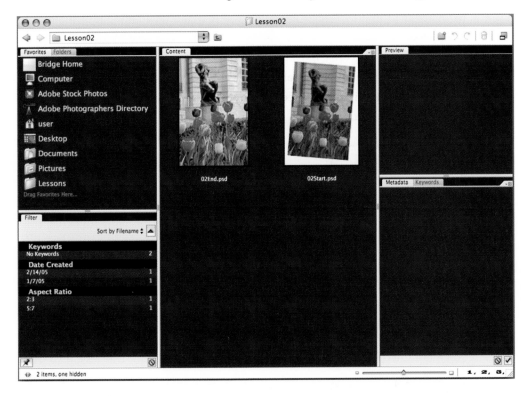

Notice that the scan is crooked, that the colors in the original scanned image are relatively dull, and the image has a red color cast. The dimensions are also larger than needed for the requirements of the magazine. You will fix all of these qualities in this lesson, starting with straightening and cropping the image.

6 Double-click the 02Start.psd thumbnail to open the file in Photoshop. If necessary, click OK to dismiss the embedded profile mismatch warning.

7 In Photoshop, choose File > Save As, rename the file **02Working.psd**, and click Save to save it in the Lesson02 folder.

Remember, when you're making permanent corrections to an image file, it's always wise to work on a copy rather than on the original. Then, if something goes horribly wrong, at least you'll be able to start over on a fresh copy of the original image.

Julieanne Kost is an official Adobe Photoshop evangelist.

TOOL TIPS FROM THE PHOTOSHOP EVANGELIST

> **The Crop tool rocks!**

Here are two little-known but great ways to use the Crop tool (Z) more effectively:

• Use the Crop tool to add canvas to any image. With an image open in Photoshop, drag to enlarge the image window so that you have gray empty space beyond the edge of the image. Then simply drag a marquee with the Crop tool, and after you release the mouse you can drag the handles outside the image area. When you apply the crop (by pressing Enter or Return), the area will be added to the canvas and filled with the background color.

• Use the dimensions of one image to crop another. Open both images in Photoshop, and make the image with the desired crop dimensions active. Select the Crop tool, and click the Front Image button in the tool options bar. This enters the image's height, width, and resolution in the respective fields in the options bar. Switch to the image that you want to crop, and drag with the Crop tool. The tool constrains the aspect ratio as you drag, and when you release and apply the crop, the image will be resized to the desired height, width, and resolution.

Straightening and cropping an image

You'll use the Crop tool to trim and scale the photograph for this lesson so that it fits the space designed for it. You can use either the Crop tool or the Crop command to crop an image. Both methods permanently delete all the pixels outside the crop selection area.

1 In the toolbox, select the Crop tool (⌗). Then, in the tool options bar (at the top of the work area), enter the dimensions (in inches) of the finished image: For Width type **2 in,** and for Height type **3 in**.

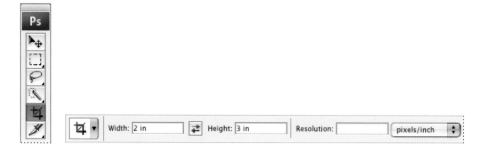

2 Draw a crop marquee around the image. Don't worry about whether the entire image is included, because you'll adjust the marquee in a moment.

As you drag, the marquee retains the same proportion as the dimensions you specified for the target size (2 x 3 inches).

When you release the mouse button, a *cropping shield* covers the area outside the cropping selection, and the tool options bar displays choices about the cropping shield.

3 In the tool options bar, make sure that the Perspective check box is *not* selected.

4 In the image window, move the pointer outside the crop marquee so that it appears as a curved double arrow (↰). Drag clockwise to rotate the marquee until it matches the angle of the picture.

5 Place the pointer inside the crop marquee, and drag the marquee until it contains all the parts of the picture you want shown to produce an artistically pleasing result. If you need to adjust the size of the marquee, drag one of the corner handles. You can also press the arrow keys to adjust the marquee in 1-pixel increments.

6 Press Enter or Return. The image is now cropped, and the cropped image now fills the image window, straightened, sized, and cropped according to your specifications.

You can use the Image > Trim command to discard a border area around the edge of the image, based on transparency or edge color.

7 Choose File > Save to save your work.

Making automatic adjustments

Photoshop contains a number of highly effective automatic features that fix many pictures with very little effort on your part. These may be all you need for certain types of jobs. However, when you want more control, you can dig down into some of the more technical features and options available in Photoshop.

Just to be a good sport about it, you'll first try the automatic adjustments to brighten the colors in the lesson image file. Then, you'll make adjustments using manual controls on another copy of the image.

1 If you didn't save your work after you cropped the image in the previous exercise, choose File > Save now.

2 Choose File > Save As, rename the cropped file **02Auto.psd**, and click Save.

3 Choose Image > Adjustments > Auto Color.

4 Choose Image > Adjustments > Shadow/Highlight.

5 In the Shadow/Highlight dialog box, drag the Highlight and Shadow sliders as needed until you think the image looks good. Make sure that Preview is checked so that you can see the changes applied to the image window as you work.

6 Click OK to close the dialog box, and then choose File > Save.

7 Close the 02Auto.psd file. Then choose File > Open Recent > 02Working.psd to open that image file.

Manually adjusting the tonal range

The tonal range of an image represents the amount of *contrast*, or detail, in the image and is determined by the image's distribution of pixels, ranging from the darkest pixels (black) to the lightest pixels (white). You'll now correct the photograph's contrast using the Levels command.

In this task, you'll use a graph in the Levels dialog box that represents the range of values (dark and light) in the image. This graph has controls that adjust the shadows, highlights, and midtones (or gamma) of the image. You'll also refer to the Histogram palette, which displays this information for you. Unless you're aiming for a special effect, the ideal histogram extends across the full width of the graph, and the middle portion has fairly uniform peaks and valleys, representing adequate pixel data in the midtones.

1 Choose Window > Histogram, or click the Histogram tab in the Navigator palette group to make the Histogram palette visible. Click the arrow in the upper right corner to display the palette menu. Then choose Expanded View from the Histogram palette menu.

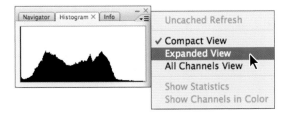

2 Choose Image > Adjustments > Levels to open the Levels dialog box.

3 Make sure that the Preview check box is selected, and then move the dialog box, if necessary, so that you can also see the image window and Histogram palette.

The left (black) triangle below the histogram represents the shadows, the middle (gray) triangle represents the midtones, or *gamma*, and the right (white) triangle represents the highlights. If your image had colors across the entire brightness range, the graph would extend across the full width of the histogram. Notice that at this point, the graphs in the Levels dialog box and the Histogram palette are identical.

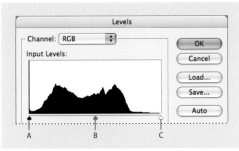

A. *Shadows* B. *Midtones, or gamma* C. *Highlights*

4 In the Levels dialog box, drag the left triangle to the right to the point where the histogram indicates that the darkest colors begin.

As you drag, the first Input Levels value (above the histogram graph) changes and so does the image itself. In the Histogram palette, the left portion of the graph now stretches to the edge of the frame. This indicates that the darkest shadow values have shifted closer to black.

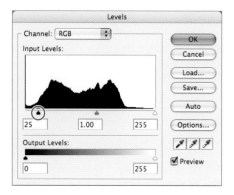

Note: *You can also scrub to change the Input Levels value: First click in the text box for the value you want to change, and then drag the pointer over the Input Levels label.*

5 Drag the right triangle to the left to the point where the histogram indicates that the lightest colors begin. Again, notice the changes in the third Input Levels value, in the image itself, and in the Histogram palette graph.

6 Drag the middle triangle a short distance to the left side to lighten the midtones.

Watch the changes in the image window and in the Histogram palette graph to determine how far to drag the middle triangle.

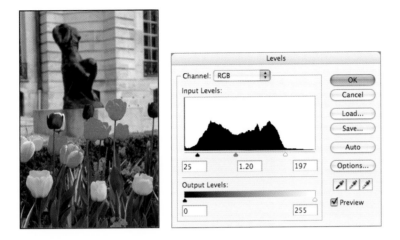

7 When the image looks good to you (we used Input Levels values of 25, 1.20, and 197), click OK to apply the changes. Then save your work.

About the Auto Contrast command

You can also adjust the contrast (highlights and shadows) and the overall mix of colors in an image automatically using the Image > Adjustments > Auto Contrast command. Adjusting the contrast maps the darkest and lightest pixels in the image to black and white. This remapping causes the highlights to appear lighter and the shadows to appear darker and can improve the appearance of many photographic or continuous-tone images. (The Auto Contrast command does not improve flat-color images.)

The Auto Contrast command clips white and black pixels by 0.5%—that is, it ignores the first 0.5% of either extreme when identifying the lightest and darkest pixels in the image. This clipping of color values ensures that white and black values are representative areas of the image content rather than extreme pixel values.

For this project, you won't use the Auto Contrast feature, but it's a feature you should know about so that you can use it in your own projects.

Removing a color cast

Some images contain color casts (imbalanced colors), which may occur during scanning or which may have existed in the original image. This photograph of the garden has a red cast. You'll use the Auto Color feature to correct this.

Note: To see a color cast in an image on your monitor, you need a 24-bit monitor (one that can display millions of colors). On monitors that can display only 256 colors (8 bits), a color cast is difficult, if not impossible, to detect.

1 Choose Image > Adjustments > Auto Color.

The red color cast goes away.

2 Choose File > Save.

About the Auto Color and Auto Correction commands

The Auto Color command adjusts the contrast and color of an image by searching the actual image rather than the channel histograms for shadows, midtones, and highlights. It neutralizes the midtones and clips the white and black pixels based on the values set in the Auto Correction Options dialog box.

The Auto Correction Options dialog box lets you automatically adjust the overall tonal range of an image, specify clipping percentages, and assign color values to shadows, midtones, and highlights. You can apply the settings during a single use of the Levels or Curves dialog boxes, or you can save the settings for future use with the Levels, Auto Levels, Auto Contrast, Auto Color, and Curves commands.

To open the Auto Correction Options dialog box, click Options in the Levels dialog box or in the Curves dialog box.

Replacing colors in an image

With the Replace Color command, you can create temporary *masks* based on specific colors and then replace these colors. (A mask isolates an area of an image so that changes affect just the selected area and not the rest of the image.) The Replace Color dialog box contains options for adjusting the hue, saturation, and lightness components of the selection: *Hue* is color, *saturation* is the purity of the color, and *lightness* is how much white or black is in the image.

You'll use the Replace Color command to change the color of one of the tulips in the image we've been correcting throughout this lesson.

1 Select the Rectangular Marquee tool (⬚), and draw a selection border around the yellow tulip in the left foreground of the image. Don't worry about making a perfect selection, but be sure to include all of the yellow flower.

2 Choose Image > Adjustments > Replace Color.

The Replace Color dialog box opens, and by default, the Selection area displays a black representation of the current selection.

Notice the three eyedropper tools in the Replace Color dialog box. One selects a color; the second adds a color to the sample; the third removes a color from the sample.

A. *Eyedropper tool*
B. *Add To Sample eyedropper*
C. *Subtract From Sample eyedropper*

3 Using the Eyedropper tool ( ), click anywhere in the yellow tulip in the image window to sample that color.

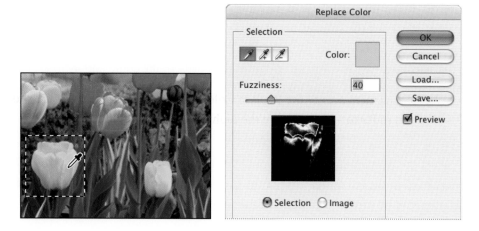

4 Then, use the Add To Sample eyedropper ( ) to sample other areas of the yellow tulip until the entire flower is selected and highlighted in the mask display in the Replace Color dialog box.

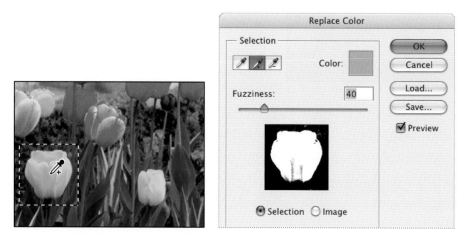

5 Drag the Fuzziness slider up to 45 to increase the tolerance level slightly.

Fuzziness controls the degree to which related colors are included in the mask.

6 If the mask display includes any white areas that are not part of the tulip, get rid of those now: Select the Subtract From Sample eyedropper (✎) and click those areas in either the image window or in the Replace Color mask display to remove those stray pixels. (It's OK if a few remain in the selection.)

7 In the Replacement area of the Replace Color dialog box, drag the Hue slider to –40, the Saturation slider to –10, and leave the Lightness slider at 0.

As you change the values, the color of the tulip changes in hue, saturation, and lightness, and the tulip becomes red.

8 Click OK to apply the changes.

9 Choose Select > Deselect, and then choose File > Save.

Adjusting lightness with the Dodge tool

You'll use the Dodge tool next to lighten the highlights and bring out the details of the sculpture in the image. The Dodge tool is based on a traditional photographer's method of holding back light during an exposure to lighten an area of the image.

1 In the toolbox, select the Dodge tool (✎).

2 In the tool options bar, do the following:

• Select a fairly large, feathered brush, such as 27 pixels, from the Brush pop-up palette (click outside the palette to close it).

• Choose Range > Highlights.

• Set Exposure to 15%.

3 Using vertical strokes, drag the Dodge tool over the sculpture to bring out the details and remove the dinginess.

You don't always need to use vertical strokes with the Dodge tool, but they work well with this particular image. If you make a mistake or don't like the results, choose Edit > Undo and try again until you are satisfied.

Original   *Result*

4 Choose File > Save.

Adjusting saturation with the Sponge tool

Next, you'll use the Sponge tool to saturate the color of the tulips. When you change the saturation of a color, you adjust its strength or purity. The Sponge tool is useful for making subtle saturation changes to specific areas of an image.

1 Select the Sponge tool (●), hidden under the Dodge tool (●).

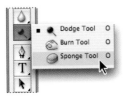

2 In the tool options bar, do the following:

- Again select a large, feathered brush, such as 27 pixels, from the Brush pop-up palette.

- Choose Mode > Saturate.

- For Flow (which sets the intensity of the saturation effect), enter **90%**.

3 Drag the sponge back and forth over the tulips and leaves to increase their saturation. The more you drag over an area, the more saturated the color becomes.

4 Save your work.

Applying the Unsharp Mask filter

The last task you may do when retouching a photo is to apply the Unsharp Mask filter. The Unsharp Mask filter adjusts the contrast of the edge detail and creates the illusion of a more focused image.

1 Choose Filter > Sharpen > Unsharp Mask.

2 In the Unsharp Mask dialog box, make sure that the Preview box is checked so that you can see the results in the image window.

You can drag inside the preview in the dialog box to see different parts of the image, or use the plus (⊞) and minus (⊟) buttons below the thumbnail to zoom in and out.

3 Drag the Amount slider to about 62% to sharpen the image.

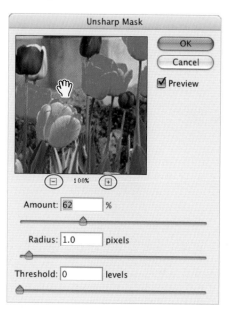

As you try different settings, toggle the Preview check box off and on to see how your changes affect the image. Or, you can click and hold the mouse button on the thumbnail preview in the dialog box to temporarily toggle the filter off. If your image is large, using the thumbnail preview can be more efficient, because only a small area is redrawn.

4 Drag the Radius slider to determine the number of pixels surrounding the edge pixels that will affect the sharpening. The higher the resolution, the higher the Radius setting should be. (We used the default value, 1.0 pixel.)

5 (Optional) Adjust the Threshold slider. This determines how different the sharpened pixels must be from the surrounding area before they are considered edge pixels and subsequently sharpened by the Unsharp Mask filter. The default Threshold value of 0 sharpens all pixels in the image. Try a different value, such as 4 or 5.

6 When you are satisfied with the results, click OK to apply the Unsharp Mask filter.

7 Choose File > Save.

About unsharp masking

Unsharp masking, or USM, is a traditional film-compositing technique used to sharpen edges in an image. The Unsharp Mask filter corrects blurring introduced during photographing, scanning, resampling, or printing. It is useful for images intended for both print and online viewing.

The Unsharp Mask locates pixels that differ from surrounding pixels by the threshold you specify and increases the pixels' contrast by the amount you specify. In addition, you specify the radius of the region to which each pixel is compared.

The effects of the Unsharp Mask filter are far more pronounced on-screen than they are in high-resolution output. If your final destination is print, experiment to determine what settings work best for your image.

Comparing automatic and manual results

Near the beginning of this lesson, you adjusted the lesson image using only automatic color and value controls. For the rest of the lesson, you painstakingly applied manual adjustments to get specific results. Now it's time to compare the two.

1 Choose File > Open Recent > 02Auto.psd, if it is available. Otherwise, choose File > Open, navigate to the Lessons/Lesson02 folder, and open the file. If necessary, click OK to dismiss the embedded profile mismatch warning.

2 Choose Window > Arrange > Tile Vertically to position the 02Auto.psd and the 02Working.psd image windows side by side.

3 Visually compare the two results.

02Auto.psd   02Working.psd

4 Close the 02Auto.psd file.

For some designers, the automatic commands may be all they'll ever need. For others with more sensitive visual requirements, manual adjustments are the way to go. The best of both worlds is when you understand the trade-offs of the two methods and can choose one or the other according to your requirements for the specific project and image.

Saving the image for four-color printing

Before you save a Photoshop file for use in a four-color publication, you must change the image to CMYK color mode in order to print your publication correctly in four-color process inks. You'll use the Mode command to change the image color mode.

For more information about converting between color modes, see Photoshop Help.

1 Choose Image > Mode > CMYK Color.

• If you use Adobe InDesign to create your publications, you can skip the rest of this process and just choose File > Save. InDesign can import native Photoshop files, so there is no need to convert the image to TIFF format.

• If you are using another layout application, you must save the photo as a TIFF file.

2 Choose File > Save As.

3 In the Save As dialog box, choose TIFF from the Format menu.

4 Click Save.

5 In the TIFF Options dialog box, select your operating system for the Byte Order and click OK.

The image is now fully retouched, saved, and ready for placement in a page layout application.

For more information about file formats, see Photoshop Help.

Review

▶ **Review questions**

1 What does *resolution* mean?

2 How can you use the Crop tool when retouching photos?

3 How can you adjust the tonal range of an image?

4 What is saturation, and how can you adjust it?

5 Why would you use the Unsharp Mask filter on a photo?

▶ **Review answers**

1 The term *resolution* refers to the number of pixels that describe an image and establish its detail. The three different types are *image resolution, monitor resolution*—both of which are measured in pixels per inch (ppi)—and *printer,* or *output, resolution,* which is measured in ink dots per inch (dpi).

2 You can use the Crop tool to trim, scale, and straighten an image.

3 You can use the black, white, and gray triangles below the Levels command histogram to control the midpoint and where the darkest and lightest points in the image begin, thus extending its tonal range.

4 Saturation is the strength, or purity, of color in an image. You can use the Sponge tool to increase the saturation in a specific area of an image.

5 The Unsharp Mask filter adjusts the contrast of the edge detail and creates the illusion of a more focused image.

YUKIMI

Adobe Photoshop includes a powerful set of cloning tools that make retouching photographs easy and intuitive. Thanks to the underlying technology supporting these features, even touchups of the human face appear so lifelike and natural that it is difficult to detect that a photograph has been altered.

3 | Retouching and Repairing

Lesson overview

In this lesson, you'll learn how to do the following:

- Use the Clone Stamp tool to eliminate an unwanted part of an image.

- Use the Spot Healing Brush tool to repair part of an image.

- Use the Healing Brush and Patch tools to blend in corrections.

- Make corrections on a duplicate layer and adjust it for a natural look.

- Backtrack within your work session using the History palette.

- Use the History brush to partially restore an image to a previous state.

- Use snapshots to preserve earlier states of your work and to compare alternative treatments of the image.

This lesson will take about 45 minutes to complete. If needed, remove the previous lesson folder from your hard drive, and copy the Lesson03 folder onto it. As you work on this lesson, you'll preserve the start files. If you need to restore the start files, copy them from the *Adobe Photoshop CS3 Classroom in a Book CD*.

Getting started

In this lesson, you'll work on three separate projects, editing three different photographs. Each of them employs the different retouching tools in unique ways, so you'll explore the strengths and special uses of the various tools.

You'll start by previewing the three images that you'll retouch in this lesson.

1 Launch Adobe Photoshop, holding down Ctrl+Alt+Shift (Windows) or Command+Option+Shift (Mac OS) to restore the default preferences. (See "Restoring default preferences" on page 6.)

2 When prompted, click Yes to confirm that you want to reset preferences, and Close to close the Welcome Screen.

3 Click the Go To Bridge button (▥) in the tool options bar to open Adobe Bridge.

4 In the Favorites panel, click Lessons, then double-click the Lesson03 folder thumbnail to preview its contents, namely, the Lesson03 Start and End files, with the letters A, B, and C.

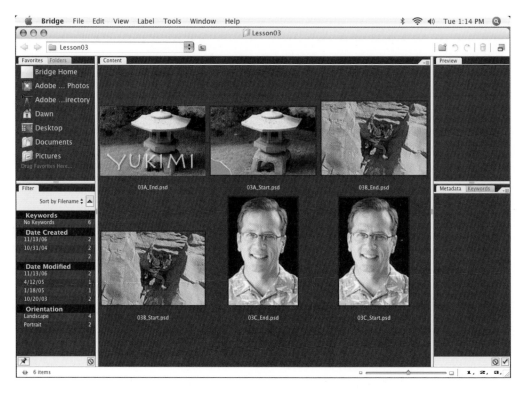

• The first project is a photograph of a Japanese stone garden lantern with semitransparent text superimposed on the foreground. You will repair a torn-off corner of the scanned image and remove some distracting areas where sprinklers in the grass appear in the background.

• The second project shows a rock climber scaling a stone wall. You will clean up the wall beside the climber to remove some graffiti and scars from old bolt holes on the surface of the rock.

• The third project is a portrait of a man. You will retouch the portrait to remove some of the fine lines from the man's forehead and around his eyes.

5 When you have finished previewing the files, double-click the 03A_Start.psd file thumbnail to open the image in Photoshop.

6 If necessary, in Photoshop, zoom in to 100% and resize the image window so that you can see the entire image.

7 Choose File > Save As, rename the file **03A_Working.psd**, and click Save. This preserves the original start file.

Repairing areas with the Clone Stamp tool

The Clone Stamp tool uses pixels from one area of an image to replace the pixels in another part of the image. Using this tool, you can not only remove unwanted objects from your images, but you can also fill in missing areas in photographs you scan from damaged originals.

You'll start by filling in the torn corner of the photograph with cloned grass from another area of the picture.

1 Select the Clone Stamp tool (🖳) in the toolbox.

2 In the tool options bar, open the Brush Preset pop-up menu in the options bar and select a large-sized brush with a soft edge, such as Soft Round 75. Then, make sure that the Sample Aligned option is selected.

3 Move the Clone Stamp tool pointer to the center of the image so that it is at the same level as the top edge of the torn corner and over grass. Then, hold down Alt (Windows) or Option (Mac OS) so that the pointer appears as target cross hairs, and click to start the sampling at that part of the image. Release the Alt or Option key.

4 Starting at the top edge of the torn corner of the photograph, drag the Clone Stamp tool over a small area at the top of the torn area of the image.

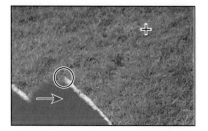

Notice the cross hairs that appear to the right of the Clone Stamp tool in the image window. The cross hairs indicate the source area of the image that the Clone Stamp tool is reproducing as you drag.

5 Release the mouse button and move the pointer to another area of the missing corner, and then start dragging again.

Notice that the cross hairs reappear not at the original source spot that you selected in Step 3, but at the same spatial relationship to the Clone Stamp tool pointer that they had when you made the first stroke. This happens because you selected the Sample Aligned option, which resets the cross hairs at that position regardless of the position of the Clone Stamp tool.

Note: When the Sample Aligned option is not selected and you make multiple brush strokes, the cross hairs and the brush maintain the same spatial relationship (distance and direction) that they had when you started your first brush stroke, regardless of the location of the original sample site.

6 Continue cloning the grass until the entire missing corner of the image is filled in.

If necessary to help make the grass appear to blend in naturally with the rest of the image, you can adjust your cloning by resetting the sample area (as you did in Step 3) and recloning. Or, you can try deselecting the Sample Aligned option and cloning again.

7   When you are satisfied with the appearance of the grass, choose File > Save.

Using the Spot Healing Brush tool

The next task to be done is to remove the sprinkler heads from the right side and upper left of the image. You could do this with the Clone Stamp tool, but instead you'll use another technique. You'll use the Spot Healing Brush to paint out the sprinklers.

Painting with the Spot Healing Brush

The Spot Healing Brush tool quickly removes blemishes and other imperfections from photos. It works similarly to the Healing Brush: It paints with sampled pixels from an image or pattern and matches the texture, lighting, transparency, and shading of the sampled pixels to the pixels being healed. But unlike the Healing Brush (which you'll use later in this lesson), the Spot Healing Brush doesn't require you to specify a sample spot. It automatically samples from around the retouched area.

The Spot Healing Brush is excellent for retouching blemishes in portraits, but it will also work nicely in this image of the sprinklers in the grass, because the grass has a uniform, muted appearance across the top of the image.

1   In the toolbox, select the Spot Healing Brush tool ( ).

2   In the tool options bar, click the Brush Preset pop-up menu and make the brush larger, about 30 pixels in diameter.

3 Drag with the Spot Healing Brush in the image window across the sprinkler head on the right side of the image, and then repeat with the left sprinkler. You can use one stroke or successive strokes; paint until you are satisfied with the results. As you drag, the stroke at first appears dark gray, but when you release the mouse, the painted area is "healed."

You'll add just one final tweak to this retouching project, and then you'll be finished.

4 In the Layers palette, click to the left of the Yukimi layer in the Show Visibility column to place an eye icon (👁) so that the text is visible in the image window.

5 Choose File > Save, and then close the 03A_Working.psd file.

Using the Healing Brush and Patch tools

The Healing Brush and Patch tools go one step beyond the capabilities of the Clone Stamp and Spot Healing Brush tools. Using their ability to simultaneously apply and blend pixels from area to area, they open the door to natural-looking touch-ups in areas that are not uniform in color or texture.

In this project, you'll touch up the stone wall, removing some graffiti and bolt holes left over from obsolete climbing techniques. Because the rock varies in color, texture, and lighting, it would be challenging to successfully use the Clone Stamp tool to touch up the damaged areas. Fortunately, the Healing Brush and Patch tools make this process easy.

If you want to review the "before" and "after" versions of this image, use Adobe Bridge as described in "Getting started" beginning on page.

Using the Healing Brush to remove flaws

Your first goal for this image is to remove the initials that mar the natural beauty of the rock wall.

1 Click the Go To Bridge button (📷) in the tool options bar, and in Bridge, double-click the 03B_Start.psd file to open it in Photoshop.

2 Choose File > Save As, rename the file **03B_Working.psd**, and click Save to save the original start file. Working on a version of the start file lets you return to the original at any time.

3 In Photoshop, select the Zoom tool (🔍) in the toolbox. Click the initials "DJ" that have been scratched into the lower left area of the rock so that you see that area of the image at about 200%.

4 In the toolbox, select the Healing Brush tool (🖌), hidden under the Spot Healing Brush tool.

5 In the tool options bar, open the Brush Preset pop-up palette, and decrease the Diameter value to 10 pixels. Then, close the pop-up palette and make sure that the other settings in the tool options bar are set to the default values: Normal in the Mode option, Sampled in the Source option, and the Sample Aligned check box deselected.

6 Hold down Alt (Windows) or Option (Mac OS) and click just above the scratched-in graffiti in the image to sample that part of the rock. Then release the Alt/Option key.

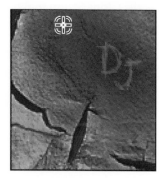

7 Starting above the graffiti "D," paint straight down over the top part of the letter, using a short stroke.

Notice that as you paint, the area the brush covers temporarily looks as if it isn't making a good color match with the underlying image. However, when you release the mouse button, the brush stroke blends in nicely with the rest of the rock surface.

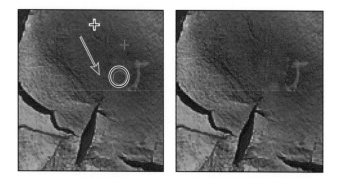

8 Continue using short strokes to paint over the graffiti, starting at the top and moving down until you can no longer detect the graffiti letters.

When you finish removing the graffiti, look closely at the surface of the rock, and notice that even the subtle striations in the stone appear to be fully restored and natural-looking in the image.

9   Zoom out to 100%, and choose File > Save.

About snapshots and History palette states

When you do retouching work, it can be easy to over-edit images until they no longer look realistic. One of the safeguards you can take to save intermediate stages of your work is to take Photoshop snapshots of the image at various points in your progress.

The History palette automatically records the actions you perform in a Photoshop file. You can use the History palette states like a multiple Undo command to restore the image to previous stages in your work. For example, to undo the most recent six actions, simply click the sixth item above the current state in the History palette. To return to the latest state, scroll back down the History palette and select the state in the lowest position on the list.

The number of items saved in the History palette is determined by a Preferences setting. The default specifies that only the 20 most recent actions are recorded. As you make more changes to the image file, the earliest states are lost as the latest ones are added to the History palette.

When you select an earlier state in the History palette, the image window reverts to the condition it had at that phase. All the subsequent actions still appear below it in the palette. However, if you select an earlier state in your work and then make a new change, all the states that appeared after the selected state are lost, replaced by the new state.

Snapshots let you try out different techniques and then choose among them. Typically, you might take a snapshot at a stage of your work that you want to keep, at least as a base point. Then, you could try out various techniques until you reach a possible completed phase. If you take another snapshot at that phase, it will be saved for the duration of the current work session on that file. Then, you can revert to the first snapshot and try out different techniques and ideas for finishing the image. When you finish the image, you could take a third snapshot, revert to the first snapshot, and try again.

Note: *Saving many previous states and snapshots is RAM-intensive. It is not recommended when you work with large or complex images, such as images with many layers, because it can slow performance. If you often work with complicated images that require maximum RAM, consider reducing the number of history states saved by changing that setting in your Photoshop preferences.*

When you finish experimenting, you can scroll to the top of the History palette to where the snapshots are listed. Then, you can select each of the final snapshots in turn and compare the results.

Once you identify the one you like best, you can select it, save your file, and close it. At that time, your snapshots and History palette listings would be permanently lost.

Note: *You can keep an Edit History Log on a Photoshop file. The Edit History Log is a textual history of what has been done to the image file. For more information, see Photoshop Help.*

Taking a snapshot

Because you are satisfied with the results of your healing the graffiti marks, now is a good time to take a snapshot. This will serve as a baseline for any future experimentation during this work session. (Remember that snapshots and history listings are discarded when you close a file.)

1 Close the Navigator, Color, and Layer palette groups—you won't use them in this lesson—and use the space to expand the History palette so that you can see as many items as possible. If necessary, scroll to the bottom of the History palette so that you can see the last change you made to the image.

2 With the most recent state in the History palette selected, click the New Snapshot button (📷) at the bottom of the History palette to create a snapshot of the current state.

3 Scroll to the top of the History palette. A new snapshot, Snapshot 1, appears at the top of the palette.

4 Double-click the words Snapshot 1, type **Post-graffiti**, and press Enter or Return to rename the snapshot.

Note: You can also take snapshots of earlier phases of your current work session. To do this, scroll to that item in the History palette, select it, and click the New Snapshot button at the bottom of the palette. After you rename the snapshot, reselect the state at which you want to continue working.

5 Make sure that either the Post-graffiti snapshot or the last state in the history list is selected in the History palette. Then, choose File > Save.

Using the Patch tool

The Patch tool combines the selection behavior of the Lasso tool with the color-blending properties of the Healing Brush tool. With the Patch tool, you can select an area that you want to use as the source (area to be fixed) or destination (area used to do the fixing). Then, you drag the Patch tool marquee to another part of the image. When you release the mouse button, the Patch tool does its job. The marquee remains active over the mended area, ready to be dragged again, either to another area that needs patching (if the Destination option is selected) or to another sampling site (if the Source option is selected).

It may be helpful to zoom in before you begin so that you can easily see the details of the image.

1 In the toolbox, select the Patch tool ( ), hidden under the Healing Brush tool ( ).

2 In the tool options bar, make sure that Source is selected.

3 Drag the Patch tool pointer around a few of the bolt holes to the right of the climber, as if you were using the Lasso tool, and then release the mouse button.

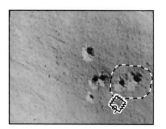

4 Drag the selection to an unblemished area of the rock, preferably—but not necessarily—one that is similar in color to the rock around the bolt holes.

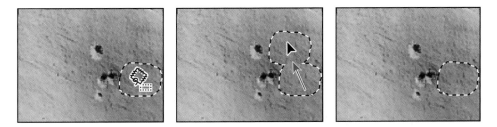

As you drag, the original selected area shows the same pixels as the lassoed selection you are dragging. When you release the mouse button, the color—but not the texture—readjust to the original color scheme of the selection.

5 Drag a new selection around some of the other bolt holes and then drag to an unblemished area of the image. Continue to patch the image until all the scars are repaired to your satisfaction. (Be sure to patch the holes on the left side of the image.)

6 Choose Select > Deselect.

7 Choose File > Save.

Using the History Brush tool to selectively reedit

Even with the best tools, retouching photographs so that they look completely natural is an art and requires some practice. Examine your rock-climber image critically to see if any areas of your work with the Healing Brush or Patch tools are now too uniform or smooth, so the area no longer looks realistic. If so, you can correct that now with another tool.

The History Brush tool is similar to the Clone Stamp tool. The difference is that instead of using a defined area of the image as the source (as the Clone Stamp tool does), the History Brush tool uses a previous History palette state as the source.

The advantage of the History Brush tool is that you can restore limited areas of the image. As a result, you can keep the successful retouching effects you've made to some areas of the image and restore other, less successfully retouched areas to their previous state so that you can make a second attempt.

1 In the toolbox, select the History Brush tool (✐).

2 Scroll to the top of the History palette and click the empty box next to the Post-graffiti snapshot to set the source state that the History Brush tool will use to paint.

3 Drag the History Brush tool over the area where the bolt holes appeared before you edited them, to start restoring that part of the image to its previous condition. The bolt holes reappear as you paint.

4 Using the tool options bar, experiment with the different settings for the History Brush tool, such as Opacity and Mode. Notice how these affect the appearance of the rock as you paint.

If you don't like the results of an experiment, choose Edit > Undo, or click an earlier action at the bottom of the History palette to revert to that state.

5 Continue working with the History Brush and Patch tools until you are satisfied with the final appearance of your image.

6 Choose File > Save, and then choose File > Close.

You've finished your work on this image.

Retouching on a separate layer

In the previous project, you safeguarded your retouching work by using snapshots and the History Brush tool. Another way to protect your original image is to do your retouching work on a duplicate layer of the original image. Then, you can retouch the duplicate layer. When you finish retouching, you can blend the two layers. This technique usually enhances the results, making your touch-up work look more natural and realistic.

Using the Healing Brush on a duplicate layer

For this project, you'll work on a portrait photograph.

1 Choose Window > Workspace > Reset Palette Locations to move, reopen, and resize any palette groups that you rearranged in the previous project.

2 Use the Go To Bridge button (▣) in the tool options bar, and double-click the 03C_Start.psd thumbnail to open the file in Photoshop.

3 Choose File > Save As, rename the file **03C_Working.psd**, and click Save.

You'll start by adding a duplicate layer for your retouching work.

4 In the Layers palette, hold down Alt (Windows) or Option (Mac OS) and drag the Background layer onto the New Layer button (▣) at the bottom of the palette to display the Duplicate Layer dialog box. Name the new layer **Retouch**, and press Enter or Return. Leave the Retouch layer selected.

5 In the toolbox, select the Healing Brush tool (✐), which may be hidden under the Patch tool (◉).

6 In the tool options bar, open the Brush Preset pop-up palette and set the brush diameter to 12 pixels; then select the Sample Aligned check box. Leave the other settings at their defaults (Normal selected as the Mode option and Sampled selected for Source).

Notice the two wrinkles running horizontally across the man's forehead. (Zoom in if necessary by pressing Ctrl+spacebar (Windows) or Command+spacebar (Mac OS) and clicking.)

7 Hold down Alt (Windows) or Option (Mac OS) and click a smooth area of the forehead, on the left side of the image, to set the sample point. Then, drag the Healing Brush tool over the lower of the two forehead wrinkles.

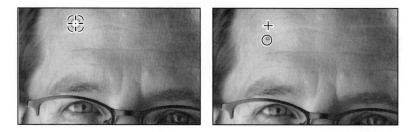

As you drag, the painted pixels don't exactly match the subject's natural skin tones. When you release the mouse button, however, the colors self-correct so that the wrinkle is covered and the skin looks quite natural.

8 Continue painting with the Healing Brush tool to remove the upper forehead wrinkle and the furrow line between the eyebrows. You can toggle between history states in the History palette to compare results.

9 Choose File > Save to save your work so far.

⭐EXTRA CREDIT *Try using the Spot Healing Brush on this image and compare the results.*

Patching and softening using the separate layer

You'll continue to do cosmetic work on the portrait image using the Patch tool and the duplicate layer (Retouch) you created in the previous exercise. Make sure that the Retouch layer is selected in the Layers palette before you begin.

1 In the toolbox, select the Patch tool (⊘), hidden under the Healing Brush tool (✐). Then, drag a marquee around the wrinkles under the subject's right eye, outside the eyeglasses.

2 Move the Patch tool inside the selected area and drag it to a smooth, similarly toned area on the man's forehead. Then, use the same technique to erase the wrinkles inside the glasses under the right eye, and inside and outside the glasses under the left eye.

3 Continue to touch up the subject's face with the Patch tool until most of the wrinkles are hidden, or at least softened. When you have finished your touch-ups, if you zoomed in, zoom out by pressing Alt+spacebar (Windows) or Option+spacebar (Mac OS) and clicking.

It is especially important that cosmetic touch-ups on the human face look as natural as possible. There's an easy way to make sure that your corrections aren't too smooth or plastic looking. You'll do that now.

4   In the Layers palette, change the Opacity value of the Retouch layer to **65%**. Now, hints of the heaviest skin creases appear in the image, giving the enhanced image a convincing realism.

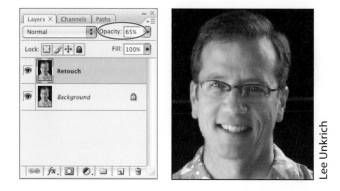

Lee Unkrich

5   Click the eye icon (👁) to toggle the Retouch layer off and on to see the difference between the original image and the corrected one.

Look at the two numbers on the status bar, just to the right of the zoom percentage, at the bottom of the image window. (If you don't see two numbers, click the right-pointing arrow and choose Show > Document Sizes.) The first number (ours is about 6.18 MB) represents the size the file would be if the two layers were flattened into one layer. The second number (ours is about 12.4 MB) shows the current size of the file with its two layers. However, after you flatten the image, you cannot separate the two layers again. When you are sure that you are satisfied with the results of your retouching efforts, it's smart to take advantage of the space-saving of flattening.

6   Choose Layer > Flatten Image, or choose Flatten Image from the Layers palette menu.

7   Choose File > Save.

Now the image has just one layer, combining the unaltered original background and the partly transparent retouched layer.

Congratulations; you've finished your work on this lesson. Close any open files.

Review

▶ **Review questions**

1 Describe the similarities and differences of the Clone Stamp tool, the Spot Healing Brush tool, the Healing Brush tool, the Patch tool, and the History Brush tool.

2 What is a snapshot and how is it useful?

▶ **Review answers**

1 As you paint with the Clone Stamp tool, it duplicates the pixels from another area of the image. You set the sample area by holding down Alt (Windows) or Option (Mac OS) and clicking the Clone Stamp tool.

The Spot Healing Brush tool removes blemishes and imperfections from a photograph. It paints with automatically sampled pixels from an image or pattern, matching the texture, lighting, transparency, and shading to the pixels being healed.

The Healing Brush tool works like the Clone Stamp tool except that Photoshop calculates a blending of the sample pixels and the painting area so that the restoration is especially subtle, yet effective.

The Patch tool works like the Healing Brush tool but instead of using brush strokes to paint from a designated area, you drag a marquee around the area to be fixed and then drag the marquee over another area to mend the flawed area.

The History Brush tool works like the Clone Stamp tool except that it paints pixels from a designated previous state or snapshot that you select in the History palette.

2 A snapshot is a temporary record of a specific stage in your work session. The History palette saves only a limited number of actions. After that, each new action you perform removes the earliest item from the History palette list. However, if you select any action listed in the History palette and take a snapshot of that state, you can continue working from that action or another one. Later in your work session, you can revert to the state recorded by the snapshot by selecting it in the History palette, regardless of how many changes you've made in the meantime. You can save as many snapshots as you please.

Learning how to select areas of an image is of primary importance— you must first select what you want to affect. Once you've made a selection, only the area within the selection can be edited. Areas outside the selection are protected from change.

4 Working with Selections

Lesson overview

In this lesson, you'll learn how to do the following:

- Make specific areas of an image active using various tools.

- Reposition a selection marquee.

- Move and duplicate the contents of a selection.

- Use keyboard-mouse combinations that save time and hand motions.

- Deselect a selection.

- Constrain the movement of a selected area.

- Adjust the position of a selected area using the arrow keys.

- Add to and subtract from a selection.

- Rotate a selection.

- Use multiple selection tools to make a complex selection.

- Erase pixels within a selection.

This lesson will take less than an hour to complete. If needed, remove the previous lesson folder from your hard drive, and copy the Lesson04 folder onto it. As you work on this lesson, you'll preserve the start file. If you need to restore the start file, copy it from the *Adobe Photoshop CS3 Classroom in a Book* CD.

About selecting and selection tools

Selecting and making changes to an area within an image in Photoshop is a two-step process. You first select the part of an image you want to change with one of the selection tools. Then, you can use another tool to make changes, such as moving the selected pixels to another location or erasing pixels within the selection. You can make selections based on size, shape, and color, using four basic sets of tools—the marquee, lasso, Magic Wand, and pen tools. The selection process limits changes to within the selected area. Other areas are unaffected.

Note: In this lesson, you'll use only the marquee tools, lasso tools, Quick Selection and Magic Wand tools to make your selections. You'll learn about the pen tools in Lesson 9, "Vector Drawing Techniques."

A. *Rectangular Marquee tool*
B. *Move tool*
C. *Lasso tool*
D. *Magic Wand tool*

The best selection tool for a specific area often depends on the characteristics of that area, such as shape or color. There are three types of selections:

Geometric selections The Rectangular Marquee tool (▭) selects a rectangular area in an image. The Elliptical Marquee tool (◯), which is hidden behind the Rectangular Marquee tool, selects elliptical areas. The Single Row Marquee tool (⇔) and Single Column Marquee tool (⇕) select either a 1-pixel-high row or a 1-pixel-wide column, respectively.

Freehand selections Drag the Lasso tool (⌿) around an area to trace a freehand selection. Using the Polygonal Lasso tool (⌿), click to set anchor points in straight-line segments around an area. The Magnetic Lasso tool (⌿) works something like a combination of the other two lasso tools, and works best when good contrast exists between the area you want to select and its surroundings.

Color-based selections The Magic Wand tool (⌿) selects parts of an image based on the similarity in color of adjacent pixels. It is useful for selecting odd-shaped areas that share a specific range of colors. The Quick Selection tool (⌿) quickly "paints" a selection by automatically finding and following defined edges in the image.

Getting started

You'll start the lesson by viewing the finished lesson file and looking at the image you will create as you explore the selection tools in Photoshop.

1 Start Adobe Photoshop and then immediately hold down Ctrl+Alt+Shift (Windows) or Command+Option+Shift (Mac OS) to restore the default preferences. (See "Restoring default preferences" on page 6.)

2 When prompted, click Yes to confirm that you want to reset preferences, and Close to close the Welcome Screen.

3 Click the Go To Bridge button (⌿) in the tool options bar to open Adobe Bridge.

4 In the upper left corner of Bridge, click the Folder tab to display its contents. Click the Lessons folder, and then double-click the Lesson04 folder in the preview area to see its contents.

5 Select the 04End.psd file and study it in the Preview palette.

The project is a collage of objects, including a lettuce head, tomato, carrot, pepper, olives, cutting board, and "Salads" logo. The challenge in this lesson is to arrange these elements, each of which is part of a multi-image scan. The ideal composition is a judgment call, so this lesson won't describe precise locations. There are no right or wrong placements of the objects.

6 Double-click the 04Start.psd thumbnail to open the image file in Photoshop.

7 Choose File > Save As, rename the file **04Working.psd**, and click Save. By saving another version of the start file, you don't have to worry about overwriting the original.

Selecting with the Magic Wand tool

The Magic Wand tool is one of the easiest ways to make a selection. You simply click a particular colored point in the image to select areas of that color. This method is most successful for selecting an area of closely similar colors that is surrounded by areas of different color. After you make the initial selection, you can add or subtract areas by using specific keyboard combinations with the Magic Wand tool.

The Tolerance option sets the sensitivity of the Magic Wand tool. This limits or extends the range of pixel similarity, so 32—the default tolerance—selects the color you click plus 32 lighter and 32 darker tones of that color. The ideal tolerance level depends on the color ranges and variations in the image.

Using the Magic Wand tool to select a colored area

The tomato in the 04Start.psd file (which should be open now) is a good candidate for using the Magic Wand tool because the image is made up of mainly of flat solid colors (red and green). For the collage you're creating in this lesson, you'll select and move just the tomato, not the shadow or background behind it.

1 Select the Magic Wand tool (✦), hidden under the Quick Selection tool.

2 In the tool options bar, scrub the Tolerance label or type **100** in the Tolerance text box to increase the number of similar tones that will be selected.

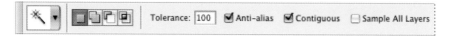

3 Using the Magic Wand, click the red part of the tomato. Most of it will be selected.

4 To select the remaining area of the tomato, hold down Shift so that a plus sign appears with the Magic Wand pointer. This indicates that whatever you click will be added to the current selection. Then, click one of the unselected areas of the tomato—the green stem.

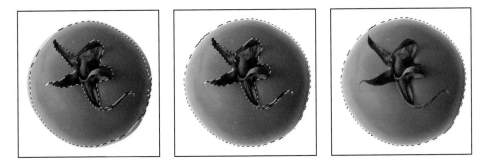

Note: When you use other selection tools, such as a marquee tool or a lasso tool, you can also use the Shift key to add to a selection. When you select the head of lettuce in the next exercise, you'll learn how to subtract from a selection.

5 Continue adding to the selection until the entire tomato is selected. If you accidentally select an area outside the tomato, choose Edit > Undo, and try again.

Leave the selection active so that you can use it in the next exercise.

Moving a selected area

Once you've selected an area of an image, any changes you make apply exclusively to the pixels within the selection marquee. The rest of the image is not affected by those changes.

To move the selected image area to another part of the composition, you use the Move tool. On a single-layer image like this one, the moved pixels replace the pixels beneath them. This change is not permanent until you deselect the moved pixels, so you can try different locations for the moved selection before you make a commitment.

1 If the tomato is not still selected, repeat the previous exercise to select it.

2 Select the Move tool (⤴). Notice that the tomato remains selected.

3 Drag the selected area (the tomato) to the lower left area of the collage so that a little less than half of the tomato overlaps the lower left edge of the cutting board.

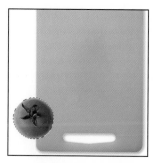

4 Choose Select > Deselect, and then choose File > Save.

In Photoshop, it's not easy to accidentally deselect. Unless a selection tool is active, stray clicks in the image will not deselect the active area. To deliberately deselect, you can use one of three methods: You can choose Select > Deselect, you can press Ctrl+D (Windows) or Command+D (Mac OS), or you can click outside the selection with one of the selection tools to start a different selection.

Using the Magic Wand with other selection tools

If a multicolored area that you want to select is set against a differently colored background, it can be much easier to select the background than the area itself. In this procedure, you'll try out this neat little technique.

1 Select the Rectangular Marquee tool (▭).

2 Drag a selection around the lettuce. Make sure that your selection marquee is set back from the edges of the head of lettuce so that a margin of white appears between the lettuce leaves and the edges of the marquee.

At this point, the lettuce and the white background area are selected. You'll subtract the white area from the selection so that only the lettuce remains in the selection.

3 Select the Magic Wand tool; then in the tool options bar, set the Tolerance to **32** to reduce the range of colors the wand will select.

4 Hold down Alt (Windows) or Option (Mac OS) so that a minus sign appears with the Magic Wand pointer, and then click in the white background area within the selection marquee.

Now all the white pixels are deselected, leaving the lettuce perfectly selected.

5 Select the Move tool (✣) and drag the lettuce to the upper left corner of the cutting board, placing it so that about a quarter of the lettuce overlaps the edge of the cutting board.

6 Choose Select > Deselect, and then save your work.

Julieanne Kost is an official Adobe Photoshop evangelist.

TOOL TIPS FROM THE PHOTOSHOP EVANGELIST

Move tool tips

If you're moving objects in a multilayer file with the Move tool (V) and you suddenly need to select one of the layers, try this: With the Move tool selected, move the pointer over any area of an image and right-click (Windows) or Control-click (Mac OS). The layers that are under the pointer appear in the context menu. Choose the one you'd like to make active.

Working with oval and circular selections

You've already had experience with the Rectangular Marquee tool, which you used to select the area surrounding the lettuce image. Now you'll use a different marquee tool.

The best part about this section is the introduction of more keyboard shortcuts that can save you time and arm motions. The repositioning techniques that you'll try here work equally well with the other marquee shapes.

Repositioning a selection marquee while creating it

Selecting ovals and circles can be tricky. It's not always obvious where you should start dragging, so sometimes the selection will be off-center, or the ratio of width to height won't match what you need. In this exercise, you'll try out techniques for managing those problems, including two important keyboard-mouse combinations that can make your Photoshop work much easier.

As you do this exercise, be very careful to follow the directions about keeping the mouse button or specific keyboard keys pressed. If you accidentally release the mouse button at the wrong time, simply start the exercise again from Step 1.

1 Select the Zoom tool (🔍), and click the bowl of olives on the lower right side of the image window to zoom in to at least 100% view (use 200% view if the entire bowl of olives will fit in the image window on your screen).

2 Select the Elliptical Marquee tool (○) hidden under the Rectangular Marquee tool.

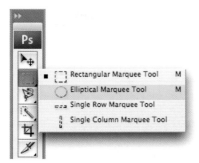

3 Move the pointer over the olive bowl, and drag diagonally across the oval bowl to create a selection, but *do not release the mouse button*. It's OK if your selection does not match the bowl shape yet.

If you accidently release the mouse button, draw the selection again. In most cases—including this one—the new selection replaces the previous one.

4 Still holding down the mouse button, press the spacebar and continue to drag the selection. The border moves as you drag.

5 Carefully release the spacebar (but not the mouse button) and continue to drag, trying to make the size and shape of the selection match the oval olive bowl as closely as possible. If necessary, hold down the spacebar again and drag to move the selection marquee into position around the olive bowl.

Note: You do not have to include absolutely all of the olive bowl, but make sure that the shape of your selection has the same proportions as the oval bowl and that the olives fit comfortably within the selection. As long as they look as if they are contained within the bowl, you're fine.

6   When the selection border is sized and positioned correctly, release the mouse button.

7   Choose View > Zoom Out or use the slider in the Navigator palette to reduce the zoom view so that you can see all of the objects in the image window.

Leave the Elliptical Marquee tool (◯) and the selection active for the next exercise.

Moving selected pixels with a keyboard shortcut

Now, you will move the olive bowl onto the cutting board using a keyboard shortcut. The shortcut allows you to temporarily access the Move tool instead of selecting it from the toolbox.

1   If the olive bowl is not still selected, repeat the previous exercise to select it.

Leave the Elliptical Marquee tool (◯) selected in the toolbox.

2   Hold down Ctrl (Windows) or Command (Mac OS), and move the Elliptical Marquee tool pointer within the selection. The pointer icon now includes a pair of scissors (✂) to indicate that the selection will be cut from its current location.

Note: When you use the Ctrl (Windows) or Command (Mac OS) keyboard shortcut to temporarily switch to the Move tool, you can release the keyboard key after you start to drag. The Move tool remains active even after you release the mouse button. Photoshop reverts to the previously selected tool when you deselect, either by clicking outside the selection or using the Deselect command.

3 Drag the oval bowl onto the cutting board so that half of the bowl overlaps the lower right edge of the cutting board. (You'll use another technique to nudge the oval bowl into the exact position in a minute.) Release the mouse button but do not deselect the olive bowl.

Moving with the arrow keys

You can make minor adjustments to the position of selected pixels using the arrow keys to nudge the olive bowl in increments of either 1 pixel or 10 pixels.

When a selection tool is active in the toolbox, the arrow keys nudge the selection border, but not the contents. When the Move tool is active, the arrow keys move the selection border and its contents.

Before you begin, make sure that the purple olive bowl is still selected in the image window.

1 In the toolbox, select the Move tool (⊹) and press the Up Arrow key (⬆) on your keyboard a few times to move the oval upward.

Notice that each time you press the arrow key, the olive bowl moves 1 pixel. Experiment by pressing the other arrow keys to see how they affect the selection.

2 Hold down Shift, and press an arrow key.

Notice that the selection now moves in a 10-pixel increment.

Sometimes the border around a selected area can distract you as you make adjustments. You can hide the edges of a selection temporarily without actually deselecting and then display the selection border once you've completed the adjustments.

3 Choose View > Show > Selection Edges or View > Extras.

Either command makes the selection border around the olive bowl disappear.

4 Use the arrow keys to nudge the olive bowl until it is positioned where you want it. Then choose View > Show > Selection Edges to toggle visibility of the selection border back on.

5 Choose Select > Deselect, or press Ctrl+D (Windows) or Command+D (Mac OS).

6 Choose File > Save to save your work so far.

Selecting from a center point

In some cases it's easier to make elliptical or rectangular selections by drawing a selection from the center point. You'll use this technique to select the salad graphic.

1 If necessary, scroll to the lower center area of the image where the salad graphic appears.

2 Select the Zoom tool (🔍) and click the salad graphic as needed to increase the magnification to about 300%. Make sure that you can see the entire salad graphic in your image window.

3 In the toolbox, select the Elliptical Marquee tool (○).

4 Move the pointer to the approximate center of the salad graphic.

5 Click and begin dragging. Then, without releasing the mouse button, hold down Alt (Windows) or Option (Mac OS) and continue dragging the selection to the outer edge of the salad graphic.

Notice that the selection is centered over its starting point.

To ensure that your selection is a perfect circle, you can also hold down Shift as you drag. If you held down Shift while using the Rectangular Marquee tool, you would constrain the marquee shape to a perfect square.

6 When you have the entire salad graphic selected, release the mouse button first and then release Alt or Option (and the Shift key if you used it). Do not deselect, because you'll use this selection in the next topic.

7 If necessary, adjust the selection border using one of the methods you learned earlier. If you accidentally released the Alt or Option key before you released the mouse button, try selecting the salad graphic again.

Moving and changing the pixels in a selection

Now you'll move the salad graphic to the upper right corner of the cutting board. Then, you'll change the its color for a dramatic effect.

Before you begin, make sure that the salad graphic is still selected. If it is not, reselect it by completing the previous exercise.

1 Choose View > Fit On Screen to adjust the magnification so that the entire image fits within the image window.

2 In the toolbox, select the Move tool (⤧).

3 Position the pointer within the salad graphic selection. The pointer becomes an arrow with a pair of scissors (⤧), which indicates that dragging the selection will cut it from its current location and move it to the new location.

4 Drag the salad graphic over the cutting board to the left of the right upper corner. If you want to adjust the position after you stop dragging, simply start dragging again. The salad graphic remains selected throughout the process.

5 Choose Image > Adjustments > Invert.

The colors making up the salad graphic are inverted so that now it is effectively a color negative of itself.

6 Leaving the salad graphic selected, choose File > Save to save your work.

Moving and duplicating simultaneously

Next, you'll simultaneously move and duplicate a selection. If your salad graphic image is no longer selected, reselect it now, using the techniques you learned earlier.

1 With the Move tool (⯬) selected, hold down Alt (Windows) or Option (Mac OS) as you position the pointer inside the salad graphic selection. The pointer becomes a double arrow, which indicates that a duplicate will be made when you move the selection.

2 Continue holding down Alt or Option, and drag a duplicate of the salad graphic down and to the right, so that it is near the upper right corner of the cutting board. You can allow the duplicate salad graphic to partially overlap the original one. Release the mouse button and the Alt or Option key, but do not deselect the duplicate salad graphic.

3 Choose Edit > Transform > Scale. A bounding box appears around the selection.

4 Hold down Shift and drag one of the corner points to enlarge the salad graphic so that it becomes about 50% larger than the original. Then, press Enter or Return to commit the change and remove the transformation bounding box.

Notice that the selection marquee also resizes, and that the resized, copied salad graphic remains selected. The Shift key constrains the proportions so that the enlarged salad graphic is not distorted.

5 Hold down Shift+Alt (Windows) or Shift+Option (Mac OS), and drag a new copy of the second salad graphic down and to the right.

Holding down Shift when you move a selection constrains the movement horizontally or vertically in 45-degree increments.

6 Repeat Steps 3 and 4 for the third salad graphic, making it about twice the size of the first one.

Shortcut: Choose Edit > Transform > Again to duplicate the salad logo and enlarge it by twice as much as the last transformation.

7 When you are satisfied with the size and position of the third salad graphic, press Enter or Return to confirm the scale, choose Select > Deselect, and then choose File > Save.

For information on working with the center point in a transformation, see "Set or move the reference point for a transformation" in Photoshop Help.

Copying selections or layers

You can use the Move tool to copy selections as you drag them within or between images, or you can copy and move selections using the Copy, Copy Merged, Cut, and Paste commands. Dragging with the Move tool saves memory because the clipboard is not used as it is with the Copy, Copy Merged, Cut, and Paste commands.

Photoshop has several copy and paste commands:

- Copy copies the selected area on the active layer.

- Copy Merged makes a merged copy of all the visible layers in the selected area.

- Paste pastes a cut or copied selection into another part of the image or into another image as a new layer.

- Paste Into pastes a cut or copied selection inside another selection in the same or a different image. The source selection is pasted onto a new layer, and the destination selection border is converted into a layer mask.

Keep in mind that when a selection or layer is pasted between images with different resolutions, the pasted data retains its pixel dimensions. This can make the pasted portion appear out of proportion to the new image. Use the Image Size command to make the source and destination images the same resolution before copying and pasting.

Selecting with the lasso tools

You can use the lasso tools to make selections that require both freehand and straight lines. You'll select the carrot for the collage using the lasso tools in this way. It takes a bit of practice to use the lasso tools to alternate between straight-line and freehand selections—if you make a mistake while you're selecting the carrot, simply deselect and start again.

1 Select the Zoom tool (⬥), and click the carrot as needed until the view enlarges to 100%. Make sure that you can see the entire carrot in the window.

2 Select the Lasso tool (⬥). Starting at the lower left of the image, drag around the rounded end of the carrot, tracing the shape as accurately as possible. *Do not release the mouse button.*

3 Hold down Alt (Windows) or Option (Mac OS), and then release the mouse button so that the lasso pointer changes to the polygonal lasso shape (▷). *Do not release the Alt or Option key.*

4 Begin clicking along the end of the carrot to place anchor points, following the contours of the carrot. Be sure to keep the Alt or Option key held down throughout this process.

The selection border automatically stretches like a rubber band between anchor points.

5 When you reach the tip of the carrot, keep the mouse button held down and then release the Alt or Option key. The pointer again appears as the lasso icon.

6 Carefully drag around the tip of the carrot, keeping the mouse button down.

7 When you finish tracing the tip of the carrot and reach the lower side of the carrot, first hold down Alt or Option again, and then release the mouse button and start clicking along the lower side of the carrot. Continue to trace the carrot until you arrive back at the starting point of your selection near the left end of the image.

8 Make sure that the click with the mouse crosses the start of the selection, and then release Alt or Option. The carrot is now entirely selected. Leave the carrot selected for the next exercise.

Rotating a selection

So far, you've moved selected images and inverted the color of a selected area. But you can do many more things with a selection. In this exercise, you'll see how easy it is to rotate a selected object.

Before you begin, make sure that the carrot is still selected.

1 Choose View > Fit On Screen to resize the image window to fit on your screen.

2 Hold down Ctrl (Windows) or Command (Mac OS), and drag the carrot selection to the lower section of the cutting board.

3 Choose Edit > Transform > Rotate. The carrot and selection marquee are enclosed in a bounding box and the pointer appears as a curved double-headed arrow (↻).

4 Move the pointer outside the bounding box and drag to rotate the carrot to a 45 degree angle. Then, press Enter or Return to commit the transformation changes.

5 If necessary, select the Move tool (▶✛) and drag to reposition the carrot. When you're satisfied, choose Select > Deselect.

6 Choose File > Save.

Selecting with the Magnetic Lasso tool

You can use the Magnetic Lasso tool to make freehand selections of areas with high-contrast edges. When you draw with the Magnetic Lasso tool, the border automatically snaps to the borders between areas of contrast. You can also control the selection path by occasionally clicking the mouse to place anchor points in the selection border.

You'll now move the yellow pepper to the center of the cutting board, using the Magnetic Lasso tool to select the yellow pepper.

1 Select the Zoom tool (🔍), and click the yellow pepper to zoom in to a 300% view.

2 Select the Magnetic Lasso tool (⌇), hidden under the Lasso tool (⌀).

3 Click once along the left edge of the yellow pepper, and begin tracing the outline of the yellow pepper by moving the magnetic lasso pointer around the outline of the yellow pepper, staying fairly close to the edge of the yellow pepper as you move.

Even though you're not holding down the mouse button, the tool snaps to the edge of the yellow pepper and automatically adds fastening points.

If you think that the tool is not following the edge closely enough (such as in low-contrast areas), you can place your own fastening points in the border by clicking the mouse button. You can add as many fastening points as seem necessary. You can also remove the most recent fastening points by pressing Delete for each anchor point you want to remove. Then, move the mouse back to the last remaining fastening point and continue selecting.

4 When you reach the left side of the yellow pepper again, double-click the mouse button to make the Magnetic Lasso tool return to the starting point, closing the selection. Or, move the Magnetic Lasso over the starting point and click once.

5 Double-click the Hand tool (🖐) to fit the image on-screen.

6 Select the Move tool ( ), and drag the yellow pepper to the middle of the cutting board.

7 Choose Select > Deselect, and then choose File > Save.

Softening the edges of a selection

You can smooth the hard edges of a selection by anti-aliasing and by feathering.

Anti-aliasing smooths the jagged edges of a selection by softening the color transition between edge pixels and background pixels. Since only the edge pixels change, no detail is lost. Anti-aliasing is useful when cutting, copying, and pasting selections to create composite images.

Anti-aliasing is available for the Lasso, Polygonal Lasso, Magnetic Lasso, Elliptical Marquee, and Magic Wand tools. (Select the tool to display its tool options bar.) You must specify the anti-aliasing option before using these tools. Once a selection is made, you cannot add anti-aliasing.

Feathering blurs edges by building a transition boundary between the selection and its surrounding pixels. This blurring can cause some loss of detail at the edge of the selection.

You can define feathering for the marquee and lasso tools as you use them, or you can add feathering to an existing selection. Feathering effects become apparent when you move, cut, or copy the selection.

• To use anti-aliasing, select a lasso tool, or the Elliptical Marquee or Magic Wand tool, and select Anti-alias in the tool options bar.

• To define a feathered edge for a selection tool, select any of the lasso or marquee tools. Enter a Feather value in the tool options bar. This value defines the width of the feathered edge and can range from 1 to 250 pixels.

• To define a feathered edge for an existing selection, choose Select > Feather. Enter a value for the Feather Radius, and click OK.

Cropping an image and erasing within a selection

Now that your composition is in place, you'll crop the image to a final size and clean up some of the background scraps left behind when you moved selections. You can use either the Crop tool or the Crop command to crop an image.

1 Select the Crop tool (⊟), or press C to switch from the current tool to the Crop tool. Then, drag diagonally across the collage composition to prepare for cropping.

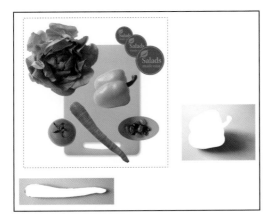

2 Adjust the crop area, as necessary:

• To reposition the crop border, position the pointer inside the cropping area and drag.

• To resize the crop area, drag a handle.

3 When you are satisfied with the position of the crop area, press Enter or Return to crop the image.

The cropped image may include some scraps of the gray background from which you selected and removed shapes. You'll fix that next.

4 Use a marquee selection tool or the Lasso tool (👄) to drag a selection marquee around a scrap of unwanted gray background. Be careful not to include any of the image that you want to keep.

5 In the toolbox, select the Eraser tool (⟋), and then make sure that the foreground and background color swatches in the toolbox are set to the defaults: black in the foreground and white in the background

Continue selecting and erasing or deleting until you finish removing all the unwanted scraps of background. When you finish, choose File > Save to save your work.

Making a quick selection

Before you finalize the composition, you'll use the Quick Selection tool to correct the color of the carrot. The Quick Selection tool lets you quickly "paint" a selection using a round brush tip of adjustable size.

1 Select the Quick Selection tool (🖌) in the toolbox.

2 In the tool options bar, click the Brushes tab in the palette well to temporarily open the Brushes palette. Set the Brush Size diameter to 21. Select the Sample All Layers option to sample from all visible layers, not just the selected one.

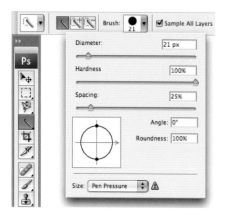

3 Position the pointer at the top of the carrot, and drag along the center of the carrot to the lower tip. As you drag, the selection expands and automatically finds and fills the defined edges of the carrot.

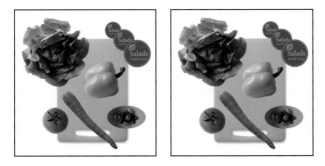

You'll save your selection by copying and pasting it onto a new layer.

4 Choose Edit > Copy and Edit > Paste. In the Layers palette, a new layer appears on top of the Background, labeled Layer 1. Double-click Layer 1 and rename the layer **Carrot**.

Next, you'll adjust the color of the carrot so that it's more orange than red.

5   Choose Image > Adjustments > Hue/Saturation. In the Hue/Saturation dialog box, slightly increase the hue and saturation. (We used +5 for Hue and +10 for Saturation).

Watch the Quick Selection QuickTime movie for a quick overview of the tool. The movie is located on the Adobe Photoshop CS3 Classroom in a Book *CD in Movies/ Quick Selection.mov. Double-click the movie file to open it; then click the Play button.*

You'll continue to organize your composition by saving selections of its individual elements. That way, your selections remain intact and easily available for editing. Now you'll save a selection of the lettuce head. The lettuce has more complicated edges than the other elements in this composition. You'll select it and then fine-tune the selection edges.

6   In the Layers palette, select the Background layer.

7 With the Quick Selection tool still selected, drag across the lettuce to select it. Because the lettuce head has several areas of different transitions, not all of the lettuce is selected.

8 In the tool options bar, click the Add To Selection button ( ).

Click near the edges of a shape to expand the selection to follow the contours of the shape edge.

9 When it appears that all of the lettuce head is selected, click Refine Edges in the tool options bar.

The Refine Edges dialog box appears with options to improve the selection edges by softening, feathering, or expanding them, or increasing their contrast. You can also view the selection edges as if masked or against various mattes, or backgrounds.

10 To create a soft edge for the shadow, enter a Feather value of **7** pixels. Set the Expand value to 5%.

By expanding the selection, the shadow you add in the next exercise will be visible outside of the edges of the object.

11 Select the Zoom tool in the dialog box, and then drag a marquee around the lettuce head to zoom in on its edges. You'll preview the shadow that you'll add to the lettuce against one of the mattes.

12 Click the center Black Matte button at the bottom of the dialog box. A black background appears under the selection and the selection edges disappear. If you'd like, try out the other preview options.

13 Increase the Expand value to add more of a shadow around the lettuce edges. We used a value of 30%.

14 When you're satisfied with the adjustments, click OK.

You've gone to a lot of work to make and refine your selection. So that you don't lose it, you'll save it. You'll learn other ways to save selections in Lesson 6, "Masks and Channels."

15 Choose Edit > Copy and Edit > Paste to paste the selection on a new layer. In the Layers palette, double-click this new layer and rename it **Lettuce**.

Watch the Refine Edges QuickTime movie for a quick overview of the feature. The movie is located on the Adobe Photoshop CS3 Classroom in a Book *CD in Movies/ Refine Edge.mov. Double-click the movie file to open it; then click the Play button.*

Isolating and saving selections

Now you'll select the remaining elements and save their selections. If you want to return to these selections in the future, it will be easy to do so.

1   In the Layers palette, select the Background layer. In the image, use the Quick Selection tool to select the yellow pepper, dragging carefully within its green stem.

You can use keyboard shortcuts to add to or subtract from a Quick Selection. Hold down Alt (Windows) or Option (Mac OS) as you "paint" with the tool to subtract from the selection; hold down Alt/Option and Shift to add to the selection.

2   Choose Edit > Copy and Edit > Paste to paste a copy of the pepper onto a new layer. In the Layers palette, double-click the layer name and rename it **Yellow Pepper**.

3 Repeat Steps 1 and 2 for the bowl of olives, tomato, and Salads logo: naming their new layers as **Olives**, **Tomato**, and **Logo**, respectively.

4 Choose File > Save.

It's good to save your selections on discrete layers—especially when you've spent time and effort creating them—so that you can easily retrieve them.

Creating a soft drop shadow

To complete your composition, you'll add a drop shadow behind the vegetables and logo. Adding the drop shadow is a simple matter of adding a layer effect.

1 In the Layers palette, select the Carrot layer.

2 At the bottom of the Layers palette, click the Add Layer Style button (fx), and from the pop-up menu, choose Drop Shadow.

3 In the Layer Styles dialog box, adjust the shadow settings to add a soft shadow. We used these values: Blend mode: Normal, Opacity: 75%, Angle: 30, Distance: 6 px, Spread 3%, Size: 15 px. Then click OK.

The carrot now has a soft drop shadow.

To replicate this shadow for the rest of the vegetables and the Salads logo, you'll simply copy the effect to their layers.

4 In the Layers palette, position the pointer on the Drop Shadow layer effect beneath the Carrot thumbnail (the pointer turns into a pointing hand).

5 Hold down Alt (Windows) or Option (Mac OS), and drag the effect down to the Lettuce layer to copy it.

Voila! You've copied the drop shadow.

6 Repeat Step 5, Alt-dragging (Windows) or Option-dragging (Mac OS) the Drop Shadow effect onto the Lettuce layer. Repeat for the remaining layers.

Note: To remove a layer effect, simply drag the effect icon to the Trash button at the bottom of the Layers palette.

7 Choose File > Save to save your work.

Good job! The collage is complete.

To quickly create multiple images from one scan, use the Crop And Straighten Photos command. Images with a clearly delineated outline and a uniform background—such as the 04Start.psd file—work best. Try it by opening the 04Start.psd file in the Lesson04 folder, and choosing File > Automate > Crop And Straighten Photos. Photoshop automatically crops each image in the start file and creates individual Photoshop files for each. Once you've tried this, simply close each file without saving.

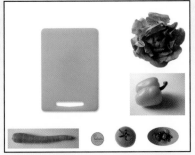

Original image

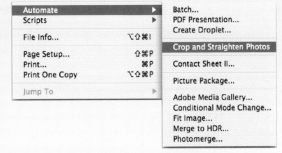

Choose File > Automate > Crop And Straighten Photos

Result

Review

▶ **Review questions**

1 Once you've made a selection, what area of the image can be edited?

2 How do you add to and subtract from a selection?

3 How can you move a selection while you're drawing it?

4 When drawing a selection with the Lasso tool, how should you finish drawing the selection to ensure that it is the shape you want?

5 How does the Magic Wand tool determine which areas of an image to select? What is tolerance, and how does it affect a selection?

6 How does the Quick Selection tool work?

▶ **Review answers**

1 Only the area within the selection can be edited.

2 To add to a selection, hold down Shift and then drag or click the active selection tool on the area you want to add to the selection. To subtract from a selection, hold down Alt (Windows) or Option (Mac OS) and drag or click the active selection tool on the area you want to remove from the selection.

3 Without releasing the mouse button, hold down the spacebar and drag to reposition the selection.

4 To make sure that the selection is the shape you want, end the selection by dragging across the starting point of the selection. If you start and stop the selection at different points, Photoshop draws a straight line between the start point of the selection and the end point of the selection.

5 The Magic Wand tool selects adjacent pixels based on their similarity in color. The Tolerance setting determines how many color tones the Magic Wand tool will select. The higher the tolerance setting, the more tones the Magic Wand selects.

6 The Quick Selection tool "paints" a selection that expands outward and automatically finds and follows defined edges in the image.

Adobe Photoshop lets you isolate different parts of an image on layers. Each layer can then be edited as discrete artwork, allowing tremendous flexibility in composing and revising an image.

5 | Layer Basics

Lesson overview

In this lesson, you'll learn how to do the following:

- Organize artwork on layers.
- Create, view, hide, and select layers.
- Rearrange layers to change the stacking order of artwork in the image.
- Apply blending modes to layers.
- Link layers to work on them simultaneously.
- Apply a gradient to a layer.
- Add text and layer effects to a layer.
- Save a copy of the file with the layers flattened.

This lesson will take about an hour to complete. If needed, remove the previous lesson folder from your hard drive, and copy the Lesson05 folder onto it. As you work on this lesson, you'll preserve the start files. If you need to restore the start files, copy them from the *Adobe Photoshop CS3 Classroom in a Book* CD.

About layers

Every Photoshop file contains one or more *layers*. New files are generally created with a *background layer,* which contains a color or an image that shows through the transparent areas of subsequent layers. All new layers in an image are transparent until you add text or artwork (pixel values).

Working with layers is analogous to placing portions of a drawing on sheets of acetate: Individual sheets of acetate may be edited, repositioned, and deleted without affecting the other sheets. When the sheets are stacked, the entire composition is visible.

Getting started

You'll start the lesson by viewing an image of the final composition.

1 Start Photoshop and then immediately hold down Ctrl+Alt+Shift (Windows) or Command+Option+Shift (Mac OS) to restore the default preferences. (See "Restoring default preferences" on page 6.)

2 When prompted, click Yes to confirm that you want to reset preferences, and Close to close the Welcome Screen.

3 Click the Go To Bridge button (▦) in the tool options bar to open Adobe Bridge.

4 In the Folders panel, click Lessons; then double-click to open the Lesson05 folder, and select the 05End.psd file to preview it.

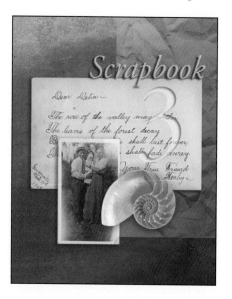

This layered composite represents the cover of a scrapbook. You will create it now, and in doing so, learn how to create, edit, and manage layers.

5 Select the 05Start.psd file and double-click it to open it in Photoshop.

6 Choose File > Save As, rename the file **05Working.psd**, and click Save. By saving another version of the start file, you don't have to worry about overwriting the original.

Using the Layers palette

The Layers palette displays all layers with the layer names and thumbnails of the images on each layer. You can use the Layers palette to hide, view, reposition, delete, rename, and merge layers. The palette thumbnails are automatically updated as you edit the layers.

1 If the Layers palette is not visible in the work area, choose Window > Layers.

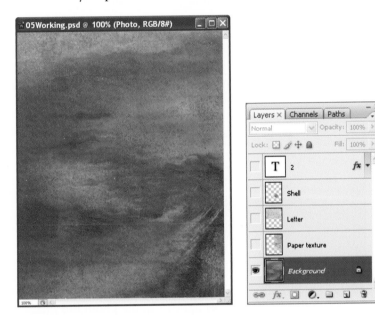

The Layers palette lists five layers for the 05Working file (from top to bottom): a type layer called 2, Shell, Letter, Paper texture, and Background.

2 Click to select the Background layer to make it active (if it is not already selected). Notice the layer thumbnail and the icons on the Background layer level:

• The lock icon (🔒) indicates that the layer is protected.

• The eye icon (👁) indicates that the layer is visible in the image window. If you click the eye, the image window no longer displays that layer.

Use the context menu to hide or resize the layer thumbnail. Right-click (Windows) or Control-click (Mac OS) on a thumbnail in the Layers palette to open the context menu, and then select No Thumbnails, Small Thumbnails, Medium Thumbnails, or Large Thumbnails.

The first task for this project is to add a sepia-toned photo to the scrapbook montage. You will retrieve it now.

3 Click the Go To Bridge button (▣) in the tool options bar, and in the Lesson05 folder, double-click the Photo.psd file to open it in Photoshop.

The Layers palette changes to display the layer information and a thumbnail for the active Photo.psd file. Notice that only one layer appears in the Photo.psd image: Layer 1, not Background. (For more information, see "About the Background layer" on the following page.)

About the Background layer

When you create a new image with a white or colored background, the bottom layer in the Layers palette is named Background. An image can have only one background. You cannot change the stacking order of a background, its blending mode, or its opacity. You can, however, convert a background to a regular layer.

When you create a new image with transparent content, the image does not have a Background layer. The bottom layer is not constrained like the Background layer; you can move it anywhere in the Layers palette, and change its opacity and blending mode.

To convert a background into a layer:

1 Double-click the name Background in the Layers palette, or choose Layer > New > Layer From Background.

2 Set layer options as desired, including renaming the layer.

3 Click OK.

To convert a layer into a background:

1 Select a layer in the Layers palette.

2 Choose Layer > New > Background From Layer.

Note: You must use this command to create a background from a regular layer; you cannot create a background simply by renaming a regular layer Background.

Renaming and copying a layer

Creating a new layer can be as simple as dragging from one file into the image window of another file. Whether you drag from the image window of the original file or from its Layers palette, only the active layer is reproduced in the destination file. Before you begin, make sure that both the 05Start.psd and Photo.psd files are open, and that the Photo.psd file is active.

First, you will give Layer 1 a more descriptive name.

1 In the Layers palette, double-click the name Layer 1, type **Photo**, and then press Enter or Return. Keep the layer selected.

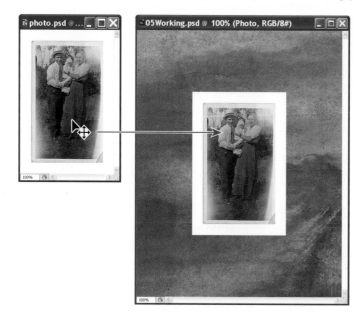

2 If necessary, drag the Photo.psd and 05Working.psd image windows so that you can see at least part of both images on-screen. Then, select the Photo.psd image so that it is the active file.

3 In the toolbox, select the Move tool (✥) and position it over the Photo.psd image window.

4 Drag the photo image and drop it into your 05Working.psd image window.

The Photo layer now appears in the 05Working.psd file image window and its Layers palette, between the Paper texture and Background layers.

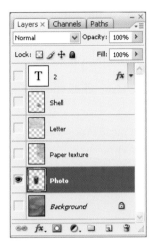

5   Close the Photo.psd file, and do not save your changes to that file.

If you hold down Shift as you drag an image from one file into another, the dragged image automatically centers itself in the target image window.

Viewing individual layers

The Layers palette shows that the 05Working.psd file now contains six layers, some of which are visible and some of which are hidden. The eye icon ( ) to the far left of a layer name in the palette indicates that that layer is visible.

1   Click the eye icon ( ) next to the Photo layer to hide the photo.

You can hide or show a layer by clicking this icon or clicking in its column—also called the Show/Hide Visibility column

2   Click again in the Show/Hide Visibility column to reveal the photo.

Selecting and removing some pixels from a layer

Notice that when you moved the photo image onto the working file, you also moved the white area around the photo. This opaque area obscures part of the blue background, because the photo layer sits on top of the blue Background layer.

Now, you'll use an eraser tool to remove the white area around the photo.

1 Make sure that the Photo layer is selected. (To select the layer, click the layer name in the Layers palette.)

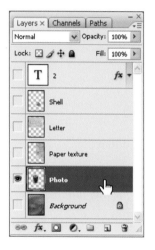

The layer is highlighted, indicating that it is active.

2 To make the opaque areas on this layer more obvious, hide all layers except the Photo layer by holding down Alt (Windows) or Option (Mac OS) and clicking the eye icon (👁) next to the Photo layer.

The blue background and other objects in the start image disappear, and the photo appears against a checkerboard backdrop. The checkerboard indicates transparent areas of the active layer.

3 Select the Magic Eraser tool (🪄), hidden under the Eraser tool (🧽).

Now you will set the tolerance for the Magic Eraser tool. If the tolerance is too low, the Magic Eraser tool leaves some white remaining around the photo. If the tolerance setting is too high, the Magic Eraser tool removes some of the photo image.

4 In the tool options bar, set the Tolerance value either by scrubbing the Tolerance label or by typing **22** in the Tolerance text box.

5 Click the white area around the photo in the image window.

The white area is replaced by the checkerboard, indicating that this area is now transparent.

6 Turn the background back on by clicking in the Show/Hide Visibility column next to its name. The blue scrapbook background now shows through where the white area on the Photo layer has become transparent.

Rearranging layers

The order in which the layers of an image are organized is called the *stacking order*. The stacking order of layers determines how the image is viewed—you can change the order to make certain parts of the image appear in front of or behind other layers.

Now, you'll rearrange layers so that the photo image is in front of another image that is currently hidden in the file.

1 Make the Shell, Letter, and Paper texture layers visible by clicking the Show/Hide Visibility column next to their layer names.

Now you can see that the photo image is partially blocked by these other images on other layers.

Note: The Photo layer is also below the 2 type layer, which is at the top of the stack, but you'll leave that layer hidden for the moment. You'll get to it later in this lesson.

2 In the Layers palette, drag the Photo layer up so that it is positioned between the Shell and Letter layers—look for a thick line between the layers in the stack—and then release the mouse button.

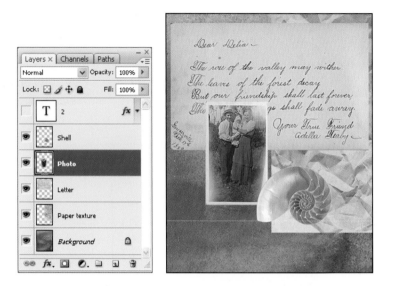

The Photo layer moves up two levels in the stacking order, and the photo image appears on top of the letter and paper texture images, but under the shell and the "2."

You can also control the stacking order of layered images by selecting them in the Layers palette and using the Layer > Arrange subcommands: Bring To Front, Bring Forward, Send To Back, and Send Backward.

Changing the opacity and mode of a layer

The opaque crinkled piece of paper blocks the blue background in the layer below it. You can reduce the opacity of any layer to let other layers show through it. You can also apply different *blending modes* to a layer, which affect how the color pixels in the opaque image blend with pixels in the layers underneath. (Currently, the blending mode is Normal.) Let's edit the Paper texture layer to let the background show through.

1 Select the Paper texture layer, and then click the arrow next to the Opacity box in the Layers palette and drag the slider to **50%**. Or, type the value into the Opacity box, or scrub the Opacity label.

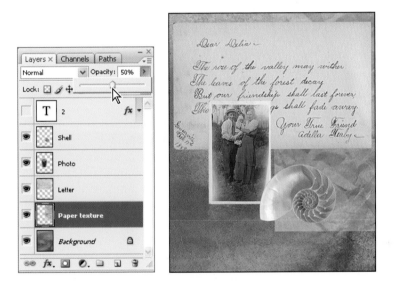

The Paper texture becomes partially transparent, and you can see the background underneath. Notice that the change in opacity affects only the image area of the Paper texture layer. The letter, photo, and shell images remain opaque.

2 To the left of the Opacity option in the Layers palette, click the Blending Mode pop-up menu to open it, and choose Luminosity.

3 Increase the Opacity to **75%**.

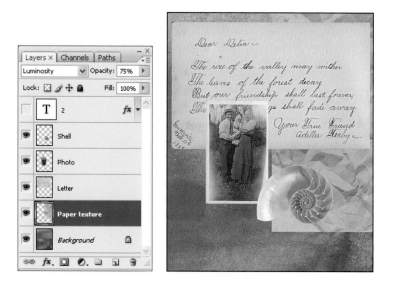

4 Choose File > Save to save your work.

For more about blending modes, including definitions and visual examples, see Photoshop Help.

Linking layers

Sometimes an efficient way to work with layers is to link two or more related layers. By linking layers together, you can move and transform them simultaneously, thereby maintaining their relative alignment.

You'll link the Photo and Letter layers, and then transform and move them as a unit.

1 Select the Photo layer in the Layers palette, and then press Shift and click to select the Letter layer.

2 Click the icon (▾≡) in the upper right of the Layers palette to display the palette menu; choose Link Layers. Or, click the Link Layers button at the bottom of the palette.

A link icon (⊜) appears next to both of the layer names in the Layers palette, indicating that they are linked.

Now, you'll resize the linked layers.

3 With the linked layers still selected in the Layers palette, choose Edit > Free Transform. A transform bounding box appears around the images in the linked layers.

4 Hold down Shift and drag a corner handle inward, scaling the photo and the letter down by about 20%.

5 Then, with the pointer inside the bounding box, drag the photo and the letter images to reposition them down and to the left in the image window so that the montage resembles the following image.

6 Press Enter or Return to apply the transformation changes.

7 Choose File > Save.

Adding a gradient layer

Next, you'll create a new layer with no artwork on it. (Adding empty layers to a file is comparable to adding blank sheets of acetate to a stack of images.) You'll use this layer to add a semitransparent gradient effect that influences the layers stacked below it.

1 In the Layers palette, select the Paper texture layer to make it active, and then click the New Layer button ( ) at the bottom of the Layers palette.

A new layer, named Layer 1, appears between the Paper texture and the Letter layer.

Note: *You can also create a new layer by choosing New Layer from the Layers palette menu or Layer > New > Layer in the Photoshop menu bar.*

2 Double-click the name Layer 1, type **Gradient**, and press Enter or Return to rename the layer.

3 In the toolbox, select the Gradient tool (▭).

4 In the tool options bar, make sure that the Linear Gradient button (▭) is selected, and then click the small downward arrow to expand the gradient picker.

5 Select the Foreground to Transparent swatch, and then click anywhere outside the gradient picker to close it.

💡 *You can list the gradient options by name rather than by sample. Just click the right-pointing palette menu button (⊙) on the gradient picker and choose either Small List or Large List. Or, hover the pointer over a thumbnail until a tooltip appears, showing the gradient name.*

6 Click the Swatches tab to bring that palette to the front of its group, and select a shade of green that appeals to you.

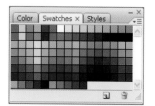

7 With the Gradient layer still active in the Layers palette, drag the Gradient tool from the lower right corner of the image to the upper left corner.

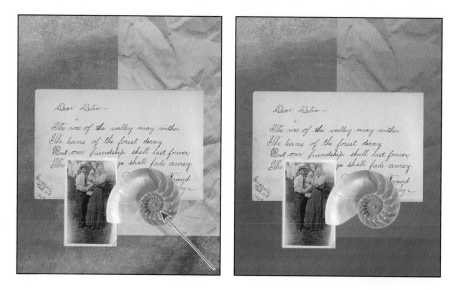

The gradient extends across the layer, starting with green on the lower right and gradually blending to transparent on the upper left. The gradient partially obscures the paper texture and background below it, so you'll change its blending mode and reduce its opacity to partially reveal those images.

8 With the Gradient layer still active, in the Layers palette choose Multiply from the Blending Mode pop-up menu and change the Opacity to **75%**; click OK. Now, the Paper texture and Background layers show through the gradient.

Adding text

Now, you're ready to create some type using the Horizontal Type tool, which places the text on its own type layer. You'll then edit the text and apply a special effect to that layer.

1 Deselect all layers in the Layers palette by clicking outside the layer names (drag to enlarge the palette to create a blank area, if necessary).

2 Set the foreground color to black by clicking the small Default Foreground and Background Colors button (▣) near the swatches in the toolbox.

3 In the toolbox, select the Horizontal Type tool (T). Then, in the tool options bar, do the following:

• Select a serif font from the Font pop-up menu (we used Adobe Garamond).

• Select a font style (we used Italic).

- Enter a large point size in the Size text box (we used **76** points), and press Enter or Return.

- Select Crisp from the Anti-aliasing pop-up menu (ªª).

- Select the Right align text (≡) option.

| T ▾ | ↓T | Adobe Garamon... ▾ | Italic ▾ | T 76 pt ▾ | ªª Crisp ▾ | ≡ ≡ ≡ | ■ | ⌐ | ▤ |

4 Click in the upper right corner of the letter area in the image window and type **Scrapbook**. Then, click the Commit Any Current Edits button (✔).

Note: If you make a mistake when you click to set the type, simply click away from the type and repeat Step 4.

The Layers palette now includes a layer named Scrapbook with a "T" thumbnail icon, indicating that it is a type layer. This layer is at the top of the layer stack.

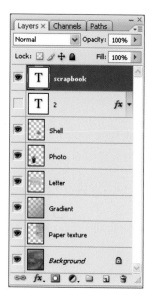

The text appears in the area of the image where you clicked, which probably isn't exactly where you want it to be positioned.

5 Select the Move tool (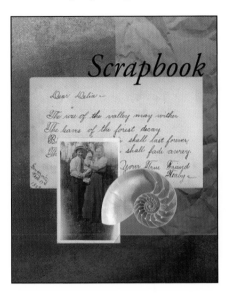), and drag the "Scrapbook" text so that the baseline aligns with the top right edge of the letter.

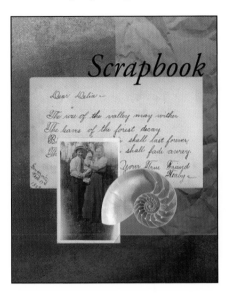

Applying a layer style

You can enhance a layer by adding a shadow, glow, bevel, emboss, or other special effects from a collection of automated and editable layer styles. These styles are easy to apply and link directly to the layer you specify.

Like layers, layer styles can be hidden by clicking eye icons (👁) in the Layers palette. Nondestructive, styles can be removed at any time. You can apply a copy of a layer style to a different layer by dragging the effect onto the destination layer.

Now, you'll make the text stand out by adding a bevel and drop shadow around the type, and coloring the text yellow.

1 With the Scrapbook type layer active, choose Layer > Layer Style > Bevel and Emboss. (The Layer Style dialog box may take a moment or two to open.)

💡 *You can also open the Layer Style dialog box by clicking the Add Layer Style button (fx) at the bottom of the Layers palette and then choosing a layer style, such as Bevel and Emboss, from the pop-up menu.*

2 In the Layer Style dialog box, make sure that the Preview option is selected, and then move the dialog box aside as needed so that you can see the Scrapbook text in the image window.

3 In the Structure area, make sure Style is Inner Bevel and Technique is Smooth. Then, set Depth at **50%**, Size to **5** pixels, and Soften to **0** pixels. Choose Up for your Direction.

4 In the left pane of the Layer Style dialog box, click the name Drop Shadow at the top of the Styles list. Photoshop automatically checks the Drop Shadow box and displays the Drop Shadow layer style options. The preview at right now includes the bevel and the default drop shadow.

5 The default Drop Shadow options are fine, so click Color Overlay in the Styles list.

6 In the Color Overlay area, click the color swatch to open the Color Picker, and then choose a shade of yellow (we used R=255, G=218, and B=47). Click OK to close the Color Picker and return to the Layer Style dialog box.

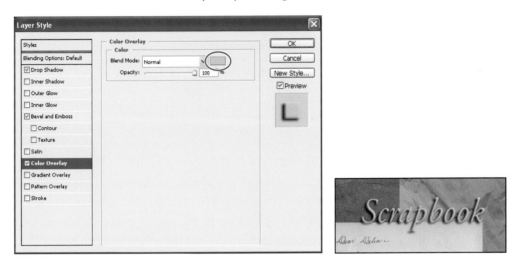

7 Examine the Scrapbook text in the image window. Then click OK to accept the settings and close the Layer Style dialog box.

8 In the Layers palette, notice the list of effects nested in the Scrapbook type layer.

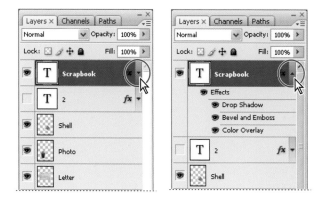

You should see four rows of information. The top row identifies them as Effects. The other three rows are the three styles that you applied to the layer: Drop Shadow, Bevel and Emboss, and Color Overlay. A visibility eye icon (👁) also appears next to each effect. You can turn off any effect by clicking its eye icon to make it disappear. Clicking this visibility box again restores both the icon and the effect. You can hide all three layer styles by clicking the eye icon for Effects.

9 Before you continue, make sure that eye icons appear for all four items nested under the Scrapbook layer.

10 To hide the layer styles listings, click the Reveal Layer Effects arrow to collapse the effects list.

Updating the layer effect

Layer effects are automatically updated when you make changes to a layer. You can edit the text and watch how the layer effect tracks the change.

1 In the Layers palette, turn on visibility for the 2 type layer and select it to make it active.

2 In the toolbox, make sure that the Horizontal Type tool (T) is still selected, but do not click in the image window yet.

3 In the tool options bar, set the font size to **225** points and press Enter or Return.

Although you didn't select the text by dragging the Type tool (as you would have to do in a word-processing program), the "2" now appears in 225-point type.

4 Using the Horizontal Type tool, select the "2" and change it to **3**.

Notice that the text formatting and layer styles remain applied.

5 Select the Move tool ( ) and drag the "3" to center it vertically between the "Scrapbook" text and the shell object.

Note: You don't have to click the Commit Any Current Edits button after typing 3, because choosing the Move tool has the same effect.

6 Choose File > Save.

Adding depth with a drop shadow

The scrapbook cover is almost done; the elements are arranged correctly in the composition. You'll finish up by adding a bit of depth to the Letter, Photo, and Shell layers using simple drop shadow effects.

1 Select the Letter layer in the Layers palette, click the Add Layer Style button (*fx*) at the bottom of the palette, and choose Drop Shadow from the pop-up menu.

2 In the Drop Shadow pane of the Layer Styles dialog box, set the Opacity to **50%**, Distance to **5** pixels, Spread to **5%**, and Size to **10** pixels. Then click OK to close the dialog box and apply the effect.

Instead of creating another drop shadow for the photo and shell images from scratch, we'll copy this one.

3 Press Alt (Windows) or Option (Mac OS) and drag the Drop Shadow layer style icon (◉) from the Letter layer onto the Photo layer.

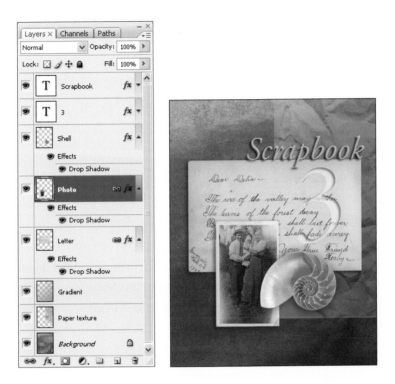

4 Repeat Step 3 to add a drop shadow to the Shell layer.

5 As a last step, to give just a bit more depth below the Shell layer, double-click its layer style icon to open the Layer Styles dialog box. Select Drop Shadow from the Styles list and change the Size to **25** pixels. Click OK to accept the change and close the dialog box.

Your final image and Layers palette should resemble the figure above.

Flattening and saving files

When you finish editing all the layers in your image, you can merge or flatten layers to reduce the file size. Flattening combines all the layers into a single background. However, you shouldn't flatten an image until you are certain that you're satisfied with all your design decisions. Rather than flattening your original PSD files, it's a good idea to save a copy of the file with its layers intact, in case you need to edit a layer later.

To appreciate what flattening does, notice the two numbers for the file size in the status bar at the bottom of the image window.

Note: Click the status bar pop-up menu arrow and choose Show > Document Sizes if the sizes do not appear in the status bar.

| 100% | | Doc: 918.5K/7.87M | ▶ |

The first number represents what the file size would be if you flattened the image. The second number represents the file size without flattening. This lesson file, if flattened, would be about 918.5 KB, but the current file is actually much larger—about 8.78 MB. So flattening is well worth it in this case.

1 If the Type tool (T) is currently selected in the toolbox, select any other tool, to be sure that you're no longer in text-editing mode. Then choose File > Save (if it is available) to be sure that all your changes have been saved in the file.

2 Choose Image > Duplicate.

3 In the Duplicate Image dialog box, name the file **05Flat.psd** and click OK.

4 Leave the 05Flat.psd file open, but close the 05Working.psd file.

5 Choose Flatten Image from the Layers palette menu.

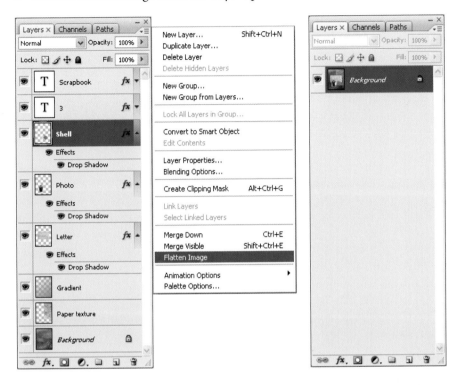

6 Choose File > Save. Even though you chose Save rather than Save As, the Save As dialog box appears.

7 Make sure that the location is the Lessons/Lesson05 folder, and then click Save to accept the default settings and save the flattened file.

You have saved two versions of the file: a one-layer, flattened copy as well as the original file, in which all the layers remain intact.

If you want to flatten only some of the layers in a file, click the eye icons to hide the layers you don't want to flatten, and then choose Merge Visible from the Layers palette menu.

About layer comps

Layer comps provide one-click flexibility in switching between different views of a multilayered image file. A layer comp is simply a definition of the settings in the Layers palette. Once you've defined a layer comp, you can change as many settings as you please in the Layers palette and then create another layer comp to preserve that configuration of layer properties. Then, by switching from one layer comp to another, you can quickly review the two designs. The beauty of layer comps becomes apparent when you want to demonstrate a number of possible design arrangements, for example. When you've created a few layer comps, you can review the design variations without having to tediously select and deselect eye icons or change settings in the Layers palette.

Say, for example, that you are designing a brochure, and you're producing a version in English as well as in French. You might have the French text on one layer, and the English text on another in the same image file. To create two different layer comps, you would simply turn on visibility for the French layer and turn off visibility for the English layer, and then click the Create New Layer Comp button on the Layer Comps palette. Then, you'd do the inverse—turn on visibility for the English layer and turn off visibility for the French layer, and click the create New Layer Comp button—to create an English layer comp.

To view the different layer comps, you click the Apply Layer comp box (⊞) for each comp to view them in turn. With a little imagination you can appreciate how much of a time-saver this would be for more complex variations. Layer comps can be an especially valuable feature when the design is in flux or when you need to create multiple versions of the same image file.

Congratulations! Your work on the scrapbook-cover montage is now complete. This lesson only begins to explore the vast possibilities and the flexibility you gain when you master the art of using Photoshop layers. You'll get more experience and try out different techniques for layers in almost every chapter as you progress forward in the book, and especially in Lesson 10, "Advanced Layer Techniques."

⭐EXTRA CREDIT *Take the blinking and bad poses out of an otherwise great family portrait with the Auto Align Layers feature. For an overview of this feature, watch the Auto Align QuickTime movie on the* Adobe Photoshop CS3 Classroom in a Book *CD in Movies/Auto Align.mov. Double-click the file to open it; then click the Play button.*

1 Open FamilyPhoto.PSD in your Lesson05 folder.

2 In the Layers palette, turn Layer 2 on and off to see the two similar photos. When both layers are visible, Layer 2 shows the tall man in the center blinking, and the two girls in the lower left looking away. You'll align the two photos, and then use the Eraser tool to brush out the parts of the photo on Layer 2 that you want to improve.

3 Make both layers visible, and Shift-click to select them. Choose Edit > Auto-Align Layers; click OK to accept the default Auto position. Now click the eye icon next to Layer 2 off and on to see that the layers are perfectly aligned.

Now for the fun part! You'll brush out the photo where you want to improve it.

4 Select the Eraser tool in the toolbox, and pick a soft, 45-point brush in the tool options bar. Start brushing in the center of the blinking-man's head to reveal the smiling face below. Repeat this erasing on the two girls looking away, until they look into the camera. You've created a natural family snapshot.

Review

► Review questions

1 What is the advantage of using layers?

2 When you create a new layer, where does it appear in the Layers palette stack?

3 How can you make artwork on one layer appear in front of artwork on another layer?

4 How can you manipulate multiple layers simultaneously?

5 When you've completed your artwork, what can you do to minimize the file size without changing the quality or dimensions?

► Review answers

1 Layers let you move and edit different parts of an image as discrete objects. You can also hide individual layers as you work on other layers by clicking to remove the eye icons (👁) for the layers you don't need to see.

2 The new layer always appears immediately above the active layer.

3 You can make artwork on one layer appear in front of artwork on another layer by dragging layers up or down the stacking order in the Layers palette, or by using the Layer > Arrange subcommands—Bring to Front, Bring Forward, Send to Back, and Send Backward. However, you cannot change the layer position of a Background layer.

4 You can link the layers by first selecting one of the layers in the Layers palette. Then you click the box to the left of the Layer name of the layer to which you want to link it. Once linked, both layers can be moved, rotated, and resized together.

5 You can flatten the image, which merges all the layers onto a single background. It's a good idea to duplicate image files with layers intact before you flatten them, in case you have to make changes to a layer later.

ZenGarden

Andrew Faulkner

Adobe Photoshop uses masks to isolate and manipulate specific parts of an image. A mask is like a stencil. The cutout portion of the mask can be altered, but the area surrounding the cutout is protected from change. You can create a temporary mask for one-time use, or you can save masks for repeated use.

6 Masks and Channels

Lesson overview

In this lesson, you'll learn how to do the following:

- Refine a selection using a quick mask.

- Save a selection as a channel mask.

- View a mask using the Channels palette.

- Load a saved mask.

- Apply filters, effects, and blend modes to a mask.

- Move an image within a mask.

- Create a layer mask.

- Paint in a mask to modify a selection.

- Make an intricate selection using the Extract feature.

- Create and use a gradient mask.

- Isolate a channel to make specific image corrections.

- Create a high-quality grayscale image by mixing channels.

This lesson will take about 90 minutes to complete. If needed, remove the previous lesson folder from your hard drive, and copy the Lesson06 folder onto it. As you work on this lesson, you'll preserve the start files. If you need to restore the start files, copy them from the *Adobe Photoshop CS3 Classroom in a Book* CD.

Working with masks and channels

Photoshop masks isolate and protect parts of an image, just like masking tape prevents a house painter from getting paint on the window glass or trim. When you create a mask based on a selection, the area not selected is *masked,* or protected from editing. With masks, you can create and save time-consuming selections and then use them again. In addition, you can use masks for other complex editing tasks—for example, to apply color changes or filter effects to an image.

In Adobe Photoshop, you can make temporary masks, called *quick masks,* or you can create permanent masks and store them as special grayscale channels called *alpha channels.* Photoshop also uses channels to store an image's color information and information about spot color. Unlike layers, channels do not print. You use the Channels palette to view and work with alpha channels.

A key concept in masking is that black hides, white reveals. As in life, rarely is anything black and white. So: shades of gray partially hide, depending on the gray levels (255 equals black (hidden), 0 equals white (revealed)).

Getting started

You'll start the lesson by viewing the finished image that you'll create using masks and channels.

1 Start Photoshop and then immediately hold down Ctrl+Alt+Shift (Windows) or Command+Option+Shift (Mac OS) to restore the default preferences. (See "Restoring default preferences" on page 6.)

2 When prompted, click Yes to confirm that you want to reset preferences, and Close to close the Welcome Screen.

3 Click the Go To Bridge button (▦) in the tool options bar to open Adobe Bridge.

4 Click the Folders tab on the left side of the Bridge window. Browse to the Lessons folder where you copied the *Adobe Photoshop CS3 Classroom in a Book* lesson files, and select the folder.

5 Choose File > Add To Favorites to add the Lessons folder to the Favorites panel on the left side of Bridge. If the folder already appears in Favorites panel, the menu item will read "Remove From Favorites," and you can skip this step.

Besides accessing folders and files from the Folder panel, you can add and retrieve them as favorites. You can also add favorite items from the Content panel. The Favorites panel lets you add icons for project files, folders, applications, and other assets you use frequently, to quickly locate them.

6 In the Favorites panel on the left side of Bridge, click the Lessons favorite, and then double-click the Lesson06 folder in the thumbnail preview area.

7 Select the 06End.psd file so that it appears in the center Content panel, and study its contents.

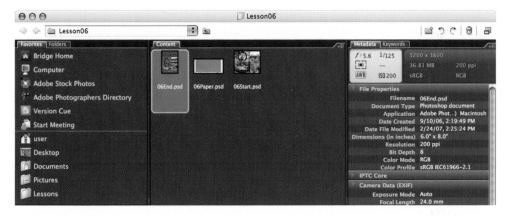

Your goal in this lesson is to create a book cover titled "Zen Garden." You will use several photos—a Buddha statue, a Japanese temple, a bamboo fence—and embossed text, and then create masks to combine the photos into one image. You'll also make intricate selections of the ripped edges of paper that will serve as the composition's background. Your final touch will be to add type to the cover that reveals the paper texture.

8 Double-click the 06Start.psd thumbnail to open it in Photoshop.

Creating a quick mask

You'll begin the lesson by using Quick Mask mode to convert a selection border into a temporary mask. Later, you will convert this temporary quick mask back into a selection border. Unless you save a quick mask as a more permanent alpha-channel mask, the temporary mask will be discarded once it is converted to a selection.

1 Choose File > Save As, rename the file as **06Working.psd**, and click Save. Click OK if a compatibility warning appears.

Saving another version of the Start file lets you return to the original if you need it.

You'll mask the Buddha statue so that you can separate it from its background and paste it in front of a new background.

2 In the Layers palette, click the Buddha layer name to select the layer.

3 Click the Quick Mask Mode button (◼) in the toolbox. (By default, you have been working in Standard mode.)

A. Standard mode
B. Change Screen mode

In Quick Mask mode, a red overlay appears as you make a selection, masking and protecting the area outside the selection the way that a rubylith, or red acetate, masked images in traditional print shops. You can apply changes only to the unprotected area that is visible and selected. Notice, too, that the selected layer in the Layers palette appears gray, indicating you are in Quick Mask mode.

4 In the toolbox, select the Brush tool (🖌).

5 In the tool options bar, make sure that the mode is Normal. Then, click the arrow to display the Brushes pop-up palette, and select a large soft brush with a diameter of 65 pixels. Click off the palette to close it.

You'll use this large brush to rough out a mask, and refine it in the next exercise.

6 In the image, drag the Brush tool to paint a mask around the halo; the brush size should match the width of the halo. A red overlay appears wherever you paint, indicating the mask you're creating.

In Quick Mask mode, Photoshop automatically defaults to Grayscale mode, with a foreground color of black, and a background color of white. When using a painting or editing tool in Quick Mask mode, keep these principles in mind:

• Painting with black adds to the mask (the red overlay) and decreases the selected area.

• Painting with white erases the mask (the red overlay) and increases the selected area.

• Painting with gray partially adds to the mask.

7 Continue painting with the Brush tool to add the Buddha statue to the mask. Don't include the background.

Don't worry if you paint outside the outline of the statue. You'll fine-tune the mask in the next exercise.

8 In the Layers palette group, click the Channels tab to bring that palette forward, or choose Window > Channels. If necessary, expand the palette by dragging its lower right corner so that you can see all of it.

In the Channels palette, the default color-information channels are listed—a full-color preview channel for the CMYK image and separate channels for cyan, magenta, yellow, and black.

Note: To hide and display individual color channels, click the eye icons (👁) in the Channels palette. When the CMYK channel is visible, eye icons also appear for all four individual channels, and vice versa. If you hide an individual channel, the eye icon for the composite (the CMYK channel) also disappears.

9 In the Channels palette, notice that this quick mask appears as a new alpha channel, named QuickMask. Remember, this channel is temporary: unless you save it as a selection, the quick mask will disappear as soon as you deselect.

Editing a quick mask

Next, you will refine the selection of the statue by adding to or erasing parts of the masked area. You'll continue to use the Brush tool to make changes to your quick mask. The advantage of editing your selection as a mask is that you can use almost any tool or filter to modify the mask. (You can even use selection tools.)

Adding to a selection by erasing masked areas

You will continue to work in Quick Mask mode. In Quick Mask mode, you do all of your editing in the image window.

1 In the tool options bar, select a smaller soft brush of 45 pixels in diameter from the Brushes pop-up menu.

You'll switch brushes several times during this lesson. For convenience, to quickly display brush choices, click the Brushes palette icon ( ) in the upper right corner of your screen to open the palette. To collapse the palette to an icon, click the double-arrow ( ) in the upper right corner of the palette.

2 Click the Switch Foreground And Background Colors button ( ) above the foreground and background color-selection boxes. To erase the mask, you paint with white.

3 Using the keyboard shortcuts, press Spacebar+Ctrl (Windows) or Spacebar+Command (Mac OS), and zoom in on the Buddha's halo.

4 Brush out any tree detail that may appear at the edge of the statue.

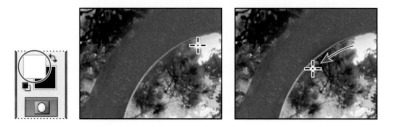

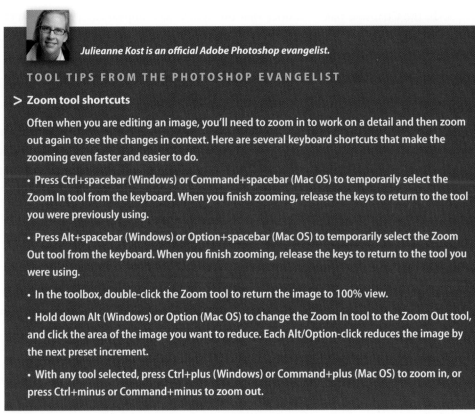

Julieanne Kost is an official Adobe Photoshop evangelist.

TOOL TIPS FROM THE PHOTOSHOP EVANGELIST

> Zoom tool shortcuts

Often when you are editing an image, you'll need to zoom in to work on a detail and then zoom out again to see the changes in context. Here are several keyboard shortcuts that make the zooming even faster and easier to do.

• Press Ctrl+spacebar (Windows) or Command+spacebar (Mac OS) to temporarily select the Zoom In tool from the keyboard. When you finish zooming, release the keys to return to the tool you were previously using.

• Press Alt+spacebar (Windows) or Option+spacebar (Mac OS) to temporarily select the Zoom Out tool from the keyboard. When you finish zooming, release the keys to return to the tool you were using.

• In the toolbox, double-click the Zoom tool to return the image to 100% view.

• Hold down Alt (Windows) or Option (Mac OS) to change the Zoom In tool to the Zoom Out tool, and click the area of the image you want to reduce. Each Alt/Option-click reduces the image by the next preset increment.

• With any tool selected, press Ctrl+plus (Windows) or Command+plus (Mac OS) to zoom in, or press Ctrl+minus or Command+minus to zoom out.

5 If you make a mistake and brush out part of the statue, click the Switch Foreground and Background Colors button (↰) above the foreground and background color-selection boxes. Then repaint any needed detail.

Shortcut: Press X to switch the foreground color to white and the background color to black, and vice versa.

6 Continue brushing along edges that are too soft or missing detail until you are satisfied with the results.

7 Click the Quick Mask Mode button (▣) in the toolbox to switch to Standard mode and see how painting in the mask alters the selected area. Notice that the selection border increases to encompass more of the statue.

💡 *For a cleaner edge, use a hard-edge, smaller brush and continue adding to and subtracting from the image until the edge is well defined. Or use the Eraser tool to remove any excess selection.*

Editing mask in Standard mode   Quick Mask selection

If any areas within the statue still appear to be selected, it means that you haven't erased all of the mask. You'll continue to refine the mask in the next steps.

Subtracting from a selection by adding masked areas

If you have erased the mask beyond the edges of the statue, part of the background will be included in the selection. You'll fix these flaws by returning to Quick Mask mode and restoring the mask to those edge areas by painting with black.

1 Click the Quick Mask Mode button (▣) to return to Quick Mask mode.

2 Press X to switch the foreground and background colors so that the black color swatch appears on top. Remember that in the image window, painting with black will add to the red overlay.

3 Choose a small, hard-edged brush, such as 9 or 13 pixels, from the Brushes pop-up palette.

4 Paint with black to restore the mask (the red overlay) to any of the background area that is still unprotected. Continue working until only the area inside the statue remains unmasked and you are completely satisfied with your mask selection.

Remember that you can zoom in and out as you work. You can also switch back and forth between Standard mode and Quick Mask mode.

Note: In Quick Mask mode, you can also use the Eraser tool to remove any excess selection.

Painting with black to restore mask

5 In the toolbox, click the Quick Mask button (⬛) to return to Standard mode and view your final statue selection.

6 Double-click the Hand tool (✋) to make the statue image fit in the window.

Saving a selection as a mask

Quick masks are temporary. They disappear as soon as you deselect. However, you can save a selection as an alpha-channel mask so that your time-consuming work won't be lost, and you can reuse the selection in this work session or a later one. You can even use alpha channels in other Photoshop image files.

To avoid confusing channels and layers, think of channels as containing an image's color and selection information; think of layers as containing painting and effects.

Note: If you save and close a file while in Quick Mask mode, the quick mask will show in its own channel the next time you open the file. If, however, you save and close your file while in Standard mode, the quick mask will be gone the next time you open your file.

1 With the (Standard mode) statue selection still active in the image window, click the Save Selection As Channel button (■) at the bottom of the Channels palette.

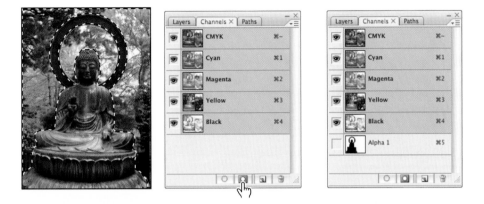

A new channel, Alpha 1, appears at the bottom of the Channels palette.

Using alpha channels

You may like to know these useful facts about alpha channels:

- An image can contain up to 56 channels, including all color and alpha channels.
- All channels are 8-bit grayscale images, capable of displaying 256 levels of gray.
- You can specify a name, color, mask option, and opacity for each channel. (The opacity affects the preview of the channel, not the image.)
- All new channels have the same dimensions and number of pixels as the original image.
- You can edit the mask in an alpha channel using the painting tools, editing tools, and filters.
- You can convert alpha channels to spot-color channels.

2 Double-click the Alpha 1 channel, type **Statue** to rename it, and press Enter or Return.

When you select the channel, Photoshop displays a black-and-white representation of the selection in the image window, and it hides all the color channels.

3 Choose Select > Deselect to deselect the statue.

4 Choose File > Save to save your work.

Masking tips and shortcuts

Here's some useful information about masks and masking.

- Masks are nondestructive, which means that you can go back and reedit the masks later without losing the pixels that they hide.

- When editing a mask, be aware of the color selected in the toolbox. Black hides, white reveals, and shades of gray partially hide or reveal. The darker the gray, the more is hidden in the mask.

- To reveal a layer's content without masking effects, turn off the mask by Shift-clicking the layer mask thumbnail or choose Layer > Layer Mask > Disable. A red X appears over the mask thumbnail in the Layers palette when the mask is disabled.

- To turn a layer mask back on, Shift-click the layer mask thumbnail with the red X in the Layers palette or choose Layer > Layer Mask > Enable. If the mask doesn't show up in the Layers palette, choose Layer > Layer Mask > Reveal All to display it.

- Unlink layers and masks to move the two independently and shift the masks' boundaries separately from the layer. To unlink a layer or group to its layer mask or vector mask, click the link icon between the thumbnails in the Layers palette. To relink them, click the blank space between the two thumbnails.

- To convert a vector mask to a layer mask, select the layer containing the vector mask you want to convert, and choose Layer > Rasterize > Vector Mask. Note, however, that once you rasterize a vector mask, you can't change it back into a vector object.

Viewing channels

You're ready to assemble a background for your book cover, using a mask to hide unwanted elements. You'll start by looking at each channel in the image, to determine which channel offers the most contrast for the mask you're about to create.

1 Drag the Layers palette by its tab to move it out of its stack and position the palette next to the Channels palette. Expand both palettes, if necessary, so that you can see all of their contents.

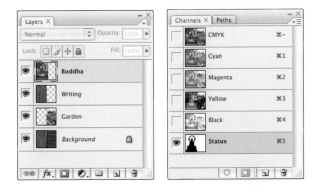

2 In the Layers palette, Alt-click (Windows) or Option-click (Mac OS) the eye icon (👁) next to the Background layer to hide all of the other layers. Select the Background layer.

3 Click the Channels palette tab to make the palette active, and then click the CMYK channel to select it.

4 In the Channels palette, click the eye icon column next to the Cyan channel. You've turned off the composite and Cyan channels, and are looking at the combination of the Magenta, Yellow, and Black channels.

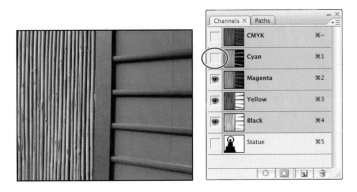

If you view a combination of channels, they appear in color, whether or not you are viewing your channels in color.

Note: You can display channels in their respective colors (red, green, and blue; or cyan, magenta, yellow, and black) by choosing Edit > Preferences > Interface (Windows) or Photoshop > Preferences > Interface (Mac OS), and then selecting the Show Channels In Color option. This can help you conceptualize how individual color channels contribute to a composite image. However, because you're working with the channel's grayscale information, to avoid distractions, leave the color view turned off.

5 Click next to the Magenta and Yellow channels to turn them off. Only the Black channel remains visible. (You can't turn off all channels in an image; at least one must remain visible.)

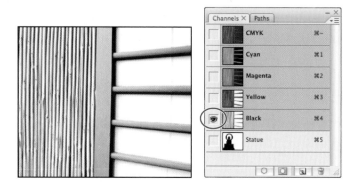

Individual channels appear in grayscale. In grayscale, you can evaluate the tonal values of the color components of the color channels, and decide which channel is the best candidate for corrections.

6 In the Channels palette, click the Yellow channel name to turn off the Black channel and turn on the Yellow channel, and then examine the contrast in the image. Repeat this step for the Magenta and Cyan channels. What you're looking for is the channel that offers the easiest selection for the blue background.

Notice that in all channels but Cyan, the panels have a vertical dark streak. The Cyan channel shows the panel background as solid black. The solid black offers the most contrast, making the Cyan channel the easiest to select.

You'll apply a levels adjustment to the channel, to make it easier to select.

Adjusting individual channels

Now that you've identified the Cyan channel as the channel with the most contrast, you'll copy it and make adjustments to the copy.

1 Make sure that only the Cyan channel is visible in the Channels palette. Drag the Cyan channel to the New Channel button (⬛) at the bottom of the Channels palette to make a copy. A channel named Cyan Copy appears in the Channels palette.

You'll isolate the black panels with a levels adjustment.

2 Choose Image > Adjustments > Levels to display the Levels dialog box. Notice the nearly flat part of the histogram: you'll isolate these values.

3 Drag the black (shadows) slider to the right to the point where the black begins to flatten out on the left side of the histogram; drag the white (highlights) slider to the left to where the black values begin to flatten out on the right side of the histogram. (We used values of 23, 1.00, and 45.) The preview shows the image as black and white. Click OK.

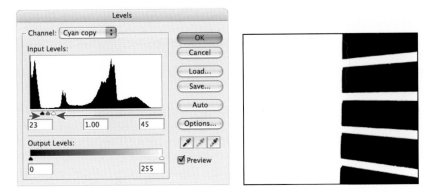

You'll name the channel to keep track of your work.

4 In the Channels palette, double-click the Cyan Copy name and rename it **Panel Mask**.

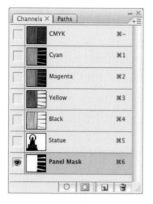

5 Choose File > Save to save your work so far.

Loading a mask as a selection

You will load the channel mask you just created as a selection, which you can then convert to a layer mask. A layer mask lets you edit the layer relative to the selection.

1 In the Layers palette, click the eye icon (👁) next to the Garden layer to make it visible, and then click the Garden layer name to select it.

2 Choose Select > Load Selection. For Channel, choose Panel Mask from the pop-up menu. Select Invert to reverse the selection to mask the panels, not the background. Click OK.

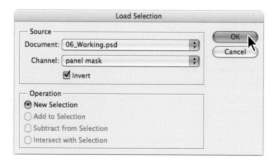

A selection marquee appears on the image.

3 With the selection active, at the bottom of the Layers palette, click the Add Layer Mask button (▣) to mask the selection.

Notice that the Channels palette displays a new channel called Garden Mask. As long as the Garden layer is selected, the Channels palette will display its mask.

4 In the Layers palette, click the Link icon (▒) between the image thumbnail and mask thumbnail to unlink the two.

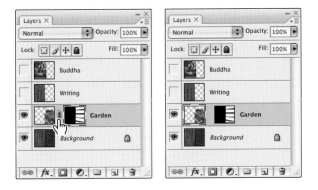

5 Click the image thumbnail to make it active.

You want to be able to reposition the temple within the mask.

6 Select the Move tool (⊕) in the toolbox. With the selection still active, drag to reposition the image within the mask, so that the peak of the temple is visible in the top panel.

7 When you are satisfied with how the image looks within the mask, in the Layers palette click the area between the image thumbnail and layer mask thumbnail to relink the two.

8 Save your work so far.

Loading a selection into an image using shortcuts

You can reuse a previously saved selection by loading it into an image. To load a saved selection using shortcuts, do one of the following in the Channels palette:

• Select the alpha channel, click the Load Channel As Selection button at the bottom of the palette, and then click the composite color channel near the top of the palette.

• Drag the channel that contains the selection you want to load onto the Load Channel As Selection button.

• Ctrl-click (Windows) or Command-click (Mac OS) the channel containing the selection you want to load.

• To add the mask to an existing selection, press Ctrl+Shift (Windows) or Command+Shift (Mac OS), and click the channel.

• To subtract the mask from an existing selection, press Ctrl+Alt (Windows) or Command+Option (Mac OS), and click the channel.

• To load the intersection of the saved selection and an existing selection, press Ctrl+Alt+Shift (Windows) or Command+Option+Shift (Mac OS), and select the channel.

Applying filters to a mask

Next, you will refine the selection of the panels by applying a filter. You worked in CMYK mode to isolate the Cyan channel. Now you'll convert the image to RGB mode to apply an RGB filter from the Filter Gallery. A limited number of filters are available in CMYK mode; Filter Gallery filters work only on RGB images.

1 In the Channels palette, make sure that the CMYK composite channel is selected.

2 Choose Image > Mode > RGB. At the alert, click Don't Flatten. The image is converted to RGB. If a compatibility alert appears, click OK.

3 Choose Filter > Filter Gallery to display the Filter Gallery dialog box.

4 In the Gallery, click the arrow to the left of the Distort folder to display its filters. Then click Glass. Set the Distortion to 2 and Smoothness to 4 to make it look like glass on a rainy day. Click OK.

Applying effects using a gradient mask

Now you'll create a gradient mask and use it to apply a filter that fades into the image.

In addition to using black to indicate what's hidden and white to indicate what's selected, you can paint with shades of gray to indicate partial transparency. For example, if you paint in a mask with a shade of gray that is at least halfway between white and black, the underlying image becomes partially (50% or more) visible.

1 In the Layers palette, click the eye icon (👁) to the left of the Writing layer to display the layer with an image of bronze lettering. Click the layer name to select the layer.

2 At the bottom of the Layers palette, click the Add Layer Mask button (▣) to add a layer mask to the Writing layer.

3 Click the Writing layer mask thumbnail to select it. A black border appears around the layer mask, indicating that it, not the image, is selected. You want to apply an effect to the mask, not the image.

4 Click the Gradient tool (▭) in the toolbox to select it. In the tool options bar at the top, make sure that the default gradient linear, and White to Black, is selected.

5 In the image window, hold down the Shift key and drag the gradient straight across from the center left side of the image to the right, where the wall meets the window. Notice that the layer mask thumbnail now displays the gradient.

This gradient will gradually reveal (where the mask is white) the filter you're about to add to the Writing image, and gradually hide the effect (where the mask is black). Gradient pixel values that decrease from 255 (black) to 0 (white) gradually reveal more of what's under the mask.

Now you will add a filter to the mask.

6 Make sure that the black border still appears around the layer mask, indicating that it, not the layer thumbnail, is selected.

7 Choose Filter > Filter Gallery. If necessary, click the left arrow button to the left of the Texture folder to expands its contents. Click Mosaic Tiles and adjust its settings. (We used Tile Size, 18; Grout Width, 4; and Lighten Grout, 1.) Click OK.

8 Choose File > Save to save your work.

Resizing the canvas

Next, you'll add canvas area to the image so that you can create a background for the cover title and byline.

1 Make sure that the background color is set to white in the toolbox. (To set it quickly, click the Default Colors button in the toolbox, and then press X to switch the colors so that the background is white.)

2 Choose Image > Canvas Size. In the Canvas Size dialog box, select Relative to add to the existing image size. Enter a Height of 2 inches. In the Anchor area, click the lower center square to add canvas centered at that spot. Click OK.

You'll perform Step 2 again to add canvas to the bottom of the image.

3 Choose Image > Canvas Size. In the Canvas Size dialog box, make sure that Relative is still selected, change the Height to 1 inch, and in the Anchor area, click the upper center square. Click OK.

Extracting the paper texture

You'll add a torn-paper background to the canvas you just created. The paper was scanned against a white background. One way to mask a delicate edge is using the Extract feature.

The Extract command provides a sophisticated way to isolate a foreground object from its background. Even objects with wispy, intricate, or undefinable edges can be clipped from their backgrounds with a minimum of effort.

1 Click the Go To Bridge button (◼) in the tool options bar to jump to Adobe Bridge, locate the 06Paper.psd image file in the Lessons/Lesson06 folder, and double-click its thumbnail preview to open it in Photoshop.

You'll start with an image that consists of only one layer. You must be working in a layer to use the Extract command. In this case, because the image has no layers—that is, it has only a background—the Extract filter will replace the Background layer with a new layer.

Note: The paper image has the same resolution as the Start file, 72 ppi. To avoid unexpected results when combining elements from multiple files, you must either use files with the same image resolution, or compensate for differing resolutions. For example, if your original image is 72 ppi and you add an element from a 144-ppi image, the additional element will appear twice as large. For information on resolutions, see "Pixel dimensions and image resolution" in Photoshop Help.

2 Choose Filter > Extract. The Extract dialog box appears with the Edge Highlighter tool (✍) selected in the upper left area of the dialog box.

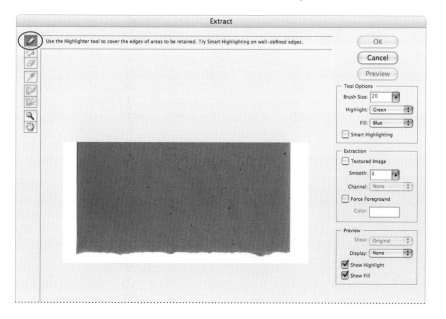

The Extract dialog box lets you highlight the edges of the object, define the object's interior, and preview the extraction. You can refine and preview the extraction as many times as you wish.

If needed, you can resize the dialog box by dragging its bottom right corner.

3 On the right side of the dialog box, locate the Brush Size option, and then type or drag the slider to 97 pixels.

4 Using the Edge Highlighter tool, brush along the white edge around the entire piece of paper, slightly overlapping the highlighter over the paper edge. The green outline should form a closed shape around the entire piece of paper.

If you make a mistake and highlight more than desired, select the Eraser tool (🖊) in the dialog box and drag over the highlight in the preview.

5 Select the Fill tool (◇), under the Edge Highlighter tool, and click inside the outlined foxtail tip to fill its interior. (You must define the object's interior before you can preview the extraction.)

The default fill color (bright blue) contrasts well with the edge highlight color (green). You can change either color if you need more contrast with the image colors using the Highlight and Fill pop-up menus in the Extract dialog box.

6 Click OK to apply the extraction. Layer 0 appears in the Layers palette, replacing the Background layer.

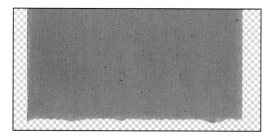

The image window displays the extracted area against the checkerboard pattern that indicates transparency.

Once you've extracted an image, you can also use the Background Eraser and History Brush tools to clean up any stray edges in the image.

7 Choose File > Save to save your work so far.

An alternative method for making intricate selections is to select areas by color. To do so, choose Select > Color Range. Then, use the eyedropper tools from the Color Range dialog box to sample the colors for your selection. You can sample from your image window or from the preview window.

Refining a selection in the Extract dialog box

To refine your selection, edit the extraction boundaries using these techniques:

• Switch between the Original and Extracted views using the Show menu.

• Click a filled area with the Fill tool to remove the fill.

• Select the Eraser tool (🖉) and drag to remove any undesired highlighting.

• Select the Show Highlight and Show Fill options to view the highlight and fill colors; deselect the options to hide them.

• Zoom in on your selection using the Zoom tool. Then, use a smaller brush size as you edit, switching between the Edge Highlighter tool and the Eraser tool as needed for more precise work.

• Toggle quickly between the Edge Highlighter and Eraser tools when one of them is selected by pressing B (Edge Highlighter) or E (Eraser).

• Switch to a smaller brush by entering a different size in the Brush Size option, and continue to refine the selection border using the Edge Highlighter tool or to erase using the Eraser tool.

Moving layers between documents

Often, you may need to move layers from one Photoshop document to another. It's very easy to do. Here, you'll move the paper texture you just extracted to the book cover composition, to add a background texture.

1 With both the your 06Working and Paper images visible on-screen, make sure that the Paper image is active.

2 Drag Layer 0 from the Paper image's Layers palette, into the center of your 06Working image. The layer is added as Layer 1, just below the top layer, Buddha.

3 In the Layers palette, select the layer name and rename it **Paper**.

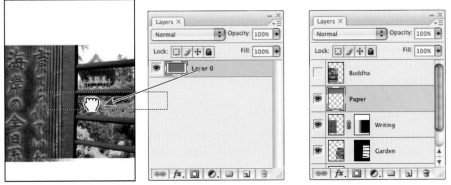

Dragging the Paper image layer into the 06Working image adds the layer to its Layers palette.

4 Choose View > Rulers. Drag a ruler guide down from the top of the document to 2¼."

5 Select the Move tool (⊕) in the toolbox. Move the paper to center it along the top of the book cover, so that the paper's bottom edge aligns with the 2¼" guide.

Colorizing with an adjustment layer

Now you'll create an adjustment layer to colorize the paper.

1 In the Layers palette, make sure that the Paper layer is selected.

2 At the bottom of the Layers palette, click the Create New Fill Or Adjustment Layer button ( ) to create an adjustment layer. Choose Hue/Saturation from the pop-up menu.

3 In the Hue/Saturation dialog box, enter these values to give the paper a violet cast: Hue: −125, Saturation −56, Lightness −18). Click OK.

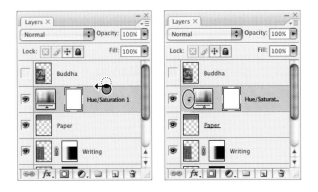

The entire image takes on a purplish cast. You can confine the effect to just the paper by creating a clipping layer.

4 Hold down the Alt (Windows) or Option (Mac OS) key, and position the pointer between the Hue/Saturation adjustment layer and the Paper layer to display a double-circle icon (⚬). Then click to create a clipping layer.

In the Layers palette, the Hue/Saturation layer indents and displays an arrow pointing to the layer beneath it, Paper, which is now underlined. This shows that the Paper layer is now clipped to the adjustment layer, meaning that the effect applies only to that layer.

5 Choose File > Save to save your work so far.

Grouping and clipping layers

You'll complete the composition by rearranging some layers and adding text.

1 In the Layers palette, turn on and select the Buddha layer. Make sure that it is at the top of the Layers palette.

2 In the Layers palette, select the Paper layer and the Hue/Saturation adjustment layer. Click the icon (▾≡) in the upper right of the Layers palette to display the Layers palette menu, and choose New Group From Layers. Name this group **Top Paper.** Click OK.

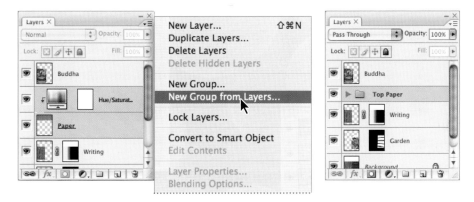

Now you'll duplicate this layer group for the bottom part of the book cover.

3 Using the Layers palette menu, choose Duplicate Group.

4 In the Duplicate Group dialog box, for Duplicate As, type **Bottom Paper**. Click OK.

5 In the Layers palette, click the triangle next to the Bottom Paper and Top Paper layers to view their contents. As you can see, the Bottom Paper layer now has the same contents as the Top Paper layer, duplicated in the same location in the image. Click the triangles again to collapse the layer contents.

6 In the Layers palette, click the eye icon next to the Top Paper layer group to hide the layer group.

7 With the Bottom Paper layer selected in the Layers palette, choose Edit > Transform > Rotate 180°.

8 Use the Move tool (↖⊕) to drag the rotated paper to the bottom of the composition, so that the top of the lower edge is at about 6½" on the ruler.

9 In the Layers palette, click in the Show/Hide Visibility column next to the Top Paper layer group to redisplay the layer group.

10 Choose View > Rulers to hide the rulers.

Applying a mask from a saved selection

Remember the beautiful mask that you created at the start of this lesson? Now it's time to retrieve it to mask out the background.

1 Select the Buddha layer at the top of the Layers palette.

2 Choose Select > Load Selection. For Channel, choose Statue. Select Invert to reverse the selection, and click OK.

3 At the bottom of the Layers palette, click the Add Layer Mask button (🔲) to mask the selection and hide the statue's background.

You can see how helpful it is to have the flexibility to apply saved alpha channels at various stages of your workflow.

Remember that you can adjust the image within the mask: In this case, you'll move the mask and the masked image together.

5 In the Layers palette with the Buddha layer selected, click its layer mask thumbnail to select the mask. In the Channels palette, notice that the Statue channel is selected. In the Document window, use the Move tool to adjust the masked image so that both the top halo and base of the statute extend about ½-inch into the paper.

Now you'll adjust how the statue appears on the paper.

6 In the Layers palette, select the Bottom Paper layer group and move it by dragging it above the Buddha layer. You want the paper to cover the base of the Buddha statue.

7 Choose File > Save to save your work.

Using type as a mask

Just as you can mask with selections, you can mask with type. Now you'll reveal the original paper texture, using type to mask the colorized paper.

1 Select the Type tool (T) in the toolbox. In the options bar, set the font to Minion Pro Regular, Center alignment, and 75 pt in size. Set black as the text color.

2   Click with the Type tool in the center of the top paper background, and type **Zen Garden**.

To add the paper texture, first you will copy it.

3   In the Layers palette, click the arrow next to the Top Paper layer group to expand its contents.

4   Press the Alt (Windows) or Option (Mac OS) key, and drag the Paper layer to just above the Zen Garden type layer. This makes a copy of the Paper layer on top of the type layer.

You must move the layer out of its layer group to be able to create a clipping group in the next step. You can clip two layers together, but you cannot clip together a layer group and a layer.

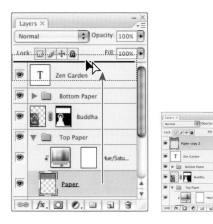

5 To clip the Paper Copy layer to the Zen Garden type layer, position the pointer between the two layers, and hold down Alt (Windows) or Option (Mac OS) to display the double-circle clipping layer icon (⊙); Click when this icon appears.

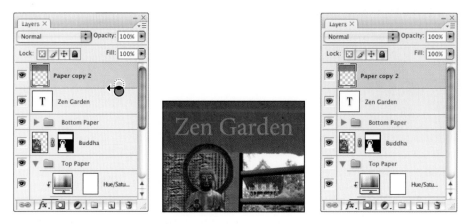

The original gold paper texture shows through the type. Now you'll make the type pop a bit more with a drop shadow.

6 To add a drop shadow, select the Zen Garden type layer. Click the Add Layer Style button (*fx*) at the bottom of the Layers palette, and choose Drop Shadow from the pop-up menu. In the Layer Style dialog box under the Drop Shadow options, select the Multiply blending mode; set the Distance to 12, Spread to 5, Size to 29. Click OK.

Note: If you make a mistake and inadvertently add the Drop Shadow effect to the Paper Copy layer, simply drag the effect to the Zen Garden type layer to apply it there.

To complete the composition and this lesson, you'll add your name as the author to the bottom paper texture.

7 In the Layers palette, make sure that the top layer is selected, so that the new type layer will be created above it.

8 To color the type, select the Eyedropper tool (✐) in the toolbox. Click a light green color from the shrubbery in the panel area to sample the color.

9 Select the Type tool (**T**) in the toolbox. In the Type tool options bar, choose Minion Pro Regular for the font, and 15 pt for the size.

10 Position the Type tool over the center of the bottom paper texture. Type the author name [**your name here**].

11 Press Ctrl (Windows) or Command (Mac OS) to get the Move tool, and drag to position the type in the center of the bottom paper.

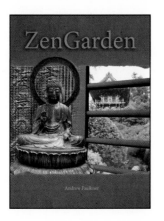

Your book cover is complete.

12 Choose File > Save.

You have completed this lesson. Although it takes some practice to become comfortable using channels, you've learned all the fundamental concepts and skills you need to get started using masks and channels.

About masks and masking

Alpha channels, channel masks, clipping masks, layer masks, vector masks—what's the difference? In some cases, they're interchangeable: a channel mask can be converted to a layer mask, a layer mask can be converted to a vector mask and vice versa.

Here's a brief description to help you keep them all straight. What they have in common is that all store selections, and all let you edit an image nondestructively and return at any time to your original.

• An **alpha channel**—also called a mask or selection—is an extra channel added to an image that stores selections as grayscale images. You can add alpha channels to create and store masks.

• A **layer mask** is like an alpha channel, just attached to a specific layer. A layer mask lets you control which part of a layer is revealed or hidden. A layer mask appears as a blank thumbnail next to the layer thumbnail in the Layers palette; a black outline indicates that its selected.

• A **vector mask** is essentially a layer mask made up of vectors, not pixels. Resolution independent, vector masks have crisp edges and are created with the pen or shape tools. They do not support transparency and so their edges cannot be feathered. Their thumbnail appears the same as layer mask thumbnails.

• A **clipping mask** applies to a layer. It lets you confine the influence of an effect to specific layers, rather than to everything below the layer in the layer stack. Using a clipping mask clips layers to a base layer: only that base layer is affected. Thumbnails of a clipped layer are indented with a right-angle arrow pointing to the layer below. The clipped base layer is underlined.

• A **channel mask** restricts editing to a specific channel (for example, a Cyan channel in a CMYK image). Channel masks are useful for making intricate, fringed, or wispy-edged selections. You can create a channel mask based on a dominant color in an image or pronounced contrast in an isolated channel, for example, between the subject and the background. An alternative to using a channel mask is the Extract command, which lets you cut out complex subjects from their backgrounds.

Review

▶ **Review questions**

1 What is the benefit of using a quick mask?

2 What happens to a quick mask when you deselect it?

3 When you save a selection as a mask, where is the mask stored?

4 How can you edit a mask in a channel once you've saved it?

5 How do channels differ from layers?

6 How do you use the Extract command to isolate an object with intricate borders from an image?

▶ **Review answers**

1 Quick masks are helpful for creating quick, onetime selections. In addition, using a quick mask is an easy way to edit a selection using the painting tools.

2 The quick mask disappears when you deselect it.

3 Masks are saved in channels, which can be thought of as storage areas for color and selection information in an image.

4 You can paint on a mask in a channel using black, white, and shades of gray.

5 Channels are used as storage areas for saved selections. Unless you explicitly display a channel, it does not appear in the image or print. Layers can be used to isolate various parts of an image so that they can be edited as discrete objects with the painting or editing tools or other effects.

6 You use the Extract command to extract an object, and the Extract dialog box to highlight the edges of the object. Then, you define the object's interior and preview the extraction. Applying the extraction erases the background to transparency, leaving just the extracted object. You can also use the Force Foreground option to extract a monochromatic or uniform-colored object based on its predominant color.

Digital photography isn't just for professionals any more. Whether you have a collection of digital images amassed for various clients or projects, or a personal collection that you want to refine, archive, and preserve for posterity, Photoshop has an array of tools for importing, editing, and archiving digital photographs.

7 | Correcting and Enhancing Digital Photographs

Lesson overview

In this lesson, you'll learn how to do the following:

*   Process a proprietary camera raw image and save it as an industry-standard digital negative.

*   Make typical corrections to a digital photograph, including removing red eye and noise and bringing out shadow and highlights detail.

*   Adjust the visual perspective of objects in an image using the Vanishing Point filter.

*   Apply optical lens correction to an image.

*   Prepare a PDF presentation of your corrected images.

*   Understand best practices for organizing, managing, and saving your images.

*   Learn about Adobe Photoshop Lightroom™, a new CS3 component that incorporates raw conversion into a single workflow, and lets you scroll through dozens of images quickly, and brand and showcase them.

This lesson will take 1½ to 2 hours to complete. If needed, remove the previous lesson folder from your hard drive, and copy the Lessons/Lesson07 folder onto it. As you work on this lesson, you'll preserve the start files. If you need to restore the start files, copy them again from the *Adobe Photoshop CS3 Classroom in a Book CD.*

Getting started

In this lesson, you will work with several images to learn about Photoshop's support for camera raw image processing and editing, as well as to explore many features that let you enhance and clean up your digital photographs. You will save each edited image in a Portfolio folder when you've finished, and at the end of the lesson, you will prepare a PDF slide show of your corrected images. You will start by viewing the before and after images in Adobe Bridge.

1 Start Photoshop and then immediately hold down Ctrl+Alt+Shift (Windows) or Command+Option+Shift (Mac OS) to restore the default preferences. (See "Restoring default preferences" on page 6.)

2 When prompted, click Yes to confirm that you want to reset preferences, and Close to close the Welcome Screen.

3 Click the Go To Bridge button (⊞) in the tool options bar to open Adobe Bridge.

4 In the Folders panel in the upper left corner of Bridge, click the Lessons folder, and then double-click the Lesson07 folder to see its contents in the preview area.

5 Make sure your thumbnail previews are large enough for a good look at the images, and locate the 07A_Start.crw and 07A_End.psd files.

Before   *After*

The original photograph of a Spanish-style church is a camera raw file, so it doesn't have the usual .psd file extension you've worked with so far in this book. It was shot with a Canon Digital Rebel camera and has the Canon proprietary .crw raw file extension instead. You will process this proprietary camera raw image to make it brighter, sharper, and clearer, and then save it as an industry-standard Digital Negative (DNG) file.

6 Locate the 07B_Start.psd and 07B_End.psd files and study their thumbnail previews.

Before

After

You are going to make several corrections to this portrait of mother and son, including bringing out shadow and highlight detail, removing red eye, and sharpening the image.

7 Locate the 07C_Start.psd and 07C_End.psd files and study their thumbnail previews.

Before

After

You are going to edit the image of this red clapboard farmhouse to add a window and remove the seasonal wreath, preserving the vanishing-point perspective as you make corrections.

8 Locate the 07D_Start.psd and 07D_End.psd files and study their thumbnail previews.

Before   *After*

You are going to correct the lens barrel distortion in this image.

About camera raw

A *camera raw* file contains unprocessed picture data from a digital camera's image sensor. Many digital cameras can save images as camera raw format files. The advantage of camera raw files is that they let the photographer—rather than the camera—interpret the image data and make adjustments and conversions. (In contrast, shooting JPEG images with your camera locks you into your camera's processing.) With camera raw, because the camera doesn't do any image processing, you can use Photoshop to set the white balance, tonal range, contrast, color saturation, and sharpening. Think of camera raw files as your photo negative. You can go back and reprocess the file anytime you like to achieve the results you want.

To create camera raw files, you set your digital camera to save files in its own, possibly proprietary, raw file format. From your camera, you download the camera raw file; it will have a file extension such as .nef (from Nikon) or .crw (from Canon). In Bridge or Photoshop, you can process camera raw files from a myriad of supported digital cameras from Canon, Kodak, Leica, Nikon, and other makers—and even process multiple images simultaneously. You can then export the proprietary camera raw files to the Digital Negative (DNG) file format, the nonproprietary Adobe format for standardizing camera raw files; or to such other formats as JPEG, TIFF, and PSD.

In Adobe Camera Raw (ACR), you can process camera raw files obtained from supported cameras. Although ACR can open and edit a camera raw image file, it cannot save an image in camera raw format.

Note: *The Photoshop Raw format (.raw extension) is a file format for transferring images between applications and computer platforms. Don't confuse Photoshop Raw with camera raw file formats.*

For a complete list of cameras supported by Adobe Camera Raw, go to www.adobe.com/products/photoshop/cameraraw.html.

Processing camera raw files

When you make adjustments to a camera raw image, such as straightening or cropping the image, Photoshop and Bridge preserve the original camera raw file data. This way, you can edit the image as you desire, export the edited image, and keep the original intact for future use or other adjustments.

Opening camera raw images

Both Adobe Bridge and Photoshop CS3 let you open and process multiple camera raw images simultaneously. They feature an identical Camera Raw dialog box, which provides extensive controls for adjusting white balance, exposure, contrast, sharpness, tone curves, and much more. If you have multiple exposures of the same shot, you can use the Camera Raw dialog box to process one of the images, and then apply the settings to all of the other shots. You will do that in this exercise.

1   In Bridge, navigate to the Lessons/Lesson07/Mission folder, which contains three shots of the Spanish church you previewed in the previous exercise.

2 Press Shift and click to select all of the images—Mission01.crw, Mission02.crw, and Mission03.crw, and then choose File > Open In Camera Raw.

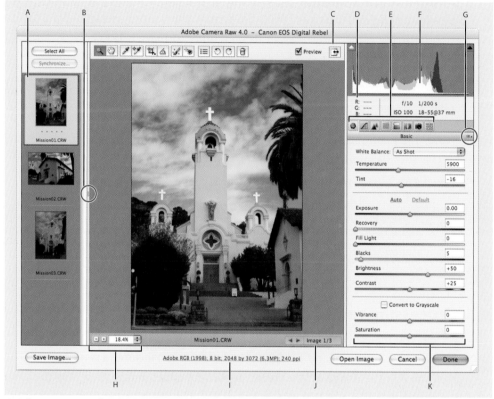

*A. Filmstrip B. Toggle Filmstrip C. Toggle full screen mode D. RGB values E. Image adjustment tabs
F. Histogram G. Camera Raw Settings menu H. Zoom levels I. Click to display workflow options
J. Multi-image navigation controls K. Adjustment sliders*

The Camera Raw dialog box displays a large preview of the first raw image, with a filmstrip down the left side of the dialog box of all open camera raw images. The histogram at top right shows the tonal range of the first image; the workflow options at the bottom center of the dialog box displays the first image's color space, bit-depth, size, and resolution. An array of tools along the top left of the dialog box lets you zoom and pan the image, select colors, crop, rotate, and more. Tabbed palettes across the right center of the dialog box let you adjust the image's white balance, tone, detail, color, lens correction, and camera calibration. You can also select a preset with predetermined settings.

You will explore these controls now, editing the first image file.

3 Click the forward arrow button under the main preview area to the right—or scroll down the filmstrip and select each thumbnail in turn—to cycle through the images, and return to Mission 01.crw.

4 Make sure that the Preview box is checked at the top of the dialog box so that you can interactively see the adjustments you're about to make.

Adjusting white balance and exposure

An image's white balance reflects the lighting conditions under which the photo was captured. A digital camera records the white balance at the time of exposure, and this is what initially appears in the Camera Raw dialog box image preview.

White balance comprises two components. The first is temperature, which is measured in kelvins and determines the level of "coolness" or "warmness" of the image—that is, its cool blue-green tones or warm yellow-red tones. The second component is tint, which compensates for magenta or green color casts in the image.

A camera's white balance usually comes close to being optimal, but you can adjust it if it's not quite right. Adjusting an image's white balance is a good way to start your corrections.

1 On the right side of the dialog box under the histogram, click the Basic button (⊙) to display the Basic pop-up menu. From the White Balance pop-up menu, choose Cloudy.

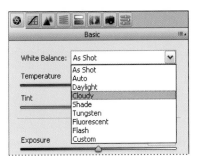

The Cloudy White Balance temperature is a little warmer than the Daylight setting and nicely suits this image, which was taken on a cloudy day.

💡 *To compare the settings, toggle Edit > Undo or press Ctrl+Z (Windows) or Command+Z (Mac OS).*

2 Change the other sliders in the Basic palette as follows:

- Set the Exposure to +1.20.
- Set Brightness to 50.
- Set Contrast to +29.
- Set Saturation to –5.

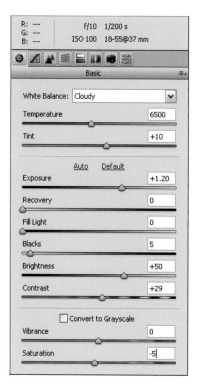

These settings help pump up the midtones of this image and make the image look bolder and more dimensional without being oversaturated.

About the camera raw histogram

The histogram in the upper right corner of the
Camera Raw dialog box simultaneously shows the
Red, Green, and Blue channels of the previewed
image, and it updates interactively as you adjust
any settings. Also, as you move any tool over the
preview image, the RGB values for the area under
the cursor appear above the histogram.

Applying sharpening

Next, you will sharpen the image to bring out more detail.

1 Zoom in to the top of the mission tower so that you can see the detail (to at least 100%).

2 Click the Detail button (▣) and drag the Sharpness slider to about 35.

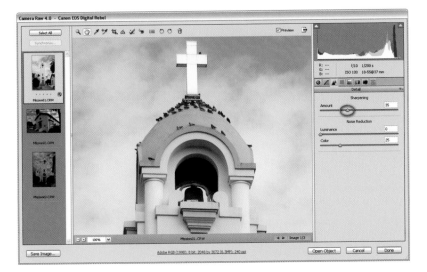

The higher sharpness value gives stronger definition to the details and edges in this
mission image.

Making adjustments from the Camera Raw dialog box preserves the original camera
raw file data. Adjustment settings are stored by image either in the Camera Raw
database file or "sidecar" XMP files (files that accompany the original camera raw image
file in the same folder). XMP files allow retaining the camera raw settings when the
image file is moved to a storage medium or another computer.

Synchronizing settings across images

Now that you've made this one mission image look stunning, you can automatically apply these camera raw settings to the other two mission images, which were shot at the same time under the same lighting conditions. You do this using the Synchronize command.

1 In the upper left corner of the Camera Raw dialog box, click the Select All button to select all of the thumbnails in the filmstrip.

2 Click the Synchronize button.

The Synchronize dialog box that appears lets you choose which settings you want to synchronize across the selected images. By default, all options (except Crop and Spot Removal) are checked. That's alright for our project, even though we didn't change all of the settings.

3 Click OK.

When you synchronize the settings across all of the selected camera raw images, the thumbnails update to reflect the changes you made. If you'd like, you can click the navigational arrows next to each preview in the left panel to cycle through a large preview of each image to see the adjustments.

Saving camera raw changes

Saving your changes so far involves two tasks: first, saving the synchronized changes to all three images and then saving one image, Mission01, for the PDF portfolio you will create later in this lesson.

1   Make sure that all three images are still selected in the Camera Raw filmstrip, and then click the Save Images button.

2   In the Save Options dialog box that appears, do the following:

- Choose the same location (the Lessons/Lesson07/Mission folder).

- Under File Naming, leave *Document Name* in the first blank field.

- Choose Format > JPEG at the bottom of the dialog box.

- Click Save.

This will save your corrected images as downsampled 72-dpi JPEGs, which can be shared with colleagues and viewed on the Web. Your files will be named Mission01.jpg, Mission02.jpg, and Mission03.jpg.

Note: Before sharing these images on the web, you would probably want to open them in Photoshop and resize them to 640 x 480 pixels. They are currently much larger, and the full-size images would not be visible on most monitors without requiring the viewer to scroll.

Bridge returns you to the Camera Raw dialog box and indicates how many images have been processed until all images are saved. The CRW thumbnails still appear in the Camera Raw dialog box—you now have JPEG versions as well as the original, unedited CRW image files, which you can continue to edit or leave for another time.

Now, you will save a copy of the Mission01 image to the Portfolio folder, where all of your portfolio images will be saved.

3 With only Mission01.crw selected in the filmstrip in the Camera Raw dialog box, click the Open Image button to open the (edited) raw image in Photoshop.

4 Choose File > Save As. In the Save As dialog box, choose Photoshop as your Format, rename the file **Mission_Final.psd**, navigate to the Lesson07/Portfolio folder, and click Save. Then close the file.

About saving camera raw files

Every camera model saves the camera raw image in a unique format, but Adobe Camera Raw can process many camera raw file formats. Adobe Camera Raw processes camera raw files with default image setting files based on built-in camera profiles for supported cameras and the EXIF data.

Choices for saving the proprietary camera raw files from your camera include DNG (the format saved by Adobe Camera Raw), JPEG, TIFF, and PSD. All of these formats can be used to save RGB and CMYK continuous-tone, bitmapped images, and all of them (except DNG) are also available in the Photoshop Save and Save As dialog boxes.

The Adobe Digital Negative (DNG) format contains raw image data from a digital camera and metadata that defines what the image data means. DNG is meant to be an industry-wide standard format for camera raw image data, helping photographers manage the variety of proprietary camera raw formats and providing a compatible archival format. (You can save this format only from the Camera Raw dialog box.)

The Joint Photographic Experts Group (JPEG) file format is commonly used to display photographs and other continuous-tone RGB images on the web. JPEG format retains all color information in an image but compresses file size by selectively discarding data. The greater the compression, the lower the image quality, and vice versa.

The Tagged Image File Format (TIFF) is used to exchange files between applications and computer platforms. TIFF is a flexible format supported by virtually all paint, image-editing, and page-layout applications. Also, virtually all desktop scanners can produce TIFF images.

The Photoshop format (PSD) is the default file format. Because of the tight integration between Adobe products, other Adobe applications such as Adobe Illustrator, Adobe InDesign, and Adobe GoLive® can directly import PSD files and preserve many Photoshop features.

Once you open a camera raw file in Photoshop, your choices of save file formats increase beyond JPEG, TIFF, and PSD. You can also save the image in such Photoshop-compatible formats as Large Document Format (PSB), Cineon, Photoshop Raw, PNG, or Portable Bit Map. (The Photoshop Raw format (RAW) is a file format for transferring images between applications and computer platforms—not to be confused with camera raw file formats.) For more information, see Photoshop Help.

Now that you know how to process a camera raw image, you will learn how to make some common corrections to a different digital photograph.

Correcting digital photographs

Photoshop contains a number of features that let you easily improve the quality of digital photographs. These include the ability to automatically bring out details in shadow and highlight areas of an image, easily remove red eye, reduce unwanted noise in an image, and sharpen an image. To explore these capabilities, you will edit a different digital image now: a portrait of a mother and a child.

Making shadow /highlight adjustments

The Shadow/Highlight command is suitable for correcting 8- or 16-bit RGB, CMYK, or Lab photos whose subjects are silhouetted against strong backlighting or are washed out from being too close to the camera flash. The adjustment is also useful for brightening areas of shadow in an otherwise well-lit image.

1 Click the Go To Bridge button ( ). In the Folder panel in Bridge, click the Lessons folder (if it is not already selected), and then double-click the Lesson07 folder. Locate the 07B_Start.psd image, and double-click to open it in Photoshop.

2 Choose Image > Adjustments > Shadow/Highlight. Photoshop automatically applies default settings to the image, lightening the background; but you will customize them next to bring out more detail in both the shadows and the highlights, and enhance the red sunset in the sky. (Make sure that the Preview box in the Shadow/Highlight dialog box is checked so that you can see the effect in the image window.)

3 In the Shadow/Highlight dialog box, check the Show More Options box, and do the following:

• In the Shadows area, set Amount to **80%** and Tonal Width to **65%**. Leave Radius at 30 pixels.

• In the Highlights area, set Amount to **5%**. Leave Tonal Width at 50% and Radius at 30 pixels.

• In the Adjustments area, drag the Color Correction slider to +45.

4 Click OK to accept your changes.

5 Choose File > Save As, rename your file **07B_Working.psd**, and click Save to save your work so far.

Correcting red eye

Red eye occurs when the retinas of a subject's eyes are reflected by the camera flash. It commonly occurs in photographs of a subject in a darkened room, because the subject's irises are wide open. Red eye is easy to fix in Photoshop. Next, you will remove the red eye from the boy's eyes in the portrait.

1 Using the Zoom tool, drag a marquee around the boy's eyes to zoom into them.

2 Select the Red Eye tool (👁), hidden under the Spot Healing Brush tool.

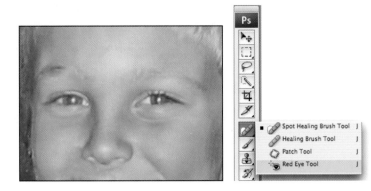

3 In the tool options bar, leave Pupil Size set to 50%, but change Darken Amount to 10%. Darken specifies how dark the pupil should be. Because this child's eyes are blue, we want the Darken Amount setting to be lighter than the default.

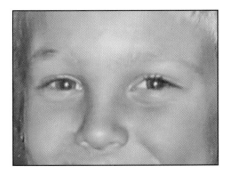

4 Click on the red area in the boy's left eye, then click the red area in his right eye. The red retinal reflection disappears.

5 Zoom back out to 100% by pressing Alt (Windows) or Option (Mac OS) and clicking on the image window with the Zoom tool.

6 Choose File > Save to save your work so far.

Reducing noise

The next correction to make on this image is to reduce the amount of noise that it contains. *Image noise* is random, extraneous pixels that aren't part of the image detail. Noise can result from using a high ISO setting on a digital camera, from underexposure, or from shooting in darkness with a long shutter speed. Scanned images may contain noise that results from the scanning sensor, or from a grain pattern from the scanned film.

There are two types of image noise: luminance noise, which is grayscale data that makes an image look grainy or patchy; and color noise, which is usually visible as colored artifacts in the image. Photoshop's Reduce Noise filter can address both types of noise in individual color channels while preserving edge detail, as well as correct JPEG compression artifacts.

You will start by zooming in to the sky to get a good look at the noise in this image.

1 Using the Zoom tool, click in the center of the sky above the woman's head and zoom in to about 300%.

The noise in this image appears as speckled and rough with uneven graininess in the sky. Using the Reduce Noise filter, we can soften and smooth out this area and give the sky more depth.

2 Choose Filter > Noise > Reduce Noise.

3 In the Reduce Noise dialog box, do the following:

• Decrease Strength to 5. (The Strength option controls the amount of luminance noise.)

• Increase Preserve Details to 70%.

• Leave the Reduce Color Noise slider at 45%.

• Increase Sharpen Details to 35%.

You don't need to check the Remove JPEG Artifact box, because this image is not a JPEG and has no JPEG artifacts.

Note: *To correct noise in individual channels of the image, you can click the Advanced button and click the Per Channel tab to adjust these same settings in each channel.*

4 To clearly see the results of your changes, click the plus button at the bottom of the dialog box to zoom in to about 300%, and then drag to position the sky in the preview area. Click and hold the mouse button down in the preview area to see the "before" image, and release the mouse button to see the corrected result. Or, make sure the Preview box is checked and watch the results in the main image window.

5 Click OK to apply your changes and to close the Reduce Noise dialog box, and then double-click the Zoom tool to return the image to 100%.

6 Choose File > Save to save your work so far.

A photographer for more than 22 years, Jay Graham began his career designing and building custom homes. Today, Graham has clients in the advertising, architectural, editorial, and travel industries. See Jay Graham's portfolio on the web at jaygraham.com.

Jay Graham

Good habits make all of the difference

A sensible workflow and good work habits will keep you enthused about digital photography, help your images shine—and save you from the night terrors of losing work you never backed up. Here's an outline of the basic workflow for digital images—books have been written on the topic—from a professional photographer with more than 22 years' experience. The guidelines that Jay Graham describes—on how to set up your camera and create a basic color workflow; what capture file formats to use; how to organize and manage your images; and how to show off images to clients, friends, and family—will help you get the most from the images you shoot.

Graham uses Adobe Bridge to organize thousands of images.

"The biggest complaint from people is they've lost their image, where is it, what does it look like?" says Graham. "So naming is important."

Start out right by setting up your camera preferences

If your camera has the option, photograph only in the Camera Raw file format, which captures all the image information you need. With one camera raw photo, says Graham, "You can go from daylight, to an indoor tungsten image without degradation" when it's reproduced.

Start with the best material

Get all the data when you capture—at fine compression and high resolution. You can't go back later.

Transfer images to your computer

Use a card reader rather than plugging your camera into the computer to download images. Card readers don't need the camera turned on; use multiple cards as needed to store your images.

Organize your files

Name and catalog your images as soon after downloading them as possible. If the camera names files, eventually it resets and produces multiple files with the same name, says Graham. Use Adobe Bridge to rename, rank, and add metadata descriptions to the photos you plan to keep; cull those you don't.

Graham names his files by date (and possibly subject). He would store a series of photos taken Dec. 12, 2006 at Stinson beach in a folder named "20061212_Stinson"; within the folder, he would name each image incrementally—"2006_1212_01" or "001" and so on. "That way it lines up on the hard drive real easily," he says. Follow Windows naming conventions to keep filenames useable on non-Macintosh platforms (32 characters maximum; only numbers, letters, underscores and hyphens).

Convert raw images to Adobe Camera Raw

Save edited the camera raw images in the DNG format. This open-source format can be read by any device, unlike many cameras' proprietary camera raw formats.

Keep a master image

Save your master in PS, TIFF, or Adobe Camera Raw format, not in JPEG. Each time a JPEG is reedited and saved, the image quality degrades due to reapplied compression.

Show off to clients and friends

Pick the best color profile for converting your work for screen or print, and set the final image resolution for quality and file size. For a comp, online display, or web photo service, use sRGB at 72 dpi resolution. For inkjet printing, use Adobe 1998 to reproduce 180 dpi and higher resolution images.

Back up your images

You've devoted a lot of time and effort to your images: don't lose them. Use a CD or DVD for backup. Even better: use an external hard drive set to back up automatically. "The question is not if your

Sharpening edges

Reducing noise can soften an image, so, as a final correction to this photograph, you will sharpen it to improve its clarity.

Photoshop has several Sharpen filters, including Sharpen, Unsharp Mask, Sharpen Edges, and Smart Sharpen. All of them focus blurry images by increasing the contrast of adjacent pixels, but some are better than others, depending on, among other things, whether all or part of an image needs to be sharpened. Smart Sharpen sharpens an image while also reducing noise and lets you specify whether the filter is applied to the overall image, to its shadows, or to its highlights.

For more on the other Sharpen filters, see Photoshop Help.

1   Choose Filter > Sharpen > Smart Sharpen.

2   In the Smart Sharpen dialog box, do the following:

•   Reduce the Amount to 40%.

•   Set the Radius to 5 pixels.

•   Choose Remove > Lens Blur.

•   Select the More Accurate check box.

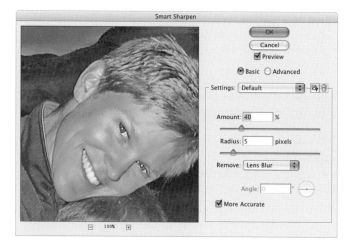

The Remove option determines the algorithm used to sharpen the image. Gaussian Blur is the same method used by the Unsharp Mask filter. Lens Blur detects the edges and detail in an image and sharpens finer detail with fewer sharpening halos. Motion Blur reduces blurring due to camera or subject movement, and includes an Angle control.

Choosing More Accurate yields more accurate sharpening, but takes longer to process.

3 To examine the results of Smart Sharpen, click and hold the mouse button in the preview area, then release. Or, toggle the Preview check box and watch the results in the main image window.

4 Click OK to apply your changes and close the Smart Sharpen dialog box.

5 Choose File > Save As. In the Save As dialog box, name the file **Portrait_Final.psd**, navigate to the Lesson07/Portfolio folder, and save the file. Then, close the image window.

Congratulations. You have made several typical corrections to a digital photograph. Next, you will try something a little more unusual—editing an image while preserving its perspective.

Editing images with a vanishing-point perspective

The Vanishing Point filter lets you define the perspective planes in an image and then paint, clone, and transform images according to that perspective. You can even create multiple planes that are related to each other by tearing off perpendicular planes from the plane you define. Then you can paint, clone, and transform across the different planes, and Photoshop will automatically scale and orient your edits in the proper perspective throughout the image.

The Vanishing Point filter works with 8-bit-per-channel images, but not with vector data. To use it, you first create a grid that defines your perspective; then you edit your image normally. Vanishing Point adjusts your editing to the defined perspective.

Defining a grid

In this exercise, you'll work with an image of a snow-covered house. You will use the Vanishing Point filter to add a window to the wall and to remove the seasonal holiday wreath, all while maintaining perspective.

1 Click the Go To Bridge button (). In the Folder panel in Bridge, click the Lessons folder (if it is not already selected), and then double-click the Lesson07 folder. Locate the 07C_Start.psd image, and double-click it to open it in Photoshop.

You will start by defining the perspective grid. Then you will create a fourth window and remove the seasonal wreath.

2 Choose Filter > Vanishing Point. Click OK if a conversion warning dialog box appears, warning that saved planes have been updated to the current version, and once saved, cannot be opened with previous versions.

An image preview appears in the Vanishing Point dialog box, which provides a variety of tools and options for creating a perspective grid.

3 Using the Create Plane tool (📖), click each of the four corner points of the main wall of the house: Click just under the white trim where the red siding meets it, and over the plant in the lower right corner, to define the size and shape of the perspective plane. As you click, a blue outline appears. When you finish, Photoshop displays a blue grid over the plane that you just defined.

Note: If you make a mistake—for example, if a red border appears and the perspective grid doesn't—either press Delete and try again, or drag the handles to adjust the grid.

4 If necessary, drag a corner or a side handle to adjust the grid.

Editing objects in the image

Now that the perspective grid is created, you can select and move the window.

1 Select the Marquee tool (▱) from the Vanishing Point dialog box's tool palette. Notice that the detailed grid disappears from the preview window, replaced by a less-distracting blue outline of the perspective grid.

2 To slightly blur the edge of the selection you're about to make, set the Feather option to 3 at the top of the dialog box. Leave Opacity set at 100 and Heal set to Off. Move Mode, which is set to Destination, should be dimmed.

Note: The Heal option determines how the selection, cloning, or paint stroke blends with the color, lighting, and shading of the surrounding pixels. Off doesn't blend the selection or stroke with the color, lighting, and shading of the surrounding pixels. Move Mode determines the behavior when moving a selection. Destination lets you move the selection marquee anywhere in the image. For more on these options, see Photoshop Help.

3 Drag a selection marquee around and a little larger than the center window. Then, press Alt (Windows) or Option (Mac OS), hold down Shift to keep the plane aligned, and drag the selected area to the right. Release the mouse when the copied window is positioned between the right window and the far end of the wall. As you drag, Photoshop scales the selection according to the perspective of the wall.

4 To prepare to remove the wreath from the wall, select the Zoom tool and drag it over the three left-most windows to get a closer view of them.

5 Switch back to the Marquee tool ( ) and drag to select the empty wall between the two left windows.

6 Once again, hold down Alt (Windows) or Option (Mac OS) and Shift, and drag the wall selection between the center and right windows, on top of the wreath.

Although the copied selection keeps perspective in its new location, it doesn't cover the whole wreath. Some of the wreath still shows in the image. You will fix this next.

7 Select the Transform tool (▦). Notice that Photoshop now displays handles on the selection.

8 Drag the transform handles to expand the selection and cover the wreath. If necessary, use the Up, Down, Right, and Left Arrow keys to nudge the selection and align the cloned clapboards.

9 Deselect the Show Edges box and zoom back out to see the results of your work. Then, then click OK to apply the Vanishing Point filter.

10 Choose File > Save As. In the Save As dialog box, name the file **Farmhouse_Final. psd** and save it in the Lesson07/Portfolio folder. Then, close the image window.

Note: Images with the Vanishing Point filter applied must be saved as PSD, TIFF, or JPEG to preserve the perspective plane information in the image.

Next, you will correct an image that contains camera lens distortion.

Watch the Vanishing Point QuickTime movie to get a quick overview of using this feature to define perspective and wrap around multiple planes. The movie is located on the Adobe Photoshop CS3 Classroom in a Book CD in Movies/Vanishing Point.mov. Double-click the movie file to open it; then click the Play button.

Correcting image distortion

The Lens Correction filter fixes common camera lens flaws, such as barrel and pincushion distortion, chromatic aberration, and vignetting. *Barrel distortion* is a lens defect that causes straight lines to bow out toward the edges of the image. *Pincushion distortion* is the opposite effect, where straight lines bend inward. *Chromatic aberration* appears as a color fringe along the edges of image objects. *Vignetting* occurs when the edges of an image, especially the corners, are darker than the center.

Some lenses exhibit these defects depending on the focal length or the f-stop used. The Lens Correction filter can apply settings based on the camera, lens, and focal length used to make the image. The filter also can rotate an image or fix image perspective caused by tilting a camera vertically or horizontally. The filter's image grid makes it easier and more accurate to make these adjustments than using the Transform command.

In this exercise, you will adjust the lens distortion in an image of a Greek temple.

1   Click the Go To Bridge button (▣). In Bridge, click the Lessons folder favorite (if it is not already selected), and then double-click on the Lesson07 folder. Locate the 07D_Start.psd image, and double-click to open it in Photoshop.

Notice how the columns bend toward the camera and appear warped. This distortion was caused because the photo was shot at too close range with a wide-angle lens.

2 Choose Filter > Distort > Lens Correction. The image appears in the Lens Correction dialog box with a large interactive preview, an alignment grid overlay, and options at right for removing distortion, correcting chromatic aberration, removing vignettes, and transforming perspective.

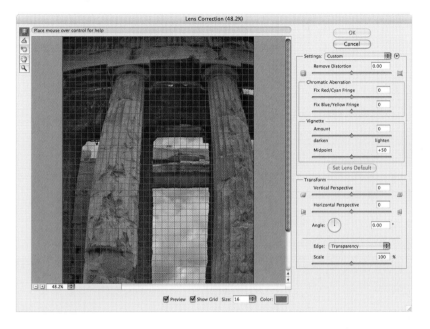

3 In the Lens Correction dialog box, do the following:

• Drag the Remove Distortion slider to about +52.00 to remove the barrel distortion in the image. Or, select the Remove Distortion tool (📷) and drag in the image preview area to accomplish this, watching the Remove Distortion slider to see when you reach +52.00.

The adjustment causes the image to bow inward; you'll correct this with the next setting.

💡 *Watch the alignment grid as you make these changes so that you can see when the vertical columns are straightened in the image.*

• Choose Edge > Transparency if it is not already chosen.

• Drag the Scale slider to 146%.

4 Click OK to apply your changes and close the Lens Correction dialog box. The curving distortion caused by the wide-angle lens and low shooting angle are eliminated.

5 (Optional) To see the effect of your change in the main image window, press Ctrl+Z (Windows) or Command+Z (Mac OS) twice to undo and redo the filter.

Now you'll save the image for your PDF portfolio.

6 Choose File > Save As. In the Save As dialog box, name the file **Columns_Final.psd** and save it in the Lesson07/Portfolio folder. Then, close the image window.

About Adobe Photoshop Lightroom

Modular and task-based, Adobe Photoshop Lightroom offers a streamlined environment from digital capture to print.

Incorporating raw conversion into a single workflow, Adobe Photoshop Lightroom speeds up the pro photographer's work. Think of Lightroom as a digital lightbox—on steroids. Click to make control panels and tools fade into the background in Lights-Out mode and place the image center stage. Use the Identity Plate feature to personally brand the application and its output, and showcase your work. Rapidly scroll through hundreds of images or instantly magnify finer points within an image.

Lightroom leverages Adobe Camera Raw technology to support more than 125 native raw file formats—including from the latest camera models. You can use Lightroom with the newest cameras, knowing that the image files will be recognized today and in the future.

Just some of the features in Lightroom:

• Intuitive image correction features, including tone curve adjustments for visually adjusting midtones, shadows, and highlights. Split-toning controls allow creating richer black-and-white images—with greater control to make adjustments and address precise image areas on the histogram.

• Time-saving ability to convert and rename imported files to Digital Negative format (DNG) or rename and segment them by folder or date.

• Quick retrieval of images with search filters and presets, and organizing options.

• Features for showcasing images via slide shows with drop shadows, borders, Identity Plates, and different colored backgrounds. The size and position of the images can be manipulated and delivered in Adobe Flash®, Adobe Portable Document Format (PDF) or HTML formats.

• Contact sheet templates that can be customized to add identity plates or produce a fine art print.

For a showcase of work by a Lightroom online community that Adobe hosts, see the Lightroom slideshow at http://www.adobe.com/products/photoshoplightroom/.

Creating a PDF portfolio

You can create an Adobe PDF slide show or a multipage PDF document from a set of Photoshop files by applying the PDF Presentation command in Photoshop or Bridge and setting the options you want. You can select which files within a folder you want to include, or simply select a folder to include all the files stored inside it. Now that you've created a portfolio of images (in the Portfolio folder), you can easily turn it into a PDF slide show to share with clients and colleagues.

1   Click the Go To Bridge button (◼). In Bridge, click the Lessons folder favorite (if it is not already selected from the previous exercise), and navigate to the Lesson07/Portfolio folder. The Portfolio folder should contain the following image files: Mission_Final.psd, Portrait_Final.psd, Farmhouse_Final.psd, and Columns_Final.psd.

2   Choose Tools > Photoshop > PDF Presentation.

The Photoshop PDF Presentation dialog box opens. Notice that the four files from the Portfolio folder already appear in the Source Files area.

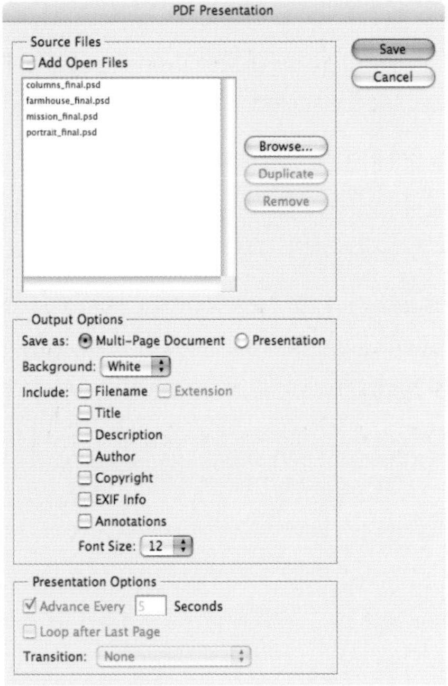

3 In the PDF Presentation dialog box, do the following:

• Under Output Options, select Presentation.

• Under Presentation Options, check the Advance Every box, and accept the default to advance every 5 seconds.

• Check the Loop after Last Page box.

• Choose Wipe Right from the Transition pop-up menu.

• Click Save.

4 In the Save dialog box that appears, type **Photography_portfolio.pdf** as the filename, and specify the location as the Lesson07 folder. (Do *not* select the Portfolio folder.) Then click Save.

5 In the Save Adobe PDF dialog box, do the following:

•   Choose Adobe PDF Preset > Smallest File Size to create a PDF document that is suitable for on-screen display.

•   Under Options, check View PDF After Saving.

•   Click Save PDF.

If you have a version of Adobe Acrobat or Adobe Reader installed on your computer, it launches automatically and starts the PDF slide-show presentation.

6   When the slide show finishes, press Esc to return to the standard Acrobat window. Then quit your Acrobat application and return to Photoshop.

Great work! You've successfully assembled a portfolio of work and shown it off.

Review

▶ **Review questions**

1 What happens to camera raw images when you edit them in Photoshop or Bridge?

2 What is the advantage of the Adobe Digital Negative file format?

3 How do you correct red eye in Photoshop?

4 Describe how to fix common camera lens flaws in Photoshop. What causes these defects?

▶ **Review answers**

1 A camera raw file contains unprocessed picture data from a digital camera's image sensor. Camera raw files give photographers control over interpreting the image data, rather than letting the camera make the adjustments and conversions. When you make adjustments to a camera raw image, Photoshop and Bridge preserve the original camera raw file data. This way, you can edit the image as you desire, export it, and keep the original intact for future use or other adjustments.

2 The Adobe Digital Negative (DNG) file format contains the raw image data from a digital camera as well as metadata that defines what the image data means. DNG is an industry-wide standard for camera raw image data that helps photographers manage proprietary camera raw file formats and provides a compatible archival format.

3 Red eye occurs when the retinas of a subject's eyes are reflected by the camera flash. To correct red eye in Adobe Photoshop, zoom in to the subject's eyes, select the Red Eye tool, and then click the red eyes. The red reflection disappears.

4 The Lens Correction filter fixes common camera lens flaws, such as barrel and pincushion distortion, in which straight lines bow out towards the edges of the image (barrel) or bend inward (pincushion); chromatic aberration, where a color fringe appears along the edges of image objects; and vignetting at the edges of an image, especially corners, that are darker than the center. Defects can occur from incorrectly setting the lens' focal length or f-stop, or by tilting the camera vertically or horizontally.

Pictures may speak a thousand words, but sometimes your image compositions need at least a few words. Luckily, Photoshop has powerful text tools that let you add type to your images with great flexibility and control.

8 | Typographic Design

Lesson overview

In this lesson, you'll learn how to do the following:

- Use guides to position text in a composition.

- Make a clipping mask from type.

- Merge type with other layers.

- Use layer styles with text.

- Preview typefaces interactively to choose them for a composition.

- Control type and positioning using advanced type palette features.

- Warp a layer around a 3D object.

This lesson will take about an hour to complete. If needed, remove the previous lesson folder from your hard drive, and copy the Lesson08 folder onto it. As you work on this lesson, you'll preserve the start files. If you need to restore the start files, copy them from the *Adobe Photoshop CS3 Classroom in a Book* CD.

About type

Type in Photoshop consists of mathematically defined shapes that describe the letters, numbers, and symbols of a typeface. Many typefaces are available in more than one format, the most common formats being Type 1 or PostScript fonts, TrueType, and OpenType (see page 266).

When you add type to an image in Photoshop, the characters are composed of pixels and have the same resolution as the image file—zooming in on characters shows jagged edges. However, Photoshop preserves the vector-based type outlines and uses them when you scale or resize type, save a PDF or EPS file, or print the image to a PostScript printer. As a result, you can produce type with crisp, resolution-independent edges, apply effects and styles to type, and transform its shape and size.

Getting started

In this lesson, you'll work on the layout for the label of a bottle of olive oil. You will start from an illustration of a bottle, created in Adobe Illustrator, and then add and stylize type in Photoshop, including wrapping the text to conform to the 3D shape. You will start with a blank label on a layer above the bottle background.

You'll start the lesson by viewing an image of the final composition.

1 Start Photoshop and then immediately hold down Ctrl+Alt+Shift (Windows) or Command+Option+Shift (Mac OS) to restore the default preferences. (See "Restoring default preferences" on page 6.)

2 When prompted, click Yes to confirm that you want to reset preferences, and Close to close the Welcome Screen.

3 Click the Go To Bridge button (▣) in the tool options bar to open Adobe Bridge.

4 In the Favorites panel on the left side of Bridge, click the Lessons favorite, and then double-click the Lesson08 folder in the Content panel.

5 Select the 08End.psd file so that it appears in the center Content panel. Enlarge the panel if necessary to get a good close-up view by dragging the right splitter bar to the right.

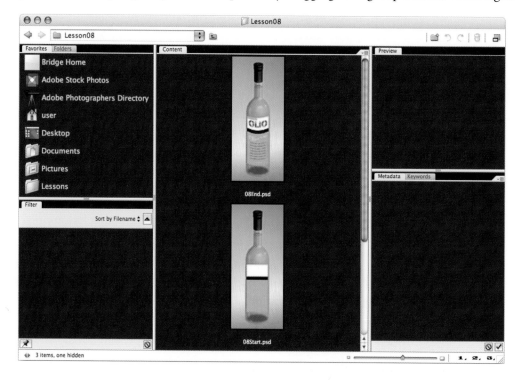

This layered composite represents a comp of packaging for a new brand of olive oil. For this lesson, you are a designer creating the comp for the product. The bottle shape was created by another designer in Adobe Illustrator. Your job is to apply the type treatment in Photoshop in preparation to present it to a client for review. All of the type controls you need are available in Photoshop, and you don't have to switch to another application to complete the project.

7   Select the 08Start.psd file and double-click it to open it in Photoshop.

8   Choose File > Save As, rename the file **08Working.psd**, and click Save.

Creating a clipping mask from type

A *clipping mask* is an object or a group of objects whose shape masks other artwork so that only areas that lie within the shape of the masking object are visible. In effect, you are clipping the artwork to conform to the shape of the object (or mask). In Photoshop, you can create a clipping mask from shapes or letters. In this exercise, you will use letters as a clipping mask to allow an image in another layer to show through the letters.

Adding guides to position type

The 08Working.psd file contains a background layer, which is the bottle, and a Blank Label layer, which will be the foundation for your typography. The Blank Label is the active layer on which you will begin your work. You'll start by zooming in on your work area and using ruler guides to help position your type.

1   Select the Zoom tool (🔍) and drag over the black-and-white portion of the blank label to zoom in to the area and center it in the image window. Repeat until you have a nice close-up view of the area, and enlarge the image window if necessary.

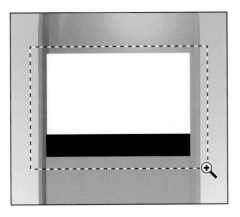

2 Choose View > Rulers to turn on guide rulers along the left and top borders of the image window. Then, drag a vertical guide from the left ruler to the center of the label (3½ inches) and release.

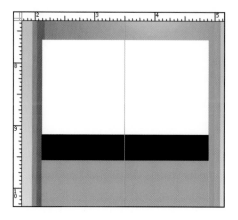

Adding point type

Now you're ready to actually add type to the composition. Photoshop lets you create horizontal or vertical type anywhere in an image. You can enter *point type* (a single letter, word, or line) or *paragraph type*. You will do both in this lesson, starting with point type.

1 Make sure that the Blank Layer is selected in the Layers palette. Then, select the Horizontal Type tool (**T**), and in the tool options bar, do the following:

- Choose a sans serif typeface, such as Myriad Pro, from the Font Family pop-up menu, and choose Bold from the Font Style pop-up menu.

- Type **79 pt** into the Size field and press Enter or Return.

- Click the Center text alignment button.

2 Click on the center guide in the white area of the label to set an insertion point, and type **OLIO** in all caps. Then click the Commit Any Current Edits button (✔) in the tool options bar.

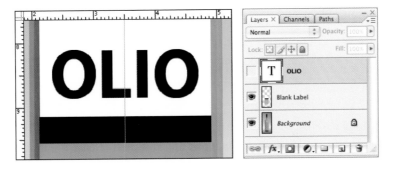

The word "Olio" is added to your label, and it appears in the Layers palette as a new type layer, OLIO. You can edit and manage the type layer as you would any other layer. You can add or change the text, change the orientation of the type, apply anti-aliasing, apply layer styles and transformations, and create masks. You can move, restack, copy, and edit layer options of a type layer as you would for any other layer.

3 Press Ctrl (Windows) or Command (Mac OS), and drag the OLIO type to visually center it vertically in the white box.

4 Choose File > Save to save your work so far.

Making a clipping mask and applying a drop shadow

Photoshop wrote the letters in black, the default text color. You want the letters to appear to be filled with an image of olives. So next you will use the letters to make a clipping mask that will allow another image layer to show through.

1 Click the Go To Bridge button () or use File > Open to open the Olives.psd file (located in the Lesson08 folder) in Photoshop. In Photoshop, arrange the image windows on-screen so that you can see both of them at once, and make sure that Olives.psd is the active image window.

2 In the Layers palette of the Olives.psd image, hold down Shift and drag the Background layer to the center of the 08Start.psd file, and then release the mouse. Pressing Shift as you drag centers the Olives.psd image in the composition.

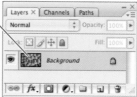

A new layer appears in the 08Working.psd Layers palette, Layer 1. This new layer contains the olives image, which you will use to show through the type. But before you make the clipping mask for it, you need make the olives image smaller, as it is too large for the composition.

3 With Layer 1 selected, choose Edit > Transform > Scale.

4 Grab a corner handle on the bounding box for the olives, and Shift-drag to make it smaller within the same proportions. You may need to move the pointer inside the box and drag to reposition the olives so that the image remains centered on the label. Resize the olives image so that it is approximately the same width as the white label.

5 Press Enter or Return to apply the transformation.

6 Double-click the Layer 1 name and change it to **Olives**. Then, press Enter or Return, or click away from the name in the Layers palette, to apply the change.

7 With the Olives layer still selected, choose Create Clipping Mask from the Layers palette menu.

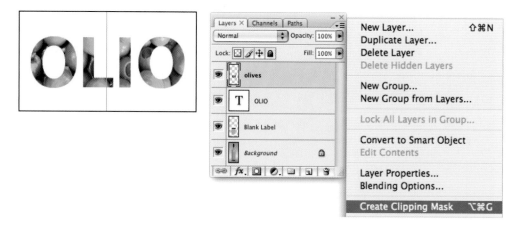

💡 *You can also make a clipping mask by holding down the Alt (Windows) or Option (Mac OS) key and clicking between the Olives and OLIO type layers.*

The olives now show through the OLIO letters. A small arrow in the Olives layer and the underlined Type layer indicate the clipping mask. Next, you will add a drop shadow to give the letters depth.

8 Select the OLIO type layer to make it active, and then click the Add Layer Style button (*fx*) at the bottom of the Layers palette and choose Drop Shadow from the pop-up menu.

9 In the Layer Style dialog box, change the Opacity to **35%**, accept all other default settings, and then click OK.

10 Choose File > Save to save your work so far, and close the Olives.psd image file without saving any changes.

Creating a design element from type

Next, you will add the vertical lines that appear at the top of the label using a type trick. These vertical lines need to be perfectly aligned, so you will use the capital "I" of a sans serif font instead of creating, copying, and moving individual lines. You will also easily adjust the size and spacing of the "lines" using the Character palette.

1 In the Layers palette, drag the lower right corner to expand the palette until some blank area is visible at the bottom. Click in the blank area to deselect all layers.

2 Select the Horizontal Type tool (T). In the tool options bar, do the following:

• Choose a sans serif typeface, preferably a narrow one such as Myriad Pro Condensed.

• Set the size to **36 pt** and press Enter or Return.

• Leave the Anti-aliasing pop-up menu set to Sharp.

• Choose Left alignment.

• Click the color swatch to open the Color Picker. Move the mouse over the olives showing through the OLIO letters to select a dark green from the photo, and click OK.

3 Click the pointer in the upper left corner of the white box and, holding down the Shift key, type **I** 12 times.

This creates a new type layer in the Layers palette.

4 Select the Move tool ( ), position it inside the box, and drag the letters so that their tops touch the top edge of the white box.

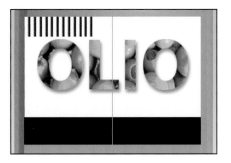

Note: Entering type in a Photoshop image window puts the Type tool in edit mode. Before you can perform other actions or use other tools, you must commit your editing in the layer—as you did with the OLIO type using the Commit Any Current Edits button. Selecting another tool or layer has the same effect as clicking the Commit Any Current Edits button in the tool options bar. You cannot commit to current edits by pressing Enter or Return; this action merely creates a new line for typing.

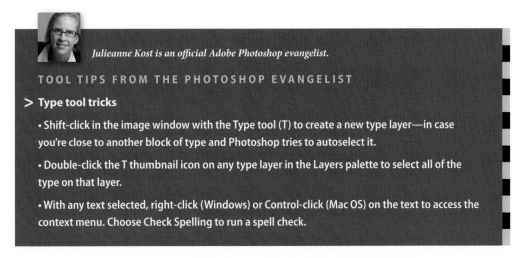

Julieanne Kost is an official Adobe Photoshop evangelist.

TOOL TIPS FROM THE PHOTOSHOP EVANGELIST

> Type tool tricks

• Shift-click in the image window with the Type tool (T) to create a new type layer—in case you're close to another block of type and Photoshop tries to autoselect it.

• Double-click the T thumbnail icon on any type layer in the Layers palette to select all of the type on that layer.

• With any text selected, right-click (Windows) or Control-click (Mac OS) on the text to access the context menu. Choose Check Spelling to run a spell check.

Now, you will adjust the tracking to space the "lines" a bit wider apart.

5 Toggle open the Character palette by choosing Window > Character.

6 Type **40** in the Tracking box, or scrub the Tracking label to set the value.

Now it is time to adjust the positioning of the OLIO letters so that they're not too close to the vertical lines. To do that, you need to link the OLIO type layer and the olive image mask layer and move them as a unit.

7 Click to select the Olives layer and then Shift-click the OLIO type layer to also select it. Then choose Link Layers from the Layers palette pop-up menu. A link icon appears next to the names of both layers.

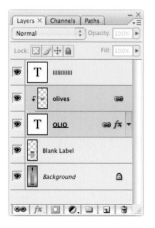

8 Select the Move tool (▶♦) and drag the type down as desired.

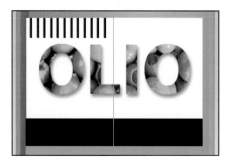

9 Choose File > Save to save your work so far.

Using interactive formatting controls

The Character palette in Photoshop contains many options to help you set beautiful type, but not all of the choices and controls are obvious—as in the trick of scrubbing the Tracking icon to choose a tracking value. In this exercise, you will make a type selection using another advanced trick for previewing type in the Character palette.

1 Click in a blank area of the Layers palette to deselect all layers.

2 Select the Horizontal Type tool (T). In the tool options bar, do the following:

• Click the Center text alignment button.

• Click the color box and choose a bright red color. Click OK to close the Color Picker.

For the moment, don't worry about which typeface or size you're using.

3 Click the pointer on the center guide in the black stripe in the label. To be sure that you don't accidentally start editing the OLIO text, make sure that the pointer has a thin dotted line around it (⌶) when you click. This means you'll create a new type layer when you type.

4 Type **EXTRA VIRGIN** in all caps.

Photoshop writes the text in whatever typeface (and size) was previously specified. But what if you want to use a different typeface? What if you're not sure which typeface you want to use?

5 Select the EXTRA VIRGIN text in the image window, and then, in the Character palette, click on the name in the Font Family pop-up menu. The name becomes highlighted.

6 Press the Up or Down Arrow key to cycle through the available fonts, and watch as Photoshop interactively previews each font in the highlighted EXTRA VIRGIN letters on-screen.

7 After experimenting, choose the sans serif typeface that you used for the OLIO letters—Myriad Pro, in our example—and then use the Tab key to jump to the Font Style box.

8 Again, use the Up and Down Arrow keys to cycle through available styles (if available) to choose one (we chose Bold), and watch as the styles preview interactively in the image window.

9 Tab to the Size box, and use the Up or Down Arrow keys to set the type at 11 points.

Press Shift as you use the Up and Down Arrow keys to change the Size increment by 10 points.

10 Tab to the Tracking field, and set the Tracking to 280: Type the value, use the Up Arrow key (press Shift as you press the key to increase the increment by 100), or scrub to set it.

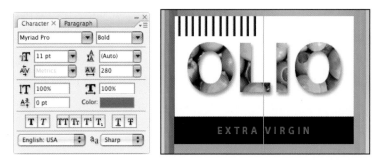

11 Select the Move tool (✛) and drag the EXTRA VIRGIN text so that it is centered in the black bar of the label.

12 Choose File > Save to save your work so far.

Warping point type

Now you will add the words "Olive Oil" to the label, and then warp them to make them more playful. *Warping* lets you distort type to conform to a variety of shapes, such as an arc or a wave. The warp style you select is an attribute of the type layer—you can change a layer's warp style at any time to change the overall shape of the warp. Warping options give you precise control over the orientation and perspective of the warp effect.

1 Scroll or use the Hand tool ( ) to move the visible area of the image window so that the orange part of the label, below the black bar, is in the center of the screen. Enlarge the image window by dragging the lower right corner, if necessary.

2 Click in a blank area of the Layers palette to deselect all layers.

3 Select the Horizontal Type tool (T), and in the Character palette, do the following:

- Choose a traditional serif typeface, such as Adobe Garamond.

- Set the size to 40 points.

- Set the tracking to 0.

- Make the color white.

4 Click and drag a text box in the upper area of the orange box, and then type **Olive Oil**. Then click the Commit Any Current Edits button ( ) in the tool options bar.

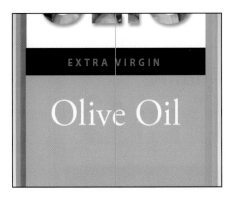

The words appear on the label, and a new layer, Olive Oil, appears in the Layers palette.

5 Right-click (Windows) or Control-click (Mac OS) on the Olive Oil layer in the Layers palette, and choose Warp Text from the context menu.

6 In the Warp Text dialog box, choose Style > Wave and click the Horizontal radio button. For Bend, specify **+77%**, Horizontal Distortion **–7%**, and Vertical Distortion **–24%**. Then click OK.

The words "Olive Oil" appear to float like a wave on the label.

Designing a paragraph of type

All of the text you've written on this label so far has been a few discrete words or lines—
point type. Often, however, many designs call for full paragraphs of text. You can design
complete paragraphs of type in Photoshop; you don't have to switch to a dedicated page-
layout program for sophisticated paragraph type controls.

Using guides for positioning

Next, you will add a paragraph of descriptive content to the label in Photoshop. You will
start by adding some guides to the work area to help you position the paragraph.

1   Drag two guides from the left vertical ruler, placing the first one at 2½ inches and the
second at 4½ inches.

2   Drag two guides down from the top horizontal ruler, placing the first one at 10¾
inches and the second at 13 inches.

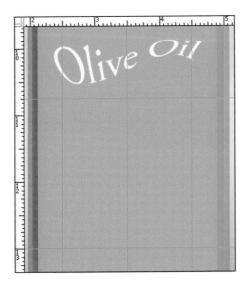

Adding paragraph type from a sticky note

Now you're ready to add the text. In a real design environment, the text might be
provided to you in the form of a word processing document, or perhaps in the body of
an e-mail, which you could copy and paste into Photoshop. Or you might have to type
it in. Another easy way to add a bit of text is for the copywriter to attach it to the image
file in a sticky note.

1 Double-click the yellow sticky note annotation in the lower right corner of the image window to open it.

Note: You may need to change the view or scroll to see the open note on-screen.

2 Drag with the pointer to select all of the text in the note, and then press Ctrl+C (Windows) or Command+C (Mac OS) to copy it to the clipboard. Then click the close button to close the sticky note window.

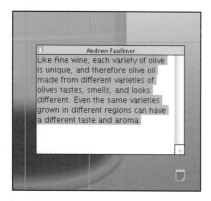

Before you paste it in, specify your type options.

3 Make sure that no layers are selected in the Layers palette.

4 Select the Horizontal Type tool (T), and in the Character palette, do the following:

• Choose a sans serif typeface, such as Myriad Pro Regular.

• Set the size to 10 points.

• Set the leading to 24 points.

• Set the tracking to 5.

• Make the color black.

4 Click the Paragraph tab to bring the Paragraph palette forward, and click the Justify All button (▤).

5 Drag with the Type tool to create a text box that matches the guides you positioned in the previous exercise, and then press Ctrl+V (Windows) or Command+V (Mac OS) to paste the text from the clipboard into the text box.

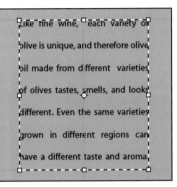

The text appears in the image window with the styles you specified, and it wraps to the dimensions of the bounding box. In our example, the second-to-last line had some unsightly gaps, so as a fine-tuning measure, we will fix that now.

💡 *If you resize the bounding box, the type will reflow within the adjusted rectangle.*

6 Position the Horizontal Type tool (T) over the second-to-last line of the paragraph, and triple-click to select the line.

7 Click the Character tab to bring the Character palette forward, and set tracking to 60.

8 Click the Commit Any Current Edits button (✔) in the tool options bar. Your paragraph text now appears as the layer named, "Like fine wine. . . ."

9 Choose File > Save to save your work so far.

OpenType in Photoshop: More fun with bottles

OpenType is a cross-platform font file format developed jointly by Adobe and Microsoft. The format uses a single font file for both Macintosh and Windows computers, so you can move files from one platform to another without fonts being substituted or text reflowing. Supported in Photoshop CS3, OpenType offers widely expanded character sets and layout features, such as swashes and discretionary ligatures, that aren't available in current PostScript and TrueType fonts. This, in turn, provides richer linguistic support and advanced typography control. For more details, watch the OpenType QuickTime movie on the *Adobe Photoshop CS3 Classroom in a Book* CD in Movies/OpenType.mov. Here are some highlights of OpenType.

The OpenType menu The Character palette menu includes an OpenType submenu that displays all available features for a selected OpenType font, including ligatures, alternates, and fractions. Grayed out features are unavailable for that typeface; checked features have been applied.

Discretionary ligatures To add a discretionary ligature to two OpenType letters, such as to a "th" in the Bickham Script Standard typeface, select them in the image, and choose OpenType > Discretionary Ligatures from the Character palette menu.

If you'd like to preview your OpenType choices before committing to them, work with the Adobe Illustrator CS3 Glyphs palette: Copy your text in Photoshop and paste it into an Illustrator document. Then, open the Glyphs palette by choosing Window > Type > Glyphs. Select the text you want to change, and choose Show > Alternates For Current Selection. Double-click a glyph to apply it, and when you've finished, copy and paste the new type into your Photoshop file.

Swashes Adding swashes or alternate characters works the same way: Select the letter, such as a capital "T" in Bickham Script, and choose OpenType > Swash to change the ordinary capital into a dramatically ornate swash T.

Creating true fractions Type fractions as usual—for example, 1-slash-2—and then select the characters, and from the Character palette menu, choose OpenType > Fractions. Photoshop applies the true fraction.

Adding the last two lines

You've almost finished adding text to the label. You just have to add two more lines.

1 With the Like fine wine. . . layer selected, click inside the paragraph of text, and then drag the handle in the middle of the lower edge of the text box down to the bottom of the edge of the label.

2 Place the type pointer at the end of the paragraph of text and press Enter or Return.

3 Type **16 FL Ounces**.

4 Triple-click to select "16 FL Ounces." In the Character palette, set the font size to 13 points and set the Baseline Shift to −10; this option moves characters up or down relative to the baseline of the surrounding text.

5 In the toolbox, click the Switch Colors button to make the type white.

6 In the Paragraph palette, click the Center text button (⬛). Then, click the Commit Any Current Edits button (✔) in the tool options bar.

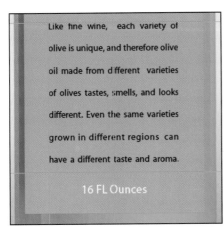

Adding vertical type

The last line will be vertical.

1 Deselect all layers in the Layers palette. Then, click and hold on the Horizontal Type tool to display the Vertical Type tool (⏐T), which is hidden under the Horizontal Type tool.

2 Drag in the orange area of the label to the right of the descriptive text to create a long, narrow text box. Start from the lower or upper right corner so that you don't accidentally select the paragraph text.

3 Type **PRODUCT OF ITALY**, all caps.

4 Select the letters either by dragging or triple-clicking them, and then, in the Character palette, do the following:

- Choose a serif typeface, such as Adobe Garamond.

- Set the size to 8 points.

- Set the tracking to 300.

- Make the color red.

5 Click the Commit Any Current Edits button (✔) in the tool options bar. Your vertical text now appears as the layer named PRODUCT OF ITALY. Use the Move tool (▸⊹) and drag to center it if necessary.

Now, you'll do a bit of clean up.

6 Click to select the annotation, and then right-click (Windows) or Control-click (Mac OS) and choose Delete Note from the context menu; click OK at the alert to delete the annotation.

7 Hide the guides by choosing the Hand tool (✋) and then pressing Ctrl+; (Windows) or Command+; (Mac OS). Then, zoom out to get a nice look at your work.

8 Choose File > Save to save your work so far.

Warping a layer

All of the text is now on the label, but there's one problem: The bottle looks three-dimensional, while the label looks unrealistically flat on its surface. So your final effect will be to warp the label and its contents to look like they realistically conform to the bottle shape.

Earlier in this lesson, you warped the words "Olive Oil" so that the letters appeared wavy. For this exercise, however, you will apply the warp transformation to a layer, rather than to individual letters. To do this, you will group the label and type layers, and then transform the new, grouped layer using the Smart Objects feature. Using Smart Objects allows you to continue to edit both the contents of the layer (the type) and to edit the warp after you apply the transformation.

Grouping layers into a Smart Object

Creating the Smart Object is a two-step process. First you have to merge the OLIO type layer and its clipping mask, then you will group all of the label's layers into the Smart Object.

1 Click to select the OLIO layer in the Layers palette, and then press Shift and click to also select the Olives layer. Then choose Merge Layers from the Layers palette pop-up menu. Photoshop combines them into one layer, Olives.

2 Click to select the Blank Label layer in the Layers palette and then Shift-click the topmost layer in the stack, PRODUCT OF ITALY. Photoshop selects the two layers and all of the layers in between. Then, choose Convert To Smart Object from the Layers palette pop-up menu.

Right-click (Windows) or Control-click (Mac OS) to display the context menu with the Merge Layers and Convert To Smart Objects commands.

Photoshop groups the selected layers into one Smart Object layer. The name for this new layer is the name of the top layer of the old stack, PRODUCT OF ITALY.

Warping with Smart Objects

Now you will warp the Smart Object layer to match the contour of the bottle. To do this, it helps to have your guides visible.

1 If the guides are not still visible, choose View > Show > Guides to display them. Then, zoom in to the label.

2 With the PRODUCT OF ITALY layer selected, choose Edit > Transform > Warp.

Photoshop lays a 3-x-3 grid over the layer in the image window, with handles and lines that you can drag to warp the layer as desired.

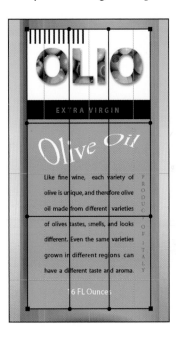

3 To help you apply the warp, drag out four horizontal guides, as follows: Place one guide at the top of the label, and one guide along the bottom of the label. Then, place two more guides one-quarter inch below each of those guides.

4 One at a time, click the center of each horizontal line of the grid and drag the line down one-quarter inch to create the curved label.

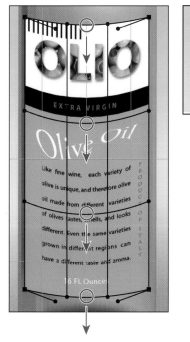

5 When you've finished, press Enter or Return to apply the warp transformation.

6 Hide the visible guides by selecting the Hand tool (🖐) and pressing Ctrl-; (Windows) or Command-; (Mac OS). Then, double-click the Hand tool to see the whole bottle composition on your screen.

Congratulations! You've added and stylized all of the type on the Olio olive oil bottle. If you'd like to experiment further with the capabilities of Smart Objects, go on to the "Extra Credit" on page 275. Otherwise, in the real world, you would flatten and save this image file for printing.

7 Choose File > Save As, rename the file as 08Start_flattened. Keeping a layered version lets you return to the file in the future to edit it—as you'll do if you complete the extra-credit section.

8 Choose Layer > Flatten Image.

9 Choose File > Save, and then close the image window.

⭐EXTRA CREDIT *You can take full advantage of your Smart Object now by editing the label's content and letting Photoshop automatically update the bottle composition.*

1   Double-click the PRODUCT OF ITALY Smart Object thumbnail in the Layers palette. (If you get a Smart Object alert dialog box, just click OK.) Photoshop opens the Smart Object in its own window.

2   Select the Horizontal type tool (**T**), and in the Smart Object image window, change the "16 FL Ounces" text and to **32 fl. ounces**. Then click the Commit Any Current Edits button (✔).

3   Click the red close button, and when prompted, click Save to save your changes.

Photoshop returns to the 08Start.psd image file and applies the Smart Object updates to the label. You can repeat this process to make more edits as often as you'd like without compromising the quality of the image or the transformation. To edit the warp effect at any time, simply choose Edit > Transform > Warp in the 08Working.psd image file, and continue to edit the transformation nondestructively.

Dancing with Type *

An excerpt from Russell Brown's Power Hour: Adobe Photoshop Tips and Techniques

Russell Brown

Dancer before

Dancer with type

Applying text to a complex path

In this fine sidebar, I'm going to demonstrate how to place text on a path. We will start with an image of a dancer. We will create a selection around the contours of her body, which we will then convert to a path. Then, we will apply the text to the path, finesse it, and voilà—you will apply text to a complex path. As you read the steps, follow along with the QuickTime movie of this tutorial that comes on the *Adobe Photoshop CS3 Classroom in a Book* CD.

—*Russell Brown*

Watch the movie! See this tutorial's detailed steps in the QuickTime movie included on the *Adobe Photoshop CS3 Classroom in a Book* CD. Browse to Movies/ DancingWithType/ DancingWithType.mov. Double-click the movie file; then click the Play button.

© Digital Vision

Step 1: Select the dancer

The evenly colored, flat background makes the Magic Wand a good selection tool to use with this image. With the Dancer layer active, click with the Magic Wand in the background to select similarly colored pixels, and then press Shift and continue clicking until everything but the dancer is selected. Then simply invert the selection by pressing Ctrl+Shift+I (Windows) or Command+Shift+I (Mac OS).

Step 2: Convert to a path

Convert the selection to a path by choosing Make Work Path from the Paths palette pop-up menu. In the Make Work Path dialog box, set Tolerance to 1.0 and click OK. The lower the tolerance, the greater detail and more control points the path will have. Because this is a complex path, we want to be sure we have enough detail.

Step 3: Place text on the path

Select the Dancing with Type layer, which contains the text. Use the Type tool to select and copy the text to the clipboard. Then hide the text layer, select the Dancer layer, click on the path, and press Ctrl+V (Windows) or Command+V (Mac OS) multiple times to paste the text all around the dancer path.

Step 4: Hide inside descenders

To finish up, we will hide the descenders that obscure the dancer. In the Paths palette, press Ctrl (Windows) or Command (Mac OS) and click on the Dancer path icon to convert the path to a selection. In the Layers palette, select the type-on-a-path layer, press Alt (Windows) or Option (Mac OS), and click the Add Layer Mask button. Ta da—the descenders are hidden!

Review

▶ **Review questions**

1 How does Photoshop treat type?

2 How is a text layer the same or different from other layers in Photoshop?

3 What is a clipping mask and how do you make one from type?

4 Describe two little-known ways to control type formatting in Photoshop.

▶ **Review answers**

1 Type in Photoshop consists of mathematically defined shapes that describe the letters, numbers, and symbols of a typeface. When you add type to an image in Photoshop, the characters are composed of pixels and have the same resolution as the image file. However, Photoshop preserves the vector-based type outlines and uses them when you scale or resize type, save a PDF or EPS file, or print the image to a PostScript printer.

2 Type that is added to an image appears in the Layers palette as a text layer that can be edited and managed in the same way as any other kind of layer. You can add and edit the text, change the orientation of the type, and apply anti-aliasing as well as move, restack, copy, and edit layer options.

3 A *clipping mask* is an object or group whose shape masks other artwork so that only areas that lie within the shape are visible. The letters on any text layer can be converted to a clipping mask by selecting both the text layer and the layer you want to show through the letters, and then choosing Create Clipping Mask from the Layers palette pop-up menu.

4 Select text in the image window, and in the Character palette or on the Type tool options bar you can do the following:

• Scrub the Size, Leading, Tracking, Kerning, Scaling, and Baseline Shift values.

• Select some type in the image window, click the font displayed in the Font Family pop-up menu, and press the up and down arrow keys to cycle through the available fonts and watch them preview interactively in the image window.

Unlike bitmap images, vector images retain their crisp edges at any enlargement. You can draw vector shapes and paths in your Photoshop images and add vector masks to control what is shown in an image. This lesson will introduce you to advanced uses of vector shapes and vector masks.

9 | Vector Drawing Techniques

Lesson overview

In this lesson, you'll learn how to do the following:

- Differentiate between bitmap and vector graphics.

- Draw straight and curved paths using the Pen tool.

- Convert a path to a selection, and convert a selection to a path.

- Save paths.

- Draw and edit layer shapes.

- Draw custom layer shapes.

- Import and edit a Smart Object from Adobe Illustrator.

This lesson will take about 90 minutes to complete. If needed, remove the previous lesson folder from your hard drive, and copy the Lesson9 folder onto it. As you work on this lesson, you'll preserve the start files. If you need to restore the start files, copy them from the *Adobe Photoshop CS3 Classroom in a Book* CD.

About bitmap images and vector graphics

Before working with vector shapes and vector paths, it's important to understand the basic differences between the two main categories of computer graphics: *bitmap images* and *vector graphics*. You can use Photoshop to work with either type of graphic; in fact, you can combine both bitmap and vector data in an individual Photoshop image file.

Bitmap images, technically called *raster images*, are based on a grid of colors known as pixels. Each pixel is assigned a specific location and color value. In working with bitmap images, you edit groups of pixels rather than objects or shapes. Because bitmap graphics can represent subtle gradations of shade and color, they are appropriate for continuous-tone images such as photographs or artwork created in painting programs. A disadvantage of bitmap graphics is that they contain a fixed number of pixels. As a result, they can lose detail and appear jagged when scaled up on-screen or if they are printed at a lower resolution than that for which they were created.

Vector graphics are made up of lines and curves defined by mathematical objects called *vectors*. These graphics retain their crispness whether they are moved, resized, or have their color changed. Vector graphics are appropriate for illustrations, type, and graphics such as logos that may be scaled to different sizes.

Logo drawn as vector art

Logo rasterized as bitmap art

About paths and the Pen tool

In Photoshop, the outline of a vector shape is a *path*. A path is a curved or straight line segment you draw using the Pen tool, Magnetic Pen tool, or Freeform Pen tool. Of these tools, the Pen tool draws paths with the greatest precision; the Magnetic Pen tool and Freeform Pen tool draw paths as if you were drawing with a pencil on paper.

Julieanne Kost is an official Adobe Photoshop evangelist.

TOOL TIPS FROM THE PHOTOSHOP EVANGELIST

> Any tool in the toolbox can be selected with a single letter shortcut key. Type the letter, get the tool. For example, press P to select the Pen tool. Pressing Shift with the key cycles though any nested tools in a group. So pressing Shift+P toggles between the Pen and Freeform Pen tools.

Paths can be open or closed. Open paths (such as a wavy line) have two distinct endpoints. Closed paths (such as a circle) are continuous. The type of path you draw affects how it can be selected and adjusted.

Paths that have not been filled or stroked do not print when you print your artwork. This is because paths are vector objects that contain no pixels, unlike the bitmap shapes drawn by the Pencil tool and other painting tools.

Getting started

You'll start the lesson by viewing a copy of the finished image that you'll create—a poster for a fictitious toy company.

1 Start Adobe Photoshop, holding down Ctrl+Alt+Shift (Windows) or Command+Option+Shift (Mac OS) to restore the default preferences. (See "Restoring default preferences" on page 6.)

2 When prompted, click Yes to confirm that you want to reset preferences, and Close to close the Welcome Screen.

3 Click the Go To Bridge button (▨) in the tool options bar to open Adobe Bridge.

4 In the Favorites palette in the upper left corner of Bridge, click the Lessons favorite, and then double-click the Lesson9 folder in the thumbnail preview area.

5 Select the 9End.psd file so that it appears in the center preview window. Enlarge the preview if needed to get a good close-up view by dragging the thumbnail slider at the bottom of the window.

To create this poster, you'll open the image of the toy space ship and practice making paths and selections using the Pen tool. Along the way, you'll learn advanced uses of path and vector masks, and ways to use Smart Objects, as you create the background shapes and type.

Note: If you open the 9End.psd file in Photoshop, you might be prompted to update type layers. If so, click Update. This notice sometimes appears when files are transferred between computers, especially between Windows and Mac OS.

6 When you've finished looking at 9End.psd, double-click the Saucer.psd file to open it in Photoshop.

7 Choose File > Save As, rename the file **09Working.psd**, and click Save.

Using paths with artwork

You'll start by using the Pen tool to make selections in the image of the flying saucer. The saucer has long, smooth, curved edges that would be difficult to select using other methods.

You'll draw a path around the saucer and create two paths inside it. After you've drawn the paths, you'll convert them to selections. Then you'll subtract one selection from the other so that only the saucer and none of the starry sky is selected. Finally, you'll make a new layer from the saucer image and change the image that appears behind it.

When drawing a freehand path using the Pen tool, use as few points as possible to create the shape you want. The fewer points you use, the smoother the curves are and the more efficient your file is.

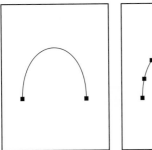
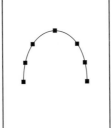

Correct number of
points

Too many points

Creating paths with the Pen tool

You can use the Pen tool to create paths that are straight or curved, open or closed. If you're unfamiliar with the Pen tool, it can be confusing to use at first. Understanding the elements of a path and how to create them with the Pen tool makes paths much easier to draw.

To create a straight path, click the mouse button. The first time you click, you set the starting point. Each time that you click thereafter, a straight line is drawn between the previous point and the current point. To draw complex straight-segment paths with the Pen tool, simply continue to add points.

To create a curved path, click to place an anchor point, drag to create a direction line for that point, and then click to place the next anchor point. Each direction line ends in two direction points; the positions of direction lines and points determine the size and shape of the curved segment. Moving the direction lines and points reshapes the curves in a path.

Smooth curves are connected by anchor points called smooth points. Sharply curved paths are connected by corner points. When you move a direction line on a smooth point, the curved segments on both sides of the point adjust simultaneously, but when you move a direction line on a corner point, only the curve on the same side of the point as the direction line is adjusted.

Path segments and anchor points can be moved after they're drawn, either individually or as a group. When a path contains more than one segment, you can drag individual anchor points to adjust individual segments of the path, or select all of the anchor points in a path to edit the entire path. Use the Direct Selection tool (λ) to select and adjust an anchor point, a path segment, or an entire path.

Creating a closed path differs from creating an open path in the way that you end the path. To end an open path, click the Pen tool ($\mathcal{Q}$) in the toolbox. To create a closed path, position the Pen tool pointer over the starting point and click. Closing a path automatically ends the path. After the path closes, the Pen tool pointer appears with a small x, indicating that your next click will start a new path.

As you draw paths, a temporary storage area named Work Path appears in the Paths palette. It's a good idea to save work paths, and it's essential if you use multiple discrete paths in the same image file. If you deselect an existing Work Path in the Paths palette and then start drawing again, a new work path will replace the original one, which will be lost. To save a work path, double-click it in the Paths palette, type a name in the Save Path dialog box, and click OK to rename and save the path. The path remains selected in the Paths palette.

Drawing the outline of a shape

In this exercise, you're going to use the Pen tool to connect the dots from point A to point N, and then back to point A. You'll set some straight segments, some smooth curve points, and some corner points.

You'll begin by configuring the Pen tool options and your work area, and then you'll trace the outline of a flying saucer using a template.

1 In the toolbox, select the Pen tool ( ).

2 In the tool options bar, select or verify the following settings:

- Select the Paths ( ) option.

- Click the arrow for Geometry Options and make sure that the Rubber Band check box is *not* selected in the Pen Options pop-up palette.

- Make sure that the Auto Add/Delete option is selected.

- Select the Add To Path Area option ( ).

A. Paths option **B.** *Geometry Options menu* **C.** *Add To Path Area option*

3 Click the Paths tab to bring that palette to the front of the Layers palette group.

The Paths palette displays thumbnail previews of the paths you draw. Currently, the palette is empty because you haven't started drawing.

4 If necessary, zoom in so that you can easily see the lettered points and red dots on the shape template that has been created for you. Make sure you can see the whole template in the image window, and be sure to reselect the Pen tool after you zoom.

5 Position the pointer on point A. Click the point and drag to its red dot to set the first anchor point and the direction of the first curve. Do the same thing at point B.

At the corner of the cockpit (point B), you'll need to make a corner point to create a sharp transition between the curved segment and the straight one.

6 Alt-click (Windows) or Option-click (Mac OS) point B to convert the smooth point into a corner point and remove one of the direction lines.

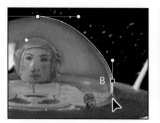

Setting a smooth point at B   Converting the smooth point
to a corner point

7 Click point C to set a straight segment (don't drag).

If you make a mistake while you're drawing, choose Edit > Undo to undo the step. Then resume drawing.

8 Click point D and drag up from point D to its red dot. Then, click point E and drag down from point E to its red dot.

9 Click point F.

10 Set curve points at G, H, and I by clicking each point and dragging from the point to its red dot, each in turn.

11 Click point J.

12 Set curve points at K and L by clicking each point and dragging from each one to its respective red dot.

13 Click point M.

14 Click point N and don't release the mouse button. Press Alt (Windows) or Option (Mac OS) and drag from point N to the red dot to add one direction line to the anchor point at N. Then, release the mouse button and the Alt or Option key.

15 Move the pointer over point A so that a small circle appears in the pointer icon, indicating that you are about to close the path. (The small circle may be difficult to see because the image is dark and the circle is faint.) Drag from point A to the red dot, and then release the mouse button to draw the last curved line.

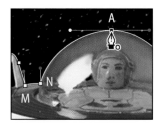

16 In the Paths palette, double-click the Work Path, type **Saucer** in the Save Path dialog box, and click OK to save it.

17 Choose File > Save to save your work.

Converting selections to paths

Now, you'll create a second path using a different method. First, you'll use a selection tool to select a similarly colored area, and then you'll convert the selection to a path. (You can convert any selection made with a selection tool into a path.)

1 Click the Layers tab to display the Layers palette, and then drag the Template layer to the Trash button at the bottom of the palette. You no longer need this layer.

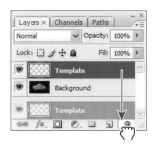

2   Select the Magic Wand tool (✳) in the tool box, hidden under the Quick Selection tool.

3   In the Magic Wand Tool options bar, make sure that the Tolerance value is **32**.

4   Carefully click the black area inside one of the saucer's vertical fins.

5   Shift-click inside the other fin to add that black area to the selection.

6   Click the Paths tab to bring the Paths palette forward. Then, click the Make Work Path From Selection button (◭) at the bottom of the palette.

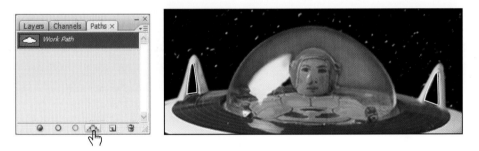

The selections are converted to paths, and a new Work Path is created.

7   Double-click the Work Path, name it **Fins**, and then click OK to save the path.

8   Choose File > Save to save your work.

Converting paths to selections

Just as you can convert selection borders to paths, so you can convert paths to selections. With their smooth outlines, paths let you make precise selections. Now that you've drawn paths for the spaceship and its fins, you'll convert those paths to a selection and apply a filter to the selection.

1   In the Paths palette, click the Saucer path to make it active.

2   Convert the Saucer path to a selection by doing one of the following:

•   From the Paths palette menu, choose Make Selection, and then click OK to close the dialog box that appears.

•   Drag the Saucer path to the Load Path As Selection button (○) at the bottom of the Paths palette.

💡 *Simply click the Load Path As Selection button (○) at the bottom of the Paths palette to convert the active path to a selection.*

Next, you'll subtract the Fins selection from the Saucer selection so that you can see the background through the vacant areas in the fins.

3 In the Paths palette, click the Fins path to make it active. Then, from the Paths palette menu, choose Make Selection.

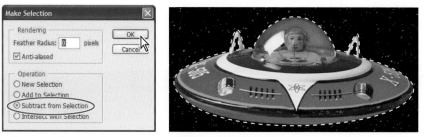

4 In the Operation area of the Make Selection dialog box, select Subtract from Selection, and click OK.

*Subtracting the Fins selection
from the Saucer selection*

Result

The Fins path is simultaneously converted to a selection and subtracted from the Saucer selection.

Leave the paths selected, because you're going to use the selection in the next procedure.

Converting the selection to a layer

Now, you'll see how creating the selection with the Pen tool can help you achieve interesting effects. Because you've isolated the saucer, you can create a duplicate of it on a new layer. Then, you can copy it to another image file—specifically, to the image that is the background for the toy store poster.

1 Make sure that you can still see the selection outline in the image window. If you can't, it was deselected and you need to repeat the previous exercise, "Converting paths to selections."

2 Choose Layer > New > Layer Via Copy.

A new layer appears in the Layers palette, Layer 1. The Layer 1 thumbnail shows that the layer contains only the image of the flying saucer, not the sky areas of the original layer.

3 In the Layers palette, double-click Layer 1, type **Saucer** to rename it, and press Enter or Return.

4 Use Adobe Bridge or the File > Open command to open the 9Start.psd file, located in the Lessons/Lesson9 folder.

This is a Photoshop image of a graduated blue background with a planet in the lower part of the image.

5 If necessary, move the image windows so that you can see at least part of both the Saucer.psd window and the 9Start.psd window on-screen. Make sure that no layers are selected in the 9Start.psd file Layers palette; then make the 09Working.psd image window active, and select the Saucer layer in the Layers palette.

6 In the toolbox, select the Move tool (), and drag from the 09Working.psd image window to the 9Start.psd image window so that the saucer appears in the sky.

7 Close the 09Working.psd image without saving changes, leaving the 9Start.psd file open and active.

Now you'll position the flying saucer more precisely in the poster background.

8 Select the Saucer layer in the Layers palette and choose Edit > Free Transform.

A bounding box appears around the saucer.

9 Position the cursor near any corner control handle until it turns into rotate cursor
(↱), then drag to rotate the saucer until it's at about a 20-degree angle. When you're
satisfied, press Enter or Return.

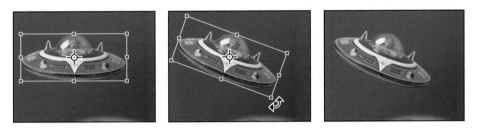

Note: *If you accidentally distort the saucer instead of rotating it, press Ctrl+. [period]
(Windows) or Command+. [period] (Mac OS) and start over.*

10 To finesse the positioning of the saucer, make sure that the Saucer layer is still
selected and use the Move tool to drag the saucer so that it grazes the top of the planet,
as in the following image.

11 Choose File > Save As, rename the file **09B_Working.psd**, and click Save.

Creating vector objects for the background

Many posters are designed to be scalable, either up or down, while retaining a crisp appearance. This is a good use for vector shapes. Next, you'll create vector shapes with paths, and use masks to control what appears in the poster. Because they're vector, the shapes can be scaled in future design revisions without a loss of quality or detail.

Drawing a scalable shape

You'll begin by creating a white kidney-shaped object for the backdrop of the poster.

1 Choose View > Rulers to display the horizontal and vertical rulers.

2 Drag the tab for the Paths palette out of the Layers palette group so that it floats independently. Since you'll be using the Layers and Paths palettes frequently in this exercise, it's convenient to have them separated.

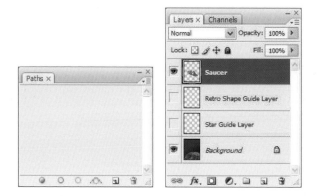

3 Hide all of the layers except the Retro Shape Guide layer and the Background layer by clicking the appropriate eye icons in the Layers palette. Select the Background layer to make it active.

 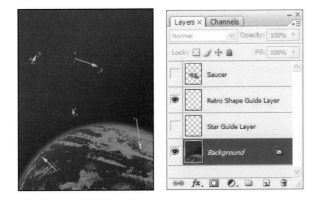

The guide layer will serve as a template as you draw the kidney shape.

4 Set the foreground and background colors to their defaults (black and white, respectively) by clicking the Default Foreground And Background Colors button (◼) in the toolbox (or type the keyboard shortcut D), and then swap the foreground and background colors by clicking the Switch Foreground And Background Colors button (↰) (or type X). Now the foreground color is white.

A. Default Foreground And Background Colors button
B. Foreground Color button
C. Switch Foreground And Background Colors button
D. Background Color button

5 In the toolbox, select the Pen tool (✎). Then, in the tool options bar, make sure that the Shape Layers option is selected.

6 Create the shape by clicking and dragging as follows:

- Click point A and drag a direction line up and to the left of point B, and then release.

- Click point C and drag a direction line toward and above point D, and then release.

- Continue to draw curved segments in this way around the shape until you return to point A, and then click on A to close the path.

Note: *If you have trouble, open the saucer image again and practice drawing the path around the saucer shape until you get more comfortable with drawing curved path segments. Also, be sure to read the sidebar, "Creating paths with the Pen tool," on page 286.*

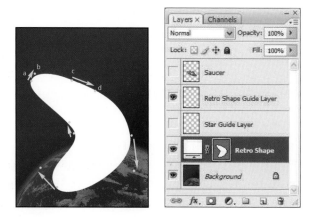

Notice as you drew that Photoshop automatically created a new layer, Shape 1, in the Layers palette.

7 Double-click the Shape 1 name, rename the shape layer **Retro Shape**, and press Enter or Return.

8 Hide the Retro Shape Guide layer by clicking its eye icon in the Layers palette.

9 Choose File > Save to save your work.

Deselecting paths

Deselecting paths is sometimes necessary to see the appropriate tool options bar when you select a vector tool. Deselecting paths can also help you view certain effects that might be obscured if a path is highlighted. Before proceeding to the next exercise, you'll make sure that all paths are deselected.

1 Select the Path Selection tool (➤), which may be hidden under the Direct Selection tool (➤).

2 In the tool options bar, click the Dismiss Target Path button (✔).

Note: You can also deselect paths by clicking in the blank area below the paths in the Paths palette.

Notice that the border between the white kidney shape and the blue background has a grainy quality. What you see is actually the path itself, which is a nonprinting item. This is a visual clue that the Retro Shape layer is still selected.

About shape layers

A shape layer has two components: a fill and a shape. The fill properties determine the color (or colors), pattern, and transparency of the layer. The shape is a layer mask that defines the areas in which the fill can be seen and those areas in which the fill is hidden.

In the layer you've just created, the fill is white. The fill color is visible within the shape you drew and is not visible in the rest of the image, so the background sky can be seen around it.

In the Layers palette, your Retro Shape layer sits above the Background layer because the background was selected when you started to draw. The shape layer has three items along with the layer name: two thumbnail images and a link icon between them.

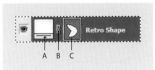

A. Fill thumbnail B. Layer mask link icon C. Mask thumbnail

The left thumbnail shows that the entire layer is filled with the white foreground color. The nonfunctioning small slider underneath the thumbnail symbolizes that the layer is editable.

The Mask thumbnail on the right shows the vector mask for the layer. In this thumbnail, white indicates the area where the image is exposed, and gray indicates the areas where the image is blocked.

The icon between the two thumbnails shows that the layer and the vector mask are linked.

Subtracting shapes from a shape layer

After you create a shape layer (vector graphic), you can set options to subtract new shapes from the vector graphic. You can also use the Path Selection tool and the Direct Selection tool to move, resize, and edit shapes. You'll add some interest to the retro shape by subtracting a star shape from it, allowing the outer space background to show through. To help you position the star, you'll refer to the Star Guide layer, which has been created for you. Currently, that layer is hidden.

1 In the Layers palette, to the far left of the Star Guide layer, click in the Show/Hide Visibility column to display the eye icon (👁) for that layer (but leave the Retro Shape layer selected). The Star Guide layer is now visible in the image window.

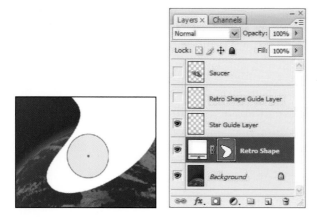

2 In the Paths palette, select the Retro Shape vector mask.

3 In the toolbox, select the Polygon tool (⬡), hidden under the Rectangle tool (▭).

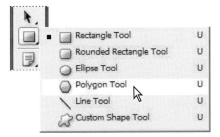

4 On the tool options bar, do the following:

• For Sides, type **11**.

• Click the Geometry Options arrow (immediately to the left of the Sides option) to open the Polygon Options. Select the Star check box, and type **50%** in the Indent Sides By option. Then click anywhere outside the Polygon Options to close it.

• Select the Subtract From Shape Area option (⬚), or press either hyphen or minus to select it with a keyboard shortcut. The pointer now appears as cross hairs with a small minus sign (✛).

5 Move the cross hairs pointer over the orange dot in the center of the orange circle in the image window, and drag outward until the tips of the star rays touch the circle's perimeter.

Note: As you drag, you can rotate the star by dragging the pointer to the side.

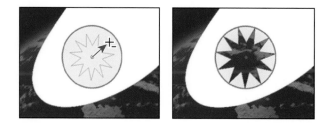

When you release the mouse, the star shape becomes a cutout, allowing the planet to show through. If the Background layer were another image, pattern, or color, you would see it inside the star shape.

Notice that the star has a grainy outline, reminding you that the shape is selected. Another indication that the shape is selected is that the Retro Shape vector mask thumbnail is highlighted (outlined in white) in the Layers palette.

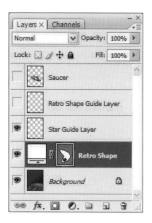

6 In the Layers palette, click the eye icon next to the Star Guide layer to hide it.

Notice how the thumbnails have changed in the palettes. In the Layers palette, the left thumbnail for the Retro Shape layer is unchanged, but the mask thumbnails in both the Layers palette and Paths palette show the retro shape with the star-shaped cutout.

7 Deselect the star and retro shape paths by selecting the Path Selection tool (✦) and clicking the Dismiss Target Path button (✔) in the tool options bar.

Your paths are now deselected, and the grainy path lines have disappeared, leaving a sharp edge between the blue and white areas. Also, the Retro Shape Vector Mask is no longer highlighted in the Paths palette.

8 Choose File > Save to save your work.

Working with defined custom shapes

Another way to use shapes in your artwork is to draw a custom or preset shape. Doing so is as easy as selecting the Custom Shape tool, picking a shape from the Custom Shape picker, and drawing in your image window. You will do so now to add checkerboard patterns to the background of your poster for the toy store.

1 Make sure the Retro Shape layer is selected in the Layers palette. Then click the New Layer button (⬛) to add a layer above it. Double-click the default Layer 1 name and rename it **Pattern**, and then press Enter or Return.

2 In the toolbox, select the Custom Shape tool (🐾), which is hidden under the Polygon tool (⬭).

3 In the tool options bar, click the pop-up arrow for the Shape option to open the Custom Shape picker.

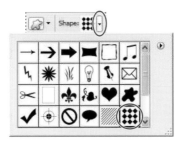

4 Locate the checkerboard preset at the bottom of the Custom Shape picker (you may need to scroll or drag the corner of the picker to see it), and double-click to select it and simultaneously close the picker.

5 In the tool options bar, select the Fill Pixels option.

6 Make sure that the foreground color is white (or select white now). Then press Shift and drag diagonally in the image window to draw and size the shape so that it's about 2-inches square. (Pressing Shift constrains the shape to its original proportions.)

7 Add five more checkerboards of various sizes until your poster resembles the following figure.

8   In the Layers palette, reduce the opacity of the Pattern layer to **20%**.

Your poster background is now complete.

9   Click the Show/Hide Visibility column next to the Saucer layer to redisplay the layer and see the whole composition.

10   Choose File > Save to save your work.

Importing a Smart Object

Photoshop offers support for Smart Objects, which lets you import vector objects from Adobe Illustrator and edit them in Photoshop without a loss of quality. Regardless of how often you scale, rotate, skew, or otherwise transform a Smart Object, it retains its sharp, precise edges. In addition, you can edit the original object in Illustrator, and the changes will be reflected in the placed Smart Object in your Photoshop image file. You learned a bit about Smart Objects in Lesson 8. You will explore them more now by placing text created in Illustrator into the toy store poster.

Adding the title

We created the toy store name for you in Illustrator. Let's add it to the poster.

1   Select the Saucer layer and choose File > Place. Navigate to the Lessons/Lesson9 folder, select the Title.ai file, and click Place. Click OK in the Place PDF dialog box that appears.

The Retro Toys text is added to the middle of your composition, inside a bounding box with adjustable handles. A new layer, Title, appears in the Layers palette.

2 Drag the Retro Toys object to the upper right corner of the poster, and then press Shift and drag a corner to make the text object proportionally larger—so that it fills the top portion of the poster, as in the following figure. When you've finished, either press Enter or Return, or click the Commit Transform button (✔) in the tool options bar.

When you commit to the transform, the layer thumbnail icon changes to reflect that the title layer is a Smart Object.

Because the Retro Toys title is a Smart Object, you can continue to edit its size and shape, if you'd like. Simply select its layer and choose Edit > Free Transform to access the control handles, and drag to adjust them. Or, select the Move tool (⊹), and check Show Transform Controls in the tool options bar. Then adjust the handles.

Finishing up

As a final step, let's clean up the Layers palette by deleting your guide template layers.

1 Make sure that the Title, Saucer, Pattern, Retro Shape, and Background layers are the only visible layers in the Layers palette.

2 Choose Delete Hidden Layers from the Layers palette pop-up menu, and then click Yes to confirm the delete action.

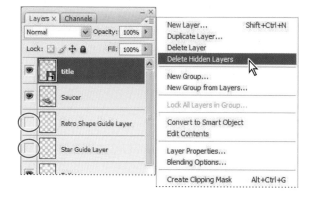

3 Choose File > Save to save your work.

Congratulations! You've finished the poster. It should look like the following image. (The title text will only be stroked if you complete the Extra Credit task.)

EXTRA CREDIT *If you have Adobe Illustrator CS or later, you can go even further with the Retro Toys text Smart Object—you can edit it in Illustrator, and it will update automatically in Photoshop. Try this:*

1 Double-click the Smart Object thumbnail in the title layer. If an alert dialog box appears, click OK. Illustrator opens and displays the Retro Toys Smart Object in a document window.

2 Using the Direct Selection tool (⬍), drag a marquee around the type to select all of the letters.

3 Select the Stroke button (▣) in the Tools panel.

4 Move the mouse over the Color panel (choose Window > Color if the panel isn't already open on-screen), until the pointer changes to an eyedropper. Use the eyedropper to choose black in the Color panel, and then, in the Stroke panel, specify a 0.5-point width.

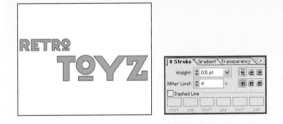

A 0.5-point black stroke appears around the Retro Toys type.

💡 *In Adobe Illustrator CS3, you can select the Stroke attribute and its color, width, and other options in the Control panel above the document window.*

5 Close the Vector Smart Object document, and click Save when prompted.

6 Switch back to Photoshop. The Retro Toys poster image window updates to reflect the stroked type.

Review

▶ **Review questions**

1 How can the Pen tool be useful as a selection tool?

2 What is the difference between a bitmap image and a vector graphic?

3 What does a shape layer do?

4 What tools can you use to move and resize paths and shapes?

5 What are Smart Objects, and what is the benefit of using them?

▶ **Review answers**

1 If you need to create an intricate selection, it can be easier to draw the path with the Pen tool and then convert the path to a selection.

2 Bitmap or raster images are based on a grid of pixels and are appropriate for continuous-tone images such as photographs or artwork created in painting programs. Vector graphics are made up of shapes based on mathematical expressions and are appropriate for illustrations, type, and drawings that require clear, smooth lines.

3 A shape layer stores the outline of a shape in the Paths palette. You can change the outline of a shape by editing its path.

4 You use the Path Selection tool (➤) and the Direct Selection tool (➤) to move, resize, and edit shapes. You can also modify and scale a shape or path by choosing Edit > Free Transform Path.

5 Smart Objects are vector objects that you can import from Adobe Illustrator and place and edit in Photoshop without a loss of quality. Regardless of how often you scale, rotate, skew, or otherwise transform a Smart Object, it retains sharp, precise edges. A great benefit of using Smart Objects is that you can edit the original object in Illustrator, and the changes will be reflected in the placed Smart Object in your Photoshop image file.

Once you've learned basic layer techniques, you can create more complex effects in your artwork using layer masks, adjustment layers, filters, and more layer styles. You can also add layers from other documents.

10 | Advanced Layering

Lesson overview

In this lesson, you'll learn how to do the following:

- Import a layer from another file.

- Clip a layer.

- Create and edit an adjustment layer.

- Use Vanishing Point 3D effects with layers.

- Set up different layer comps to showcase your work.

- Manage layers.

- Flatten a layered image.

- Merge and stamp layers.

This lesson will take less than an hour to complete. If needed, remove the previous lesson folder from your hard drive, and copy the Lesson10 folder onto it. As you work on this lesson, you'll preserve the start file. However, if you need to restore the start file, copy it from the *Adobe Photoshop CS3 Classroom in a Book* CD.

Getting started

In this lesson, you'll combine an image with two layers with one that has four, to create a cell phone package. You'll create three different, multilayered designs, which you can display selectively using layer comps. You'll get more experience with adjustment layers, layer effects, layer masks, and layer filters. Beyond this lesson, the best way to learn how to work with layers is by experimenting and being creative with combining the many filters, effects, layer masks, and layer properties in new ways.

1 Start Photoshop and then immediately hold down Ctrl+Alt+Shift (Windows) or Command+Option+Shift (Mac OS) to restore the default preferences. (See "Restoring default preferences" on page 6.)

2 When prompted, click Yes to confirm that you want to reset preferences, and click Close to close the Welcome Screen.

3 Click the Go To Bridge button (▣) in the tool options bar to open Adobe Bridge.

4 In the Favorites panel in the upper left corner of Bridge, click the Lessons favorite, and then double-click the Lesson10 folder to preview its contents in the Content panel.

5 Select the 10End.psd file and study it. If necessary, drag the thumbnail slider at the bottom of the window to enlarge the preview and get a good look.

Your goal in this lesson is to create a package prototype by assembling artwork from various files, layering the artwork, adding perspective, and then refining the design. You'll create several layer comps to show the design to your client.

6 Double-click the 10Start.psd file to open it in Photoshop. Choose File > Save As, rename the file **10Working.psd**, and click Save.

7 Drag the Layers palette by its tab to move it out of its group, to the top of the work area. Drag the corner of the Layers palette group to elongate it so that you'll be able to see about 10 layers without scrolling.

The palette has three layers, two of which are visible—the gray three-dimensional box displayed in the image window, and the background stacked underneath it. The Full Art layer is hidden.

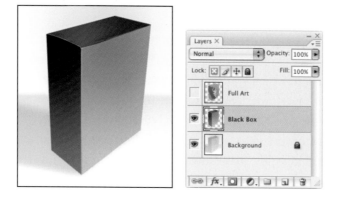

8 In the Layers palette, select the Full Art layer. Notice that even though the layer is selected, it remains hidden.

Clipping a layer to a shape

You will start building a composite image by opening the file that has some of the artwork you will use to create the box design.

1 Switch to Adobe Bridge by clicking the Go To Bridge button (▣) in the tool options bar.

2 In the Bridge Content panel, double-click the Phone_art.psd file to open it. This is some of the art that will go on your box.

This file has two layers, one labeled Phone Art and the other named Mask. You will clip the phone art image so that it fits within the freeform shape in the Mask layer below it.

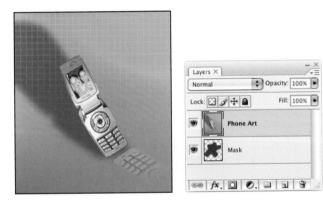

3 In the Layers palette, make sure that the Mask layer is below the Phone Art layer. A clipping shape must be below the image that you will clip.

4 Make sure that the Phone Art layer is selected. Then hold down the Alt (Windows) or Option (Mac OS) key, and position the pointer between the Phone Art layer and the Mask layer to display a double-circle icon (•⊛), and click.

The thumbnail of the clipped layer, Phone Art, is indented in the Layers palette, and a right-angle arrow points to the layer beneath it, which is now underlined.

You will import this new image into the Start file. But first, you need to flatten the image to one layer.

5 With the Phone Art layer selected, click the icon (▾☰) in the upper right of the Layers palette to display the palette menu. Then choose Merge Down from the palette menu.

You can merge the layers other ways, for example, by choosing the Merge Visible command, either in the Layer menu or from the Layers palette menu. But don't choose Layer > Flatten Image, because it would remove the transparency already set up in the file.

Now you'll see how easy it is to add artwork from another file, simply by dragging and dropping.

6 Drag the merged Mask layer from the Layers palette into the 10Working.psd image window. The layer appears above the selected layer (the Full Art layer, which you selected at the end of the previous procedure) and at the top of the 10Working.psd Layers palette. The artwork covers the box.

7 In the 10Working.psd Layers palette, select the Mask layer name, and type **Shape Art** to rename it.

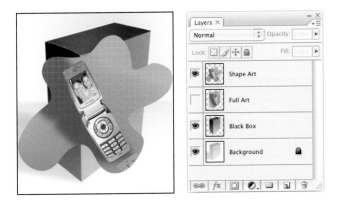

8 Choose File > Save to save your work so far.

9 Close the Phone_Art.psd file without saving your changes.

Setting up a Vanishing Point grid

The artwork you've added sits on top of the box—not exactly the effect you want. You'll fix that by making the artwork appear in perspective, wrapped around the box.

1 With the Shape Art layer selected in the Layers palette, press Ctrl+A (Windows) or Command+A (Mac OS) to select all of a layer's contents.

2 Press Ctrl+X (Windows) or Command+X (Mac OS) to cut the contents to the clipboard. Now only the box is visible, not the artwork.

3 Choose Filter > Vanishing Point. The Vanishing Point dialog box appears, where you can draw a perspective plane that matches the dimensions of the box.

4 Using the Create Plane tool (▦), click the upper right corner of the front of the box to begin defining the plane. It's easiest to define planes when you can use a rectangular object in the image as a guide.

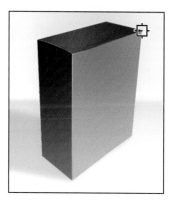

5 Continue drawing the plane by clicking each corner of the box front. Click the last corner to complete the plane. When you complete the plane, a grid appears on the front face and the Edit Plane tool (▶) is automatically selected. You can adjust the size of this grid at the top of the dialog box using the Edit Plane tool.

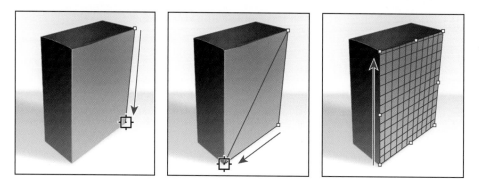

6 Use the Edit Plane pointer to adjust corner points to refine your plane, as needed.

Now you'll extend the grid to the top and sides of the box to complete the perspective.

7 With the Edit Plane tool selected, press Ctrl (Windows) or Command (Mac OS) and drag to select the top center point along the top edge of the plane, and move it back towards the top back side of the box. This extends the perspective plane along the top of the box, and displays a grid on the top of the box; the grid on the front face disappears, but the blue border remains.

8 Use the Edit Plane pointer to adjust any corner points along the top side, as needed.

9 When you are satisfied with the grid's placement, repeat Steps 7 and 8 to extend the grid down the side panel.

Note: The final grid doesn't have to match the box dimensions exactly.

If you were applying perspective to many planes, you might want to create a separate layer for each plane. Putting the Vanishing Point results in a separate layer preserves your original image and lets you use the layer opacity control, styles, and blending modes.

You're ready to add the artwork and give it perspective.

10 Press Ctrl+V (Windows) or Command+V (Mac OS) to paste the contents of the clipboard onto the grid. This action automatically selects the Marquee tool in the Vanishing Point dialog box.

11 Using the Marquee tool (▯), select the contents and drag it to the center of the front perspective plane so that most of the artwork appears on the front panel, but wraps around the side and top. It's important to place the artwork on the front panel, so that it wraps correctly.

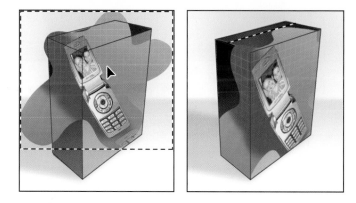

12 When you're satisfied with the positioning, click OK.

13 Choose File > Save to save your work so far.

Creating your own keyboard shortcuts

As you build your composite image in this lesson, you will place several images created in Adobe Illustrator CS3. To make your work more efficient, you will start by creating a keyboard shortcut for the Place function.

1 Choose Edit > Keyboard Shortcuts. The Keyboard Shortcuts dialog box appears.

2 In the dialog box under Application Menu Command, click the triangle to the left of File to expand its contents. Scroll down to Place, and select it.

3 Press the F13 key on the keyboard to assign that key as a new shortcut. An alert appears, warning you that the F13 key can be assigned to actions, overriding this command.

4 Click Accept, and then click OK.

Placing imported artwork

Now you'll take advantage of the keyboard shortcuts you set up at the beginning of this lesson to add more artwork to your package. The imported artwork contains the words *ZX-Tel cellular,* originally created with the Type tool in Illustrator, but then converted to a graphic. You can no longer edit the text with the Type tool. However, you don't have to worry about whether others working on the file can see the type correctly if they don't have the same font installed.

1 Press F13 to open the Place dialog box.

2 Select the ZX-Tel logo.ai file in the Lesson10 folder. Click Place. The Place PDF dialog box appears.

3 Leave the settings at their defaults, and click OK to place the file.

The Place command adds a photo, art, or any Photoshop-supported file as a Smart Object to your document.

You may remember from your work in Lesson 9 that Smart Objects are layers that contain image data from raster or vector images, such as Photoshop or Illustrator files. Smart Objects preserve an image's source content with all its original characteristics, enabling you to edit the Smart Object layer nondestructively. You can scale, position, skew, rotate, or warp Smart Objects without affecting their precise edges.

4 Drag the logo over to the front panel, and then drag the corner points to resize the logo to roughly the width of the box front. Don't worry about being exact: you'll use the Vanishing Point filter to position the logo in perspective in a short while.

5 When you are satisfied with the positioning, press Enter or Return to place the file.

The placed image appears as the ZX-Tel layer at the Top of the Layers palette. The icon in the lower right of the layer thumbnail indicates that it is a Smart Object.

6   Choose File > Save to save your work so far.

Filtering Smart Objects

You'll apply the text you just placed to the three-dimensional box, and transform and stylize it so that it looks realistic and in perspective. You'll start by converting the vector data in the Smart Object layer to pixels. Rasterizing the Smart Object lets you apply filters or painting tools to it.

1   In the Layers palette, right-click (Windows) or Control-click (Mac OS) the ZX-Tel layer name, and choose Rasterize Layer from the context menu. This converts the Smart Object to a flat, raster layer.

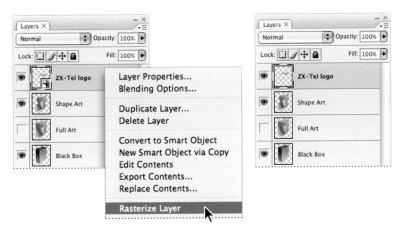

2   Press Ctrl+I (Windows) or Command+I (Mac OS) to invert the color from black to gray. This will make it easier to read the text when it's added to the box.

3 In the Layers palette, Ctrl-click (Windows) or Command-click (Mac OS) the ZX-Tel layer icon to select this layer.

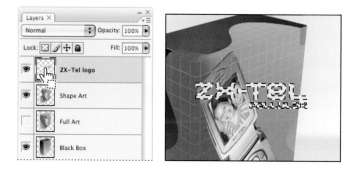

4 Press Ctrl+X (Windows) or Command+X (Mac OS) to cut the contents of the layer and place it on the clipboard.

5 Choose Filter > Vanishing Point to return to the perspective plane, with the three-dimensional box with the cell phone artwork.

Now you'll apply a filter to the Smart Object. Filters applied to Smart Objects become Smart Filters, which let you continue to edit filter effects without overwriting the original image data or affecting the image quality. You can revert to the original image data, if you want to.

6 Press Ctrl+V (Windows) or Command+V (Mac OS) to paste the logo onto the perspective plane, and drag it into position on the front of the box.

7 Press Ctrl+T (Windows) or Command+T (Mac OS) to get the free transform handles. Drag the handles to adjust the logo so that it matches the perspective of the box.

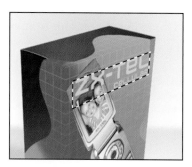

8 Press the Alt (Windows) or Option (Mac OS) key, and drag a (cloned) copy of the logo directly upwards and onto the top of the box. When you are satisfied with the positioning, click OK.

9 Choose File > Save to save your work.

Adding a layer style

Now you'll add a layer style to give the logo some depth. Layer styles are automated effects that you can apply to a layer.

1 In the Layers palette, select the ZX-Tel logo layer.

2 Choose Layer > Layer Style > Bevel and Emboss. Leave the settings at their default, and click OK.

Now the logo has sharp, deep edges, to give the box the appearance of more depth.

Placing the side panel artwork

To complete the package, you'll add product copy to the side panel of the box.

1 Press F13 and select the Side Box Copy.ai file. Click Place. In the Place PDF dialog box, leave the settings at their defaults, and click OK.

2 Press the Shift key and drag to size the placed image down to roughly the size of the side panel. Then press Enter or Return to place the artwork.

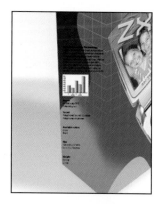

3 In the Layers palette, right-click (Windows) or Control-click (Mac OS) the Side Box Copy layer name, and choose Rasterize Layer from the context menu.

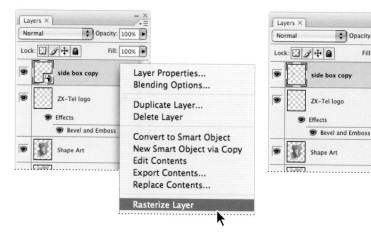

You will select the type and change its color to make it more legible.

4 Choose the Polygonal Lasso tool (🔽) in the toolbox, hidden under the Lasso tool.

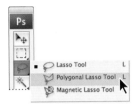

5 Click with the Polygonal Lasso pointer to draw a box around the top block of text. Then hold down the Shift key, and draw another box around the bottom block of text to add to the selection. You don't want to include the graph.

You used the Polygonal Lasso tool because the lines of text form a slightly irregular shape. You could also use the Rectangular Marquee tool.

6 Press Ctrl+I (Windows) or Command+I (Mac OS) to invert the color from black to white.

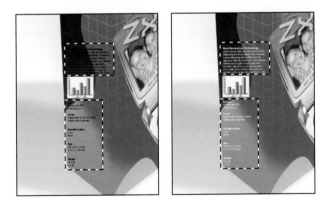

Adding more artwork in perspective

Now you'll add the copy from the side panel to your three-dimensional box.

1 With the Side Box Copy layer selected, press Ctrl+A (Windows) or Command+A (Mac OS) to select all of the Box Copy contents.

2 Press Ctrl+X (Windows) or Command+X (Mac OS) to cut the contents to the clipboard.

3 Choose Filter > Vanishing Point.

4 Press Ctrl+V (Windows) or Command+V (Mac OS) to paste the side copy artwork onto the perspective plane.

5 Position the artwork so that it fits along the side panel. If necessary, press Ctrl+T (Windows) or Command+T (Mac OS), and use the free transform handles to adjust the artwork so that it fits properly.

6 When you are satisfied with how the side copy artwork looks, click OK.

Now you'll repeat this procedure one more time to place the last piece of artwork and add it to the box in perspective.

7 Press F13, and select and place the Special Offer.ai file. Click OK to close the dialog box. Size the artwork down to fit in the lower left corner of the box front, and then press Enter or Return to place the file. Position the artwork in the lower left corner of the front panel.

8 In the Layers palette, right-click (Windows) or Control-click (Mac OS) the Special Offer layer name, and choose Rasterize Layer from the context menu.

9 Place the Special Offer on the box in perspective, following the same procedure you used to add the box artwork, text, and side copy:

• In the Layers palette, Ctrl-click (Windows) or Command-click (Mac OS) the Special Offer layer thumbnail to select all of its contents.

• Press Ctrl+X (Windows) or Ctrl+X (Mac OS) to cut the contents to the clipboard.

• Choose Filter > Vanishing Point.

• Press Ctrl+V (Windows) or Ctrl+V (Mac OS) to paste the contents from the clipboard.

• Position the artwork in the lower left corner of the front panel, and then click OK.

10 Choose File > Save to save your work.

Adding an adjustment layer

To enhance the realism of the package, you'll add an adjustment layer to create a shadow over the side panel.

Adjustment layers can be added to an image to apply color and tonal adjustments without permanently changing the pixel values in the image. For example, if you add a Color Balance adjustment layer to an image, you can experiment with different colors repeatedly, because the change occurs only on the adjustment layer. If you decide to return to the original pixel values, you can hide or delete the adjustment layer.

Here, you'll add a Levels adjustment layer to increase the tonal range of the selection, in effect increasing the overall contrast. An adjustment layer affects all layers below it in the image's stacking order.

1 In the Layers palette, select the Side Box Copy layer.

2 Select the Polygonal Lasso tool ( ) in the toolbox, and draw a rectangular shape around the side panel.

3 Choose Layer > New Adjustment Layer > Levels. Type **Shadow** to name this adjustment layer, and click OK.

4 In the Levels dialog box, make sure that the Preview option is selected. Under Output Levels, drag the right slider to about 210 to decrease the brightness, and click OK.

5 Choose File > Save to save your work.

6 Experiment by clicking the Show/Hide Visibility button for the Side Copy layer, to turn the layer off and on and see the effect of the adjustment layer on the other layers. When you finish, make sure that all layers are visible.

Side Box copy original

Shadow adjustment layer added

Working with layer comps

Next, you'll save this configuration as a layer comp. Layer comps let you easily switch between various combinations of layers and effects within the same Photoshop file. A layer comp is a snapshot of a state of the Layers palette.

1 On the right side of your screen, next to the palette dock, notice the row of palette icons. Click the Layers Comp icon (▦) to display the Layers Comp palette, or choose Window > Layer Comps.

2 At the bottom of the Layer Comps palette, click the New Layer Comp button. Name the new layer comp **Black Box**, and type a description of its appearance: **3D box, black top and side shape with full-color art**. Click OK.

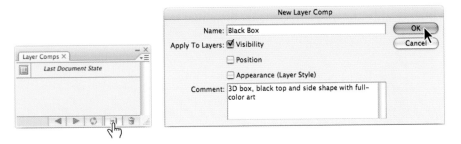

Now you'll make some changes and save the new look as a different layer comp.

3 In the Layers palette, click the eye icon next to the Black Box layer to turn off its visibility. Click in the Show/Hide Visibility column next to the Full Art layer to show this layer.

4 In the Layers palette, click the eye icon next to the Shape Art layer to turn off its visibility. Click in the Show/Hide Visibility column next to the Full Art layer to show this layer.

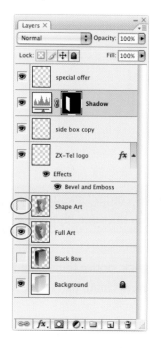

You'll save this version as a new layer comp.

5 At the bottom of the Layer Comps palette, click the New Layer Comp button. Type **Full Image**, and enter a description, **3D box, blue top with full-color art**. Click OK.

6 In the Layer Comps palette, toggle the visibility icons to show and hide your two layer comps and view the differences.

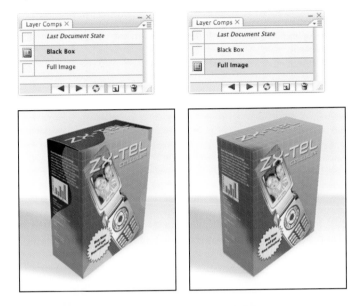

You can also use layer comps to record the layer position in the document or the layer appearance—whether a layer style is applied to the layer and the layer's blending mode.

7 Choose File > Save to save your work.

Managing layers

With layer comps, you learned a great way to present different design options for a package. It is also helpful to be able to group your layers by content. In these next steps you will organize your type and art elements by creating a separate group for each.

1 In the Layers palette, Ctrl-click (Windows) or Command-click (Mac OS) to select the Special Offer, Side Box Copy, and ZX-Tel Logo layers.

2 In the upper right of the Layers palette, click the icon to display the palette menu, and choose New Group From Layers. Type **Box Type** for the name, and click OK.

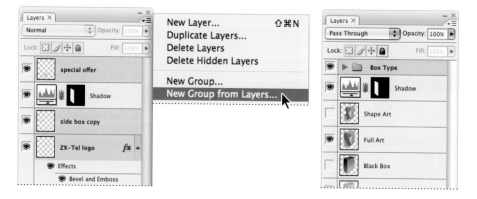

3 Shift-click the Shadow adjustment layer, Shape Art layer, and Full Art layer to select them, and then repeat Step 2. In the New Group From Layers dialog box, name this group **Box Artwork**. Then click OK.

Layer sets help you organize and manage individual layers by grouping them. You can then expand the layer set to view the layers contained in it, or collapse the set to simplify your view. You can change the stacking order of layers within a layer set.

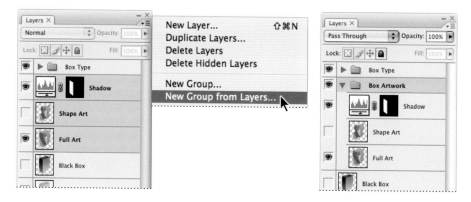

4 Click the eye icon next to each layer group to toggle off their visibility and test how the layers are grouped together. Click in the Show/Hide Visibility column again to turn the layer groups on.

Layer sets can function like layers in a number of ways, so you select, duplicate, and move entire sets of layers, as well as apply attributes and masks to the entire layer set. Any changes you make at the layer-set level apply to all the layers within the set.

Flattening a layered image

As you've done in previous lessons of this book, you'll now flatten the layered image. When you flatten a file, all layers are merged into a single background, greatly reducing the size of the file. If you plan to send a file out for proofs, it's a good idea to save two versions of the file—one containing all the layers so that you can edit the file if necessary, and one flattened version to send to the print shop.

1 First, note the values in the lower left corner of the image or application window. If the display does not show the file size (such as "Doc: 5.01M/31.8M"), click the arrow and choose Show > Document Sizes.

The first number is the printing size of the image, which is about the size that the saved, flattened file would be in Adobe Photoshop format. The number on the right indicates the approximate document size of the file as it is now, including layers and channels.

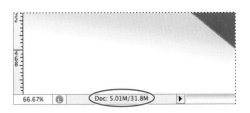

2 Choose Image > Duplicate, name the duplicate file **10Final.psd**, and click OK.

3 From the Layers palette menu, choose Flatten Image. The layers for the 10Final.psd file are combined onto a single background layer.

Now the file sizes shown in the lower left area of the work area or image window are almost the same smaller number that you saw earlier (our files were 5.01M/5.99M). Note that flattening fills transparent areas with white.

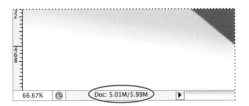

4 Choose Edit > Undo.

You'll try another way to merge layers and reduce the file size.

Merging layers and layer groups

Unlike flattening a layered image, merging layers allows you to select however many layers you want to flatten or leave unflattened.

You'll merge together all the elements of the box, while keeping the Box Type layer group and Background layer untouched. This way, you can return to the file and reuse the Background and Box Type layers at any time.

1 In the Layers palette, click the eye icon next to the Box Type Group to hide these layers.

2 Select the Box Art layer group in the Layers palette.

3 Choose Layer > Merge Visible. Any layers that aren't visible in the layer group will remain, unmerged, in the Layers palette.

4 Choose Edit > Undo.

You'll try another way to merge layers and reduce the file size.

Stamping layers

You can combine the benefits of flattening an image yet still keep some layers intact by stamping the layers. Stamping flattens two or more layers and places the flattened image into a new layer, while leaving other layers intact. This is useful if you need to use a flattened image but also need to keep some layers intact for your work.

1 In the Layers palette, select the layers you want to flatten by selecting the Box Artwork group.

2 Hold down the Alt (Windows) or Option (Mac OS) key, and choose Layer > Merge Group. The Layers palette displays a new layer that includes your merged image.

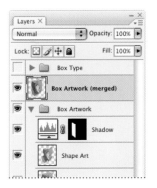

3 Choose File > Save. In the Save As dialog box that appears, click Save to save the file in Photoshop format.

Good work! You've created a three-dimensional composite image and tried out various ways to save the final artwork to complete the lesson.

Clone Movie Source*

* Highlights from Russell Brown's video demonstartion of the Clone Source feature

Watch the movie!
See the detailed steps of this tutorial in the CloneSource QuickTime movie included on the *Adobe Photoshop CS3 Classroom in a Book* CD. Browse to Movies/CloneSource/CloneSource.mov. Double-click the movie file to open it; then click the Play button.

Now use Photoshop to create animation effects!

Hey, Photoshop enthusiasts!

Russell Brown here, the official Photoshop Nutty Professor. Back at my lab, I've concocted some fun Photoshop tutorials that will appeal to movie-makers and nutty professors around the globe.

In this sidebar we will feature highlights from my short video demonstration found on this CD. You will learn how to paint over time into an Animation timeline window.

Russell Brown

The image files used in this exercise are located in Russell's Video Assets folder on the *Adobe Photoshop CS3 Classroom in a Book* CD in the Movies/CloneSource folder.

Step 1: Create a new video layer

In Bridge, navigate to Movies/CloneSource/Video Assets folder, and double-click Spray Paint Start.psd to open it. This Photoshop file contains an imported QuickTime movie. In Photoshop, create a new video layer by choosing Layer > Video Layers > New Blank Video Layers. With this new layer selected, define a custom brush by opening the Custom Brush.jpg file in the Video Assets folder. Choose Edit > Define Brush Presets, and click OK.

Step 2: Select a clone source

Select a moment in time when you want to start painting, by choosing Window > Animation and selecting a frame in the Animation (Timeline) palette. Choose Window > Close Source to open the Clone Source palette, and select the Clone tool in the toolbox. Now you'll open a second window to clone from: Open the Dr. Brown image in your Video Assets folder. Press Alt (Windows) or Option (Mac OS) and click the image to store it in the Clone Source palette.

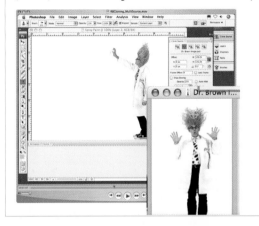

Step 3: Show overlay and spray

You're ready to start cloning. In the Clone Source palette, select the Show Overlay option. In the image, move your pointer into position where you will begin spraying with the image. Click to set your first spray point.

Step 4: Copy frames and spray

Return to the Clone Source palette, and deselect the Show Overlay option. Now you'll duplicate the frame and spray-paint again, and keep repeating this step until the image is complete. Choose Layer > Video Layers > Duplicate Frame to add a new frame and then click to spray the image; continue repeating this process of duplicating the frame and spray-painting again until the image is complete.

Review

▶ **Review questions**

1 Why would you use layer sets?

2 What are clipping path layers?

3 How do adjustment layers work, and what is the benefit of using them?

4 What are layer styles, and why would you use them?

5 What is the difference between flattening, merging, and stamping layers?

▶ **Review answers**

1 Layer sets allow you to organize and manage layers. For example, you can move all the layers in a layer set as a group and then apply attributes or a mask to them as a group.

2 A clipping path is when you configure the artwork on the base layer as a mask for the layer above it. In this lesson, you used the Mask layer (which had a freeform shape) as a clipping path for the Phone Art layer, so that the cell phone image appeared only in the freeform shape.

3 An adjustment layer is a special type of Photoshop layer that works specifically with color and tonal adjustments. When you apply an adjustment layer, you can edit an image repeatedly without making a permanent change to the colors or tonal range in the image.

4 Layer styles are customizable effects that you can apply to layers. You can use them to apply changes to a layer, and you can modify or remove them at any time.

5 Flattening an image merges all layers into a single background, greatly reducing the size of the file. Merging layers lets you choose which layers to flatten; this technique combines all selected or visible layers in one layer. Stamping combine the benefits of flattening an image while keeping some layers intact; it flattens two or more layers and places the flattened image into a new layer, while leaving other layers intact.

With the huge assortment of filters available for Adobe Photoshop, you can transform ordinary images into extraordinary digital artwork. You can select filters that simulate a traditional artistic medium—a watercolor, for example—or you can choose from filters that blur, bend, sharpen, or fragment images. In addition to using filters to alter images, you can use adjustment layers and painting modes to vary the look of your artwork.

11 | Advanced Compositing

Lesson overview

In this lesson, you'll learn how to do the following:

- Record and play back an action to automate a series of steps.
- Add guides to help you place and align images precisely.
- Save selections and load them as masks.
- Apply color effects only to unmasked areas of an image.
- Add an adjustment layer to color-correct a selection.
- Apply filters to selections to create various effects.
- Add layer styles to create editable special effects.

This lesson will take about 90 minutes to complete. If needed, remove the previous lesson folder from your hard drive, and copy the Lessons/Lesson11 folder onto it. As you work on this lesson, you'll preserve the start files. If you need to restore the start files, copy them from the *Adobe Photoshop CS3 Classroom in a Book* CD.

Getting started

You'll start the lesson by viewing the final lesson file, to see what you'll accomplish.

1 Start Photoshop and then immediately hold down Ctrl+Alt+Shift (Windows) or Command+Option+Shift (Mac OS) to restore the default preferences. (See "Restoring default preferences" on page 6.)

2 When prompted, click Yes to confirm that you want to reset preferences, and Close to close the Welcome Screen.

3 Click the Go To Bridge button () in the tool options bar to open Adobe Bridge.

4 In the Favorites palette in the upper left corner of Bridge, click the Lessons favorite, and then double-click the Lesson11 folder in the preview area.

5 Select the 11A_End.psd thumbnail and examine it in the Content panel. If necessary, enlarge the Content panel so that you can get a good look.

This end file is a montage that comprises four pictures. Each quadrant has had a specific filter or effect applied to it.

6 Double-click the 11Start.jpg thumbnail to open it in Photoshop.

Automating a multistep task

An *action* is a set of one or more commands that you record and then play back to apply to a single file or a batch of files. In this exercise, you'll see how actions can help you save time by applying a multistep process to the four images you'll use in this project.

Using actions is one of several ways that you can automate tasks in Adobe Photoshop. To learn more about recording actions, see Photoshop Help.

Opening and cropping the images

You'll start by resizing four images. Since this part of the task involves aesthetic choices about where and how much of the image to crop, you'll do these steps manually rather than record them with the Actions palette.

1 Click the Info tab in the Navigator palette group to bring that palette forward.

2 In the toolbox, select the Crop tool (⧉). Hold down Shift to constrain the shape to a square, and drag around the word "Flowers." When you finish dragging, be careful to release the mouse button first and then the Shift key.

Dragging and pressing Shift

3 Examine the width (W) and height (H) values in the Info palette. If you've drawn a perfect square, the pixel counts will be identical.

4 If necessary, make any adjustments to the selection so that all of the word "Flowers" is selected and the cropping marquee is aligned with the top of the image.

• If the width and height are not equal, drag a corner until the W and H values in the Info palette are identical. (Do not hold down Shift.)

• To move the marquee, click inside it and drag until it is positioned properly.

• To resize the marquee, hold down Shift and drag one of the corners to make the marquee larger or smaller.

• To start over, press Esc or click the Cancel button (⊘) in the options bar, and then repeat Steps 2 through 4.

5 When you are satisfied with the crop selection, double-click inside the crop area, or press Enter or Return to apply the cropping.

Cropped image

Because you're working with a number of files, you'll rename the 11Start.jpg file with a descriptive name so that it will be easy to identify. You'll also save the file in the Photoshop format, because each time you edit and then resave a JPEG file, its quality degrades.

6 Choose File > Save As, choose Photoshop for the Format, and save the cropped image as **Museum.psd** in your Lesson11 folder.

7 Using Adobe Bridge, open these three JPEG images in the Lesson11 folder: Flower_orange.jpg, Flower_white.jpg, and Flower_yellow.jpg.

8 Choose File > Save As, choose Photoshop for the format, rename the Flower_orange.jpg file as **Orange.psd**, and save it in the Lesson 11 folder. Repeat the step for the Flower_white.jpg and Flower_yellow.jpg files, renaming them as **White.psd** and **Yellow.psd**, respectively.

9 Repeat Steps 2 through 5 for each file you just opened. The choose File > Save to save each of the files.

Note: It is not necessary to make all the cropped images the same size. You will adjust their sizes again later in this lesson.

Cropped versions of the yellow flower, white flower, and orange JPEG files

Leave all the newly cropped files open for the next procedures.

Preparing to record an action

You use the Actions palette to record, play, edit, and delete individual actions. You also use the Actions palette to save and load action files. You'll start this task by opening a new document and preparing to record a new action in the Actions palette.

1   Click the Actions tab in the History palette group to bring the Actions palette forward, or choose Window > Actions to accomplish the same thing.

2   At the bottom of the Actions palette, click the Create New Set button (🗀). Or, create a new set by choosing New Set from the Actions palette menu.

3   In the New Set dialog box, type **My Actions**, and click OK.

4   Choose Window > White.psd to make that file active.

5   Select the marquee tool in the toolbox. This deselects the Crop tool, which you longer need.

Recording a new action set

For this project, you want each image to be the same size and to have a narrow white border. You'll perform those tasks now on the white flower image. You'll start by setting the image dimensions to a specific number of pixels, and then you'll apply a stroke to the image. As you work, you'll set up the Actions palette to record each step of the process.

Note: It is important that you finish all steps in this procedure without interruption. If you become distracted and need to start over, skip ahead to Step 10 to stop the recording; then delete the action by dragging it onto the Trash button ( ) in the Actions palette. To clear any actions applied to the image, use the History palette to delete any states after the crop. Then start again at Step 1.

1 In the Actions palette, click the New Action button ( ) or choose New Action from the Actions palette menu.

2 In the New Action dialog box, type **Size & Stroke** in the Name field and make sure that My Actions is selected from the Set pop-up menu. Then click Record.

Note: Take all the time you need to do this procedure accurately. The speed at which you work has no influence on the amount of time required to play a recorded action.

3 Choose Image > Image Size.

4 Make sure that both the Constrain Proportions and the Resample Image check boxes are selected at the bottom of the Image Size dialog box. For the Width, type **500**, and make sure that pixels is selected as the unit of measurement. Then click OK.

5 Choose Select > All.

6 Choose Edit > Stroke.

7 In the Stroke dialog box, make sure that the following options are selected, or select them now:

• Width should be **1** pixel.

• In the Color swatch, use white, or select it by clicking the swatch to open the Color Picker, selecting white (C, M, Y, and K = 0), and clicking OK to close the picker.

• For Location, leave Center selected.

• For Blending, leave Mode set to Normal and Opacity set at 100%.

Stroke dialog box settings and resulting border on image

8 Click OK to apply the settings and close the Stroke dialog box.

9 Choose Select > Deselect.

10 In the Actions palette, click the Stop button (■) at the bottom of the palette to stop recording steps. Save your work.

Your action is now saved in the Actions palette. You can click the arrows to the left of the My Actions set, the Size & Stroke action, and beside each step of that action to expand and collapse them at your convenience. With these expanded, you can examine each recorded step and the specific selections you made. When you finish reviewing the action, click the arrows to collapse the steps.

Playing an action on an individual file

Now that you've recorded the process of setting the image size and stroke characteristics for the white flower image, you can use the action as an automated task. You'll apply the Stroke & Size action to one of the other three image files that you cropped earlier in this lesson.

1 If the Yellow.psd, Museum.psd, and Orange.psd files are not still open, use Adobe Bridge or choose File > Open and open them now.

2 Choose Window > Document > Orange.psd to make that image active.

3 In the Actions palette, select the Size & Stroke action in the My Actions set, and then click the Play button (▶), or choose Play from the Actions palette menu.

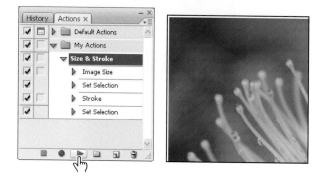

The Orange.psd image is automatically resized and given a stroke so that it now matches the White.psd image for these properties.

4 Choose File > Save.

Batch-playing an action

Applying actions is a time-saving process for performing routine tasks on files, but you can streamline your work even further by applying actions to all open files. Two more files in this project need to be resized and given strokes, so you'll apply your automated action to them simultaneously.

1 Close the White.psd and Orange.psd files, saving the changes if you're prompted. Make sure that only the Museum.psd and Yellow.psd files are open.

2 Choose File > Automate > Batch.

3 Under the Play section of the Batch dialog box, make sure that My Actions is chosen for Set, and that Size & Stroke is chosen for Action.

4 In the Source pop-up menu, choose Opened Files.

5 Leave Destination set as None, and click OK.

The action is applied to both the museum and yellow flower images, so the files have identical dimensions and strokes.

6 Choose File > Save and then File > Close for each of the two open files.

In this exercise, you batch-processed two files instead of making all the same changes in each of them; this was a mild convenience. But creating and applying actions can save significant amounts of time and tedium when you have dozens or even hundreds of files that require any routine, repetitive work.

7 Click the close button at the top of the Actions palette to close the palette.

Applying Smart Filters

Unlike regular filters, which permanently change an image, Smart Filters are nondestructive: they can be adjusted, turned off and on, and deleted. However, they can be applied only to a Smart Object layer, so the layer itself can no longer be edited—just its Smart Filter effects.

1   Using Adobe Bridge, open the Background.jpg image in the Lesson11 folder.

You'll begin by turning the image that will be used as the background into a Smart Object, and then apply several filters to it.

2   Choose Filter > Convert For Smart Filters. Click OK at the alert that the layer will be converted to a Smart Object.

In the Layers palette, notice the icon in the lower right corner of the layer thumbnail. This icon indicates the layer is now a Smart Object. Now you are free to apply as many filters you want to the image and adjust them at any time.

3 With the image layer still selected in the Layers palette, choose Filter > Texture > Stained Glass. Select Cell Size: 11; Border Thickness: 1; and Light Intensity: 3. Click OK.

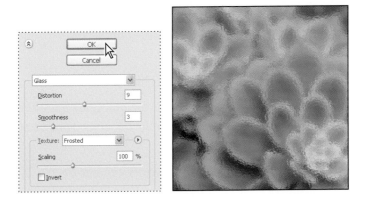

Smart Filters appear in the Layers palette beneath the Smart Object layer to which they are applied. Layers that have filter effects display an icon to the right of the layer name.

4 Apply another filter of your choice. (We chose Filter > Distort > Glass, with Distortion: 9, Smoothness: 3, Texture: Frosted, Scaling: 100%.) When you are satisfied with the results, click OK.

You can mix and match Smart Filters and turn them off and on.

5 In the Layers palette, double-click the Glass Smart Filter effect. In the Filter dialog box, click the Ocean Ripple thumbnail to select the filter, adjust the settings as desired, and then click OK. (We set both the ripple size and magnitude to 9.)

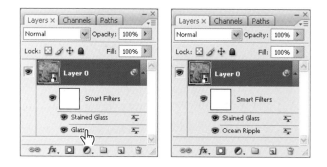

Notice that the name of the filter effect in the Layers palette has changed to the filter you just applied, Ocean Ripple.

6 In the Layers palette, drag the Stained Glass Smart Filter above the Ocean Ripple Smart Filter to see how the effect changes.

7 Click the eye icon (👁) next to the Stained Glass Smart Filter effect to turn off the effect.

You can apply any filter (including third-party filters)—except for Extract, Liquify, Pattern Maker, and Vanishing Point—as a Smart Filter. In addition, you can apply the Shadow/Highlight adjustment as a Smart Filter.

8 Play around with the filters until you find one to your liking.

9 When you have finished experimenting, redisplay the Stained Glass Smart Filter effect by clicking in the Show/Hide Visibility column to the left of its name to redisplay it and its eye icon.

10 Choose File > Save As, choose Photoshop for the format, rename the file **11Working.psd**, and save the file in your Lesson11 folder. Keep the file open. You'll continue to use it in the next exercise.

Watch the Smart Filters QuickTime movie to get a quick overview of how these nondestructive filters work. The movie is located on the Adobe Photoshop CS3 Classroom in a Book *CD in Movies/Smart Filters.mov. Double-click the movie file to open it; then click the Play button.*

Setting up a four-image montage

Now that you've finished preparing the background and the four images, you'll place them together in a new composite image. Using guides, you'll be able to align the images precisely without a lot of effort.

Adding guides

Guides are nonprinting lines that help you align elements in your document, either horizontally or vertically. You can choose a Snap To command so that the guides behave like magnets: When you drag an object close to a guide, it will snap into place along the guide when you release the mouse button.

1 With the 11Working.psd file active, choose View > Rulers. A vertical ruler appears along the left side of the window and a horizontal ruler appears along the top of the window.

Note: If the ruler units are not inches, choose Edit > Preferences > Units And Rulers (Windows) or Photoshop > Preferences > Units And Rulers (Mac OS); choose Rulers > Inches; and then click OK.

2 If the Info palette is not visible, click the Info tab or choose Window > Info to bring it forward in its palette group.

3 Drag down from the horizontal ruler to the middle of the image window, watching the Info palette to see the Y coordinate as you drag. Release the mouse when Y = 3.000 inches. A blue guide line appears across the middle of the window.

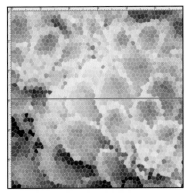

4 Drag another guide from the vertical ruler to the middle of the image and release the mouse when X = 3.000 inches.

5 Choose View > Snap To, and make sure that the Guides command is checked, or select it now.

6 Choose View > Rulers to hide the rulers again.

Snapping images into position

Your guides are in place, so you're ready to arrange your four cropped images in the montage.

1 Choose File > Open Recent > Museum.psd. The museum image opens in a separate image window.

2 In the toolbox, select the Move tool (⊹).

3 Click the Move tool anywhere in the museum image and drag from that image window to the larger 11Working.psd window, and then release the mouse button. If a warning appears about a color profile mismatch, click OK.

4 Still using the Move tool, drag the museum image into the upper left quadrant of the montage image so that its lower right corner snaps into place against the intersection of the two guides at the center of the window.

In the Layers palette, you'll notice that the museum image is on a new layer, Layer 1.

5 Choose Window > Museum.psd to make it active again, and then close it, either by clicking the red close button or by choosing File > Close.

6 Repeat Steps 1 through 5 for the three other cropped files, placing the yellow flower image in the upper right quadrant, the white flower in the lower left quadrant, and the orange flower in the lower right quadrant. All the images should snugly abut the intersection of the guides in the center of the window.

7 Choose View > Show > Guides to hide the guides.

8 In the Layers palette, double-click the layer name at the top of the palette and name it according to its image (for example, "Yellow Flower"). Repeat the step for each image. Rename Layer 0 as **Background**.

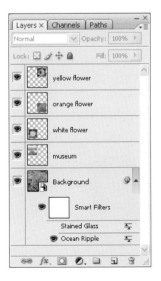

⭐ *EXTRA CREDIT It was easy to align the four images using centered guides, but for greater precision, Smart Guides are an excellent way to align photos and objects. Using your working file as it is after the "Snapping images into position" exercise, you can try another way to align these photos; or continue with your lesson and try this technique some other time.*

1 Select the White Flower layer in the Layers palette. In the image window, use the Move tool to move the image out of alignment. Repeat for the Yellow Flower and Orange Flower layers.

2 Choose View > Show > Smart Guides.

3 Select the Orange Flower layer in the Layers palette, and (still using the Move tool) drag in the image window to line up the orange flower's left edge with the right edge of the white flower image. Pink Smart Guides appear when the images are aligned.

4 Next, select the White Flower layer in the Layers palette; then Shift-click to also select the Orange Flower layer. Use the Move tool in the image window to move them together to align the top of the white flower image with the bottom of the stamp image.

5 Select the Yellow Flower layer in the Layers palette. Drag in the image window to square it up with the other three images, as shown below. Smart Guides will show you when each image is aligned in Steps 3, 4, and 5.

6 Choose View > Show > Smart Guides to turn off the Smart Guides when you've finished.

Saving selections

Next, you'll select the museum façade and save the selection. Later in this lesson, you'll use your saved selections to colorize the museum façade and add a special effect.

1 In the Layers palette, select the Museum layer.

2 In the toolbox, select the Zoom tool (🔍), and drag a marquee around the "Flowers" text to magnify your view. Make sure that you can see all of the letters in the image window.

3 In the toolbox, select the Magic Wand tool (🪄), hidden under the Quick Selection tool. Set the tolerance to 20, and make sure that the Anti-alias and Contiguous options are checked.

4 Click on the letter "f" in "Flowers."

5 Hold down the Shift key and click on the letter "l" in "Flowers." Continue Shift-clicking each letter until all of the letters in the word "Flowers" are selected.

6 Choose Select > Save Selection. Name the selection **Letters**, and click OK to save the selection in a new channel.

7 Choose Select > Deselect to deselect "Flowers" in the image.

8 To see your saved selection, click the Channels tab to open the palette. Scroll down, if necessary, to the Letters channels. Click each channel name in turn to display the channel masks in the image window.

9 When you're ready to continue working, scroll to the top of the Channels palette and click the RGB channel to select it. If necessary, click the eye icon (👁) next to the Letters channel to hide it, and double-click the Hand tool (✋) to zoom out.

Hand-coloring selections on a layer

You'll start to add special effects to your montage by hand-coloring the museum façade, beginning with the superimposed letters. To select the façade, you'll create a selection named "wall." Next, you'll remove the color from the selection so that you can color it by hand. Then, you'll add a new layer above the façade that you'll use to apply the color. In this way, you can simply erase the layer and start over if you don't like the results.

Desaturating a selection

You'll use the Desaturate command to remove the color from the museum façade. Saturation is the presence or absence of color in a selection. When you desaturate a selection within an image, you create a grayscale-like effect without affecting the colors in other parts of the image.

1 Click the Layers tab to bring that palette forward. In the palette, select the Museum layer containing the museum image.

2 Create a selection marquee around the museum layer by Ctrl-clicking (Windows) or Command-clicking (Mac OS) the layer thumbnail in the Layers palette.

3 To avoid selecting the image's white outline, choose Select > Modify > Contract. Click OK to shrink the selection by the default amount of 1 pixel. You don't want to accidentally colorize the outline in the next steps when you paint the layer.

Now you'll protect the areas that you don't want to desaturate by loading the Letters selection and subtracting it from the selection of the background.

4 Choose Select > Load Selection. In the Load Selection dialog box, choose Letters from the Channel pop-up menu, select Subtract From Selection, and click OK.

You'll rename this combined selection.

5 Choose Select > Save Selection, Name the channel **Wall**, and click OK.

6 Choose Image > Adjustments > Desaturate. The color is removed from the selection.

7 Choose Select > Deselect.

8 Choose File > Save to save your work. If you get a compatibility warning, click OK.

Creating a layer and choosing a blending mode

Now, you'll add a layer and specify a layer blending mode for painting the desaturated museum façade. By painting on a separate layer, you won't permanently alter the image. This makes it easy to start over if you aren't satisfied with the results.

Layer blending modes determine how the pixels in a layer blend with underlying pixels on other layers. By applying modes to individual layers, you can create a variety of special effects.

1   In the Layers palette, click the New Layer button (⬛) to add a layer to the image, just above Museum layer in the palette. Select the new layer name in the palette, and rename the layer **Paint**.

2   In the Layers palette, with the Paint layer active, choose Color from the Blending Mode pop-up menu to the left of the Opacity text box.

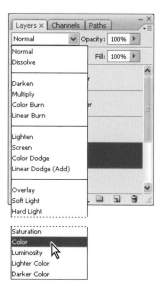

Note: If you ever want to delete a layer, you can drag it to the Trash button (🗑) at the bottom of the Layers palette. Or, simply select the layer you want to delete and then click the Trash button and, when prompted, confirm that you want to delete the layer.

You can use the Color mode to change the hue of a selection without affecting the highlights and shadows. This means that you can apply a variety of color tints without changing the original highlights and shadows of the background.

Applying painting effects

To begin painting, you must load the selection that you created earlier named Wall. By loading the Wall channel, you protect the unselected areas of the image as you apply colors, making it easy to paint within the lines.

1 With the Paint layer active in the Layers palette, choose Select > Load Selection.

In the Load Selection dialog box, notice that the color-mode change you just made also was saved as a selection, called Paint Transparency. In the dialog box, choose Wall from the Channel pop-up menu, and click OK.

2 Select the Brush tool (✐) in the toolbox. Then, in the tool options bar, set the Opacity to about 50%.

💡 *Change the brush opacity by pressing a number on the keypad from 0 to 9 (where 1 is 10%, 9 is 90%, and 0 is 100%).*

3 In the Brush pop-up palette, select a large soft-edged brush, such as the Soft Round 35-pixel brush. Close the palette by clicking a blank area of the tool options bar.

4 Hold down Alt (Windows) or Option (Mac OS) to get the Eyedropper tool, and click a green swatch from anywhere in the collage to select the color for the painting.

5 Drag the brush over the letters "E" and "R" and "S."

6 Using the Eyedropper tool again, Alt/Option-click a yellow-orange color in the yellow flower's petals to select the color. Drag the brush over the letters "O" and "W."

7 Now select a rich orange-red color from the orange flower image by Alt/Option-clicking again. Drag the brush over the letters "F" and "L." When you've finished coloring the letters, choose a color to paint the image of the building, and then paint it.

8 When you are satisfied with your results, choose Select > Deselect, and then choose File > Save.

Merging layers

The next task, merging layers, helps you to keep the file size relatively small. However, after you merge, you cannot easily go back and restore the image or start the process over, so be sure that you are happy with your results before you choose a merge command.

1 In the Layers palette, make sure that the Paint layer is selected.

2 Choose Layer > Merge Down to merge the Paint layer with the Museum layer below it.

Now the two layers are fused as one layer, Museum.

3 Double-click the Hand tool (🖑) so that the entire image fits in the image window, or double-click the Zoom tool (🔍) to set the view to 100%.

4 Choose File > Save.

Changing the color balance

Now, you'll use an adjustment layer to adjust the color balance on the yellow flower image.

Altering the color for a channel or a regular layer permanently changes the pixels on that layer. However, with an adjustment layer, your color and tonal changes reside only within the adjustment layer and do not alter any pixels in the layers beneath it. The effect is as if you were viewing the visible layers through the adjustment layer above them. By using adjustment layers, you can try out color and tonal adjustments without permanently changing pixels in the image. You can also use adjustment layers to affect multiple layers at once.

1 In the Layers palette, press Ctrl (Windows) or Command (Mac OS) and click the yellow flower layer to select its contents.

2 Choose Select > Modify > Contract. Accept the default value of 1 px, and click OK. This subtracts the image's white border from your selection.

3 Choose Layer > New Adjustment Layer > Color Balance.

4 In the New Layer dialog box, select the Use Previous Layer To Create Clipping Mask check box, which ensures that your adjustment layer will affect only the yellow flower image, not the other three sections of the montage. Then click OK to create the adjustment layer with the default name, Color Balance 1.

The Color Balance dialog box opens, where you can change the mixture of colors in a color image and make general color corrections. When you adjust the color balance, you can keep the same tonal balance, which you'll do here. You can also focus changes on the shadows, midtones, or highlights.

5 Move the dialog box so that you can see the flower in the image window and make sure that the Preview check box is selected.

6 Experiment with different Color Levels for the image, such as 12, 1, and -59.

7 When you are happy with the result, click OK.

Adjustment layers act as layer masks, which can be edited repeatedly without permanently affecting the underlying image. You can double-click an adjustment layer thumbnail to display the last settings used, and you can adjust adjustment layers as often as you like. You can delete an adjustment layer by dragging it to the Trash button (🗑) at the bottom of the Layers palette.

8 Choose Select > Deselect, and then save your work.

Applying filters

Next, you'll apply two filters to the yellow flower and white flower images. Because there are so many filters for creating special effects, the best way to learn about them is to try out different filters and filter options.

Improving performance with filters

Some filter effects can be memory-intensive, especially when applied to a high-resolution image. You can use these techniques to improve performance:

• Try out filters and settings on a small portion of an image.

• Apply the effect to individual channels—for example, to each RGB channel—if the image is large and you're having problems with insufficient memory. (With some filters, effects vary if applied to the individual channel rather than the composite channel, especially if the filter randomly modifies pixels.)

• Free up memory before running the filter by using the Purge commands.

• Allocate more RAM to Photoshop (Mac OS). You can also close other open applications to make more memory available to Photoshop.

• Try changing settings to improve the speed of memory-intensive filters such as Lighting Effects, Cutout, Stained Glass, Chrome, Ripple, Spatter, Sprayed Strokes, and Glass filters. For example, with the Stained Glass filter, increase cell size. With the Cutout filter, increase Edge Simplicity, decrease Edge Fidelity, or both.

• If you plan to print to a grayscale printer, convert a copy of the image to grayscale before applying filters. However, applying a filter to a color image and then converting to grayscale may not have the same effect as applying the filter to a grayscale version of the image.

Applying the Paint Daubs filter

The Paint Daubs filter lets you choose from various brush sizes and types—such as rough, sharp, blurry, or sparkle—for a painterly effect.

1 In the Layers palette, press Ctrl (Windows) or Command (Mac OS) and click the yellow flower image thumbnail to select its layer contents. Be sure to select the layer itself, not the adjustment layer.

Now you'll exclude the image's 1-pixel white stroke outline from the filter effect.

2 Choose Select > Modify > Contract. The default is 1 pixel. Click OK to subtract the image's 1-pixel white stroke outline from the selection.

3   Choose Filter > Artistic > Paint Daubs. In the upper right corner of the Paint Daubs dialog box, set Brush Size to 8, Sharpness to 7, and Brush Type to Simple. Then click OK to close the dialog box.

Using filters

To use a filter, choose the appropriate submenu command from the Filter menu. These guidelines can help you in choosing filters:

• The last filter chosen appears at the top of the Filter menu.

• Filters are applied to the active, visible layer.

• Filters cannot be applied to bitmap-mode or indexed-color images.

• Some filters work only on RGB images.

• Some filters are processed entirely in RAM.

• See "Using filters" in Photoshop Help for a list of filters that can be used with 16- and 32-bit-per-channel images.

Applying the Twirl filter

Next, you'll use the Twirl filter to create the impression that the white flower is spinning.

1   In the Layers palette, select the white flower layer.

2   In the toolbox, select the Elliptical Marquee tool (○), which is hidden behind the Rectangular Marquee tool (▭).

3 Begin dragging across the white flower image, and then hold down the Shift+Alt (Windows) or Shift+Option (Mac OS) keys to keep the selection circular as you select most of the white petals. Do not extend the selection to the borders of the image.

The selection restricts the area that the filter will affect within the white flower-image layer. If the selection is too large, the border will also become wavy and start to overlap the other quadrants of the montage image.

4 Choose Filter > Distort > Twirl.

5 In the angle box, enter 100. Adjust the zoom so that you can see the flower.

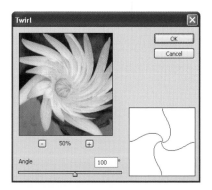

6 When you are satisfied with the result, click OK.

7 Choose Select > Deselect, and then File > Save to save your work.

For specific information on individual filters, see Photoshop Help.

Julieanne Kost is an official Adobe Photoshop evangelist.

TOOL TIPS FROM THE PHOTOSHOP EVANGELIST

> **Using filter shortcuts**

Try powerful shortcuts to help save time when working with filters:

• To reapply the most recently used filter with its last values, press Ctrl+F (Windows) or Command+F (Mac OS).

• To display the dialog box for the last filter you applied, press Ctrl+Alt+F (Windows) or Command+Option+F (Mac OS).

Moving a selection

Your next task is simple: Move the selection of letters to another area of the image. This sets the stage for the final work, creating a different effect in the shape of the letters.

1 Choose Select > Load Selection. In the Load Selection dialog box, choose Letters from the Channel pop-up menu. Click OK.

2 Use the Zoom tool (🔍) to zoom out so that you can see all of the image.

3 Select the Rectangular Marquee tool (⬚), which may be hidden under the Elliptical Marquee tool (◯).

4 Move the pointer inside the Letters selection and then drag the selection marquee (not the letters) into the lower right quadrant, centering it over the orange flower image.

If you want to move the selection at exactly a 45-degree angle, start dragging and then hold down Shift. Release the mouse button first, then the Shift key.

Be careful not to deselect yet, because you'll need this selection for the next exercise.

Creating a cutout effect

Next, you'll use your selection and some layer styles to create the illusion of a cutout in the orange flower image. Make sure that the letters-shaped selection is still active. If you have accidentally deselected, you'll have to start this process over, beginning with "Moving a selection" on the previous page.

1 In the Layers palette, select the Orange Flower layer.

2 Choose Layer > New > Layer Via Copy to create a new layer above the original Orange Flower layer, based on your combined selection. The new layer, named Layer 1, automatically becomes the active layer in the Layers palette, and the letters-shaped marquee disappears.

You can quickly create a selection marquee around a layer by Ctrl-clicking (Windows) or Command-clicking (Mac OS) the layer thumbnail in the Layers palette. You can try this with the new Paint layer to make the letters marquee reappear. Before you continue with this lesson, choose Select > Deselect.

3 At the bottom of the Layers palette, click the Add Layer Style button (*fx*) and then choose Pattern Overlay from the pop-up menu.

4 Drag the Layer Style dialog box aside, as needed, so that you can see both the dialog box and the image window.

5 Next to the Pattern thumbnail, click the arrow to the right of the thumbnail to open the pattern picker. The picker displays smaller thumbnails of an assortment of patterns.

6 Click the arrow button (⊙) to open the palette menu for the pattern picker, and choose Load Patterns.

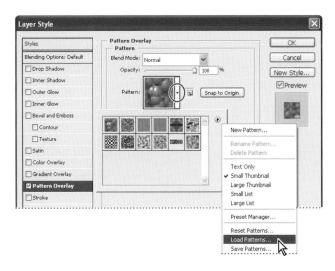

7 In the Load dialog box, go to the Lessons/Lesson11 folder and select the Effects.pat file. Click Load. Notice the new pattern that appears as the last thumbnail in the pattern picker.

8 Select the pattern thumbnail you added in Step 7. The pattern replaces the default pattern inside your Letters selection. At this point, you can drag the pattern in the image window to adjust the area of the pattern that appears in the selection—even with the Layer Style dialog box open.

9 On the left side of the Layer Style dialog box, under Styles, select Inner Shadow to add that effect to the selection, and adjust the Inner Shadow options to your liking. (The example uses Multiply for Blend Mode, 100% for Opacity, 120 for Angle, 5 px for Distance, 0% for Choke, and 5 px for Size.)

10 Continue to experiment with other styles and settings until you create results that you think are interesting. When you are satisfied with the results, click OK.

11 Choose File > Save to save your work.

Matching color schemes across images

In this final task, you'll harmonize the color schemes in the four images by matching the target image to the dominant colors in a source.

1 Scroll down the Layers palette to the Background layer and click the eye icon (👁) to hide that layer. If the Background layer is selected, select any other layer.

2 From the Layers palette menu, choose Merge Visible.

The Layers palette is reduced to two layers: Background and a merged layer with the same name as the layer that was selected at the end of Step 1.

Next, you have to open the document that will be the source for the color match adjustment—the 11A_End.psd file that you previewed at the beginning of the lesson. It has all of the unmerged layers intact.

3 Use Adobe Bridge or the File > Open command to open the 11A_End.psd file, located in the Lesson11 folder.

4 Make 11Working.psd the active image file, and then choose Image > Adjustments > Match Color. In the Match Color dialog box, do the following:

• Select the Preview option, if it is not already selected.

• Choose 11A_End.psd from the Source pop-up menu.

• From the Layer pop-up menu, choose the Museum layer that contains the museum image; look at the thumbnail to the right of the menu to identify it. Observe the effect of your selection on the 11Working.psd image window.

- One by one, choose the other layers and study the results in the image window. You can also experiment with the Image Options by adjusting the sliders for Luminance, Color Intensity, and Fade, with or without the Neutralize check box selected.

5 When you find the color scheme that you think does the best job of unifying the image and giving it the look you want, click OK to close the Match Color dialog box. (We used the Museum layer and the default Image Options settings.)

6 In the Layers palette, make the Background layer visible again by clicking its Visibility column.

7 Choose File > Save.

You can use Match Color with any source file to create interesting and unusual effects. The Match Color feature is also useful for certain color corrections (such as skin tones) in some photographs. The feature can also match the color between different layers in the same image. See Photoshop Help for more information.

You have completed Lesson 11, and you can close the 11Working.psd and 11A_End.psd files.

⭐ *EXTRA CREDIT Here's an easy way to frame an image. Using the image you finished at the end of Lesson 11 (or use the 11A_End.psd file), you'll turn it into a stamp. (To view the final image, open the 11B_End.psd file located in the Lesson11 folder.)*

1   Click the Default Foreground and Background colors Colors button in the toolbox to reset them to Black and White, respectively.

2   Choose Layer > Flatten Image.

3   Choose File > Save As, and rename the file **11Stamp.psd**.

4   Choose Image > Canvas Size. Select Relative to add canvas to the existing image, and set both the Width and Height to 2 inches. Click OK.

5   In the Layers palette, Alt/Option-click the New Layer button, and name it **Border**; click OK. Double-click the Background to convert it to a layer, name it **Montage**, and click OK. Drag the Montage layer above the empty Border layer.

6   With the Montage layer still selected, select the Magic Wand tool in the toolbox. Click to select the white canvas area around the montage image. Press Delete so that only the montage image remains. Deselect.

7   In the Layers palette, select the empty Border layer. Choose View > Rulers to display the rulers. Using the Rectangular Marquee tool and the rulers as guides, drag a square selection around the montage that is ½-inch larger than the artwork. Choose View > Rulers to hide the rulers.

8   Choose Edit > Fill, choose White for Contents, and click OK to fill the selection with white paint.

9   In the Layers palette, click the Add Layer Style button and choose Drop Shadow from the pop-up menu to apply a drop shadow to the layer. The settings for the shadow don't matter, as long as some shadow appears around the entire image. Click OK.

To create the stamp border, you'll create a path and stroke it in the shape of semicircle cutouts.

10   Select the object in the Border layer by pressing Ctrl (Windows) or Command (Mac OS) and clicking the Border layer thumbnail in the Layers palette.

11 Select the Pen tool in the toolbox. Click the Paths palette tab to bring the palette forward. Click the icon in the upper right of the palette to display the palette menu. Choose Make Work Path. In the dialog box, set the path to 1 pixel and click OK.

12 Select the Eraser tool in the toolbox. In the tool options bar, click the arrow next to the Brush Preset picker. Set the Master Diameter to 50 px and Hardness to 100%.

You'll set brush options to create the knockout.

13 On the right side of the image window, click the Brushes palette icon to expand the Brushes palette. From the palette menu, choose Expanded View. On the left side of the expanded palette, click Brush Tip Shape to display additional options; in the lower right, set Spacing to about 200%.

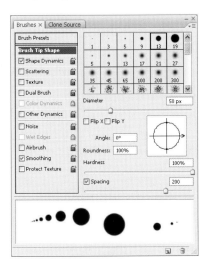

14 In the Paths palette, choose Stroke Path from the palette menu. In the Stroke Path dialog box, choose Eraser. Make sure that Simulate Pressure is not selected. Click OK.

Half circles are knocked out around the white Border layer, in the shape of a stamp edge.

15 In the Paths palette, click in an empty area of the palette to deselect the Work Path and hide the black stroke around the artwork.

16 Choose File > Save to save your work.

Review

► Review questions

1 What is the purpose of saving selections?

2 Describe one way to isolate color adjustments to an image.

3 Describe one way to remove color from a selection or from an image for a grayscale effect.

4 What are the differences between using a Smart Filter and a regular filter to apply effects to an image?

5 Describe one use for the Match Color feature.

► Review answers

1 By saving a selection, you can create and reuse time-consuming selections and uniformly select artwork in an image. You can also combine selections or create new selections by adding to or subtracting from existing selections.

2 You can use adjustment layers to try out color changes before applying them permanently to a layer.

3 You can choose Image > Adjustments > Desaturate to desaturate, or remove the color, from a selection.

4 Smart Filters are nondestructive: they can be adjusted, turned off and on, and deleted, at anytime. In contrast, regular filters permanently change an image; one applied, they cannot be removed. Smart Filters can be applied only to a Smart Object layer, so the layer itself can no longer be edited—just its Smart Filter effects.

5 You can use the Match Color feature to match color between different images, such as to adjust the facial skin tones in photographs—or to match color between different layers in the same image. You can also use the feature to create unusual color effects.

Part of the fun of navigating websites and web pages is clicking linked graphics to jump to another site or page, and activating built-in animations. This lesson shows how to prepare files for the web in Photoshop, by adding slices to link to other pages or sites, and creating rollovers and animations.

12 | Preparing Files for the Web

Lesson overview

In this lesson, you'll learn how to do the following:

- Slice an image in Photoshop.
- Distinguish between user slices and auto slices.
- Link user slices to other HTML pages or locations.
- Define rollover states to reflect mouse actions.
- Preview rollover effects.
- Create simple animated GIFs using a layered file.
- Use the Layers and Animation palettes to create animation sequences.
- Create animations based on changes in position, layer visibility, and layer effects.
- Use the Tween command to create smooth transitions between different settings for layer opacity and position.
- Preview animations in a web browser.
- Optimize images for the web and make good compression choices.
- Distinguish between GIF and JPEG optimization.
- Export large, high-resolution files that tile, for zooming and panning.

This lesson will take about 90 minutes to complete. If needed, remove the previous lesson folder from your hard drive, and copy the Lessons/ Lesson12 folder onto it. As you work on this lesson, you'll preserve the start files. If you need to restore the start files, copy them again from the *Adobe Photoshop CS3 Classroom in a Book* CD.

In addition, for this lesson, you will need to use a web browser application such as Netscape, Internet Explorer, or Safari. You do not need to connect to the Internet.

Getting started

In this lesson you'll fine-tune graphics for the home page of a Spanish art museum's website.

You'll add hypertext links to the topics, to link them to different, prebuilt pages on the site. Website visitors will be able to click a link to open a different linked page. You'll also add rollovers to alter how the web page looks without switching the user to a different web page, and you'll animate the Museo Arte logo in the upper left corner.

Let's start now by viewing the finished HTML page that you will create, based on a single PSD file. Several areas of the artwork react to mouse actions. For example, some areas of the image change appearance when the pointer "rolls over" them, or when you click one of the links.

1 Start Adobe Photoshop, holding down Ctrl+Alt+Shift (Windows) or Command+Option+Shift (Mac OS) to restore the default preferences. (See "Restoring default preferences" on page 6.)

2 When prompted, click Yes to confirm that you want to reset preferences, and Close to close the Welcome Screen.

3 Click the Go To Bridge button (▣) in the tool options bar to open Adobe Bridge.

4 In Bridge, click Lessons in the Favorites panel in the upper left corner of the browser window. Double-click the Lesson12 folder in the preview area; double-click the 12End folder; then double-click the site folder.

5 Right-click (Windows) or Control-click (Mac OS) the home.html file, and choose Open With from the context menu. Choose a web browser to open the HTML file.

6 Notice the logo animate in the upper left corner. The logo animates once when the browser opens.

Note: *If you don't see the logo animate when you open your browser, use your browser controls to refresh or reload the page.*

7 Move the mouse pointer over the topics on the left side of the web page and over the images. Look for changes in the appearance of the pointer, from an arrow to a pointing hand.

8 Click the angel in the lower center of the image to view the Zoomify window. Try out the Zoomify controls by clicking them to see how they zoom in and out of the image.

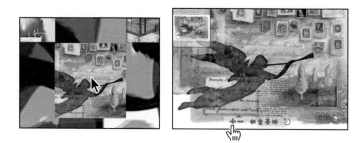

9 To get back to the home page, close the Zoomify window.

10 Click one of the other images to get a closer look at it in its own window. Close its browser windows when you have finished.

11 On the home page, click the topics to jump to their linked page. To get back to the home page, click "Museo Arte" just below the logo in the upper left of the window.

12 When you have finished viewing the web page, quit the web browser and return to Bridge.

In the preceding steps, you experienced two different types of links: slices (in the topics on the left side of the page) and images (the boy, Spanish Masters page, and angel).

Slices are rectangular areas in an image that you define based on layers, guides, or precise selections in the image, or by using the Slice tool. When you define slices in an image, Photoshop creates an HTML table or Cascading Style Sheet to contain and align the slices. If you want, you can generate and preview an HTML file that contains the sliced image along with the table or Cascading Style Sheet.

You can also add hypertext links to images. A website visitor can then click the image to open a linked page. Unlike slices, which are always rectangular, images can be any shape.

Setting up a Web Design workspace

As the leading application for preparing images for websites, Photoshop also has some basic, built-in HTML creation tools. To make it easier to get to these tools for your web design tasks, you can customize the default arrangement of palettes, toolbars, and windows, using one of the predefined workspaces in Photoshop.

1 In Bridge, click the Go Up button (📷) twice to go up two levels to the 12Start folder, and then double-click the 12Start.psd thumbnail to open it in Photoshop.

You'll customize your workspace now, and turn it into a working web page.

2 Choose Window > Workspace > Web Design. In the alert dialog box stating that changes will affect menu and keyboard shortcuts, click Yes.

3 In the main menu, click different menu items to display their options, and view the options that are highlighted in purple. These are the options you typically would use in Web Design mode.

4 Choose File > Save As, and rename the file **12Working.psd** to save your workspace. Click OK in the Maximize Compatibility dialog box.

Creating slices

When you define a rectangular area in an image as a slice, Photoshop creates an HTML table to contain and align the slice. Once you create a slice, you can turn slices into buttons, and program those buttons to make the web page work.

You can't create just one slice—unless you create a slice that includes the whole image, which would be fairly useless. Any new slice you create within an image (a *user slice*) automatically creates other slices (*auto slices*) that cover all the area of the image outside the user slice.

Selecting slices and setting slice options

You'll start by selecting a premade slice in the Start file. We created the first slice for you, so that it matches the pixel size exactly of the animation you'll add to the slice at the end of the lesson.

1   In the toolbox, select the Slice Select tool ( ) tool, hidden under the Slice tool.

2   In the upper left corner of the image, click the slice numbered 01 with the small blue rectangle. A gold bounding box appears, indicating that the slice is selected.

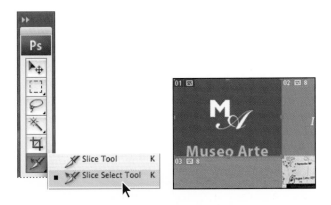

The rectangle numbered 01 includes the upper left corner of the image; it also has a small icon, or *badge*, that resembles a tiny mountain. The blue color tells you that the slice is a user slice, a slice we created in the Start file.

Also notice the gray slices—02 to the right, and 03 just below slice 01. The gray color tells you that these are auto slices, automatically created by making a user slice. The symbol indicates that the slice contains image content. See "About slice symbols" on the next page for a description of the various slice symbols.

About slice symbols

The blue and gray slice symbols, or badges, in the Photoshop image window and Save For Web And Devices dialog box can be useful reminders if you take the time to learn how to read them. Each slice can contain as many badges as are appropriate. The following badges appear under the stated conditions:

(🔲) The number of the slice. Numbers run sequentially from left to right and top to bottom of the image.

(🖼) The slice contains image content.

(🖾) The slice contains no image content.

(🔳) The slice is layer based; that is, it was created from a layer.

(🔹) The slice is linked to other slices (for optimization purposes).

3 Using the Slice Select tool, double-click slice 01. The Slice Options dialog box appears. By default, Photoshop names each slice based on the filename and the slice number—in this case, 12Start_01.

Slices aren't particularly useful until you set options for them. Slice options include the slice name and the URL that opens when the user clicks the slice.

Note: You can set options for an auto slice, but doing so automatically promotes the auto slice to a user slice.

4 In the Slice Options dialog box, for the name, type **Logo Animation**. For URL, type **#.** The pound sign lets you preview a button's functionality without programming an actual link. It's very helpful in the early stages of website design, when you want to see how a button will look and behave.

5 Click OK to apply the changes. Later in the lesson, you will create an animated version of this sliced image to replace it on the final website.

Creating navigation buttons

Now you'll slice the navigation buttons on the left side of the page, so that you can turn them into rollovers. You could select each button at a time and add navigation properties to it. But you can do the same thing a faster way.

1 In the toolbox, switch to the Slice tool (✐) or press Shift+K to use the shortcut.

Notice the guides set up above and below the words on the left side of the image.

2 Using the guides on the left side of the image, draw diagonally from the upper left above "About Museo Arte," to the bottom guide below "Contact," to enclose all five words.

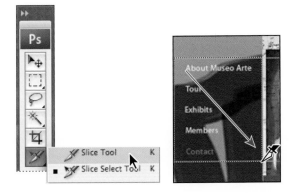

A blue rectangle, similar to the one for slice 01, appears in the upper left corner of the slice you just created, numbered slice 04. The blue color tells you that this is a user slice, not an auto slice.

The original gray rectangle for auto slice 03 remains unchanged, but the area included in slice 03 is smaller, covering only a small rectangle above the text.

The gold bounding box indicates the bounds of the slice and that it's selected.

3 With the Slice tool still selected, press Shift+K to toggle to the Slice Select tool. The Slice options in the tool bar above the image window change, and a series of alignment buttons appear.

Now you'll slice your selection into five separate buttons.

4 Click the Divide button in the tool options bar above the image window.

5 In the Divide Slice dialog box, select Divide Horizontally Into, and type **5** for Slices Down, Evenly Spaced. Click OK.

Now you will name each slice and add a corresponding link.

6 Using the Slice Select tool, double-click the top slice, labeled About Museo Arte, to open the Slice Options dialog box.

7 In the Slice Options dialog box, name the slice **About**; type **about.html** for URL; and type **_self** for Target. (Be sure to include the underscore before the letter *s*.) Click OK.

The Target option controls how a linked file opens when the link is clicked. The _self option displays the linked file in the same frame as the original file.

8 Repeat Steps 6 and 7 for the remaining slices in turn, starting from the second top slice, as follows:

• For the second top slice, name it **Tour**; type **tour.html** for URL; type **_self** for Target.

• For the third slice, name it **Exhibits**; type **exhibits.html** for URL; type **_self** for Target.

• For the fourth slice, name it **Members**; type **members.html** for URL; type **_self for** Target.

• For the fifth, bottom slice, name it **Contact**; type **contact.html** for URL; type **_self** for Target.

Important: Name the HTML pages exactly as shown, to match the premade pages with these names, to which you will link the buttons.

9 Choose File > Save to save your work so far.

If you find the indicators for the auto slices distracting, select the Slice Select tool and then click the Hide Auto Slices button in the tool options bar. You can also hide the guides by choosing View > Show > Guides, because you won't need them again.

Creating slices based on layers

You can also create slices based on layers rather than with the Slice tool. The advantage of using layers for slices is that Photoshop creates the slice based on the dimensions of the layer, and includes all its pixel data. When you edit the layer, move it, or apply a layer effect to it, the layer-based slice adjusts to encompass the new pixels.

1 In the Layers palette, select the Image 1 layer. If you can't see all of the contents of the Layers palette, drag the palette from its dock and expand the palette by dragging its lower right corner.

2   Choose Layer > New Layer Based Slice. In the image, a blue rectangle numbered 04 appears. It is numbered according to its position in the slices, starting from the top left corner of the image.

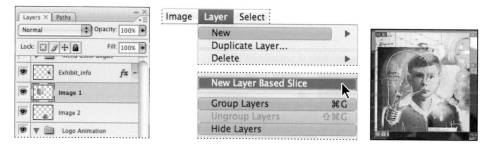

3   Using the Slice Select tool, double-click the slice and name it **Image 1**. For URL, type **image1.html** for URL. Type **_blank** for Target. The _blank Target option opens the linked page in a new instance of the web browser. Click OK.

Be sure to enter these options exactly as indicated, to match the pages we've created with links to this slice.

Now you'll create another slice for the Exhibit Info layer.

4   In the Layers palette, select the Exhibit Info layer.

5   Choose Layer > New Layer Based Slice; the new slice is numbered 08. In the image window, double-click this new layer using the Slice Select tool. In the Slice Options dialog box, name it **Exhibit Info**; for URL, type **exhibitinfo.html** for URL, and type **_blank** for Target. Click OK.

6   Repeat Steps 4 and 5 for the Image 2 layer. (The new slice is numbered 18.) Name it **Card**, type **card.html** for URL, and type **_blank** for Target. Click OK.

You may have noticed that the dialog box contains more options than the three you specified for these slices. For more information on how to use these options, see Photoshop Help.

7   Choose File > Save to save your work so far.

About creating slices

Here are other methods for creating slices that you can try on your own.

• You can create No Image slices, and then add text or HTML source code to them. No Image slices can have a background color and are saved as part of the HTML file. The primary advantage of using No Image slices for text is that the text can be edited in any HTML editor, saving you the trouble of having to go back to Photoshop to edit it. However, if the text grows too large for the slice, it will break the HTML table and introduce unwanted gaps.

• If you use custom guides in your design work, you can instantly divide up an entire image into slices with the Slices From Guides button on the Slice tool options bar. Use this technique with caution, however, because it discards any previously created slices and any options associated with those slices. Also, it creates only user slices, and you may not need that many of them.

• When you want to create identically sized, evenly spaced, and aligned slices, try creating a single user slice that precisely encloses the entire area. Then, use the Divide button on the Slice Select tool options bar to divide the original slice into as many vertical or horizontal rows of slices as you need.

• If you want to unlink a layer-based slice from its layer, you can convert it to a user slice. Simply double-click it with the Slice Select tool, and select options for it.

Adding animation

In Photoshop, you create animations from a single image using animated GIF files. An *animated GIF* is a sequence of images, or frames. Each frame varies slightly from the preceding frame, creating the illusion of movement when the frames are viewed in quick succession—just like movies. You can create animation in several ways:

• By using the Duplicate Selected Frame button in the Animation palette to create animation frames, and then using the Layers palette to define the image state associated with each frame.

• By using the Tween feature to quickly create new frames that warp text or vary a layer's opacity, position, or effects to create the illusion of an element in a frame moving or fading in and out.

• By opening a multilayer Adobe Photoshop or Adobe Illustrator file for an animation, with each layer becoming a frame.

In this lesson, you'll try out the first two techniques.

Files for animations must be saved in GIF format or as QuickTime movies. You cannot create animations as JPEG or PNG files.

Creating an animated GIF

To add interest to the web page, you'll animate the Museo Arte logo so that it seems to dance across the left corner. You'll animate the type by using the Animation and Layers palettes in tandem, as you continue to work in the Web Design workspace (Window > Workspace > Web Design).

1 In the Layers palette, click the triangle next to the Logo Animation group to expand its contents. The group consists of three components—an *M*, and *A*, and the text *Museo Arte*—on separate layers.

You will create an animation showing the two letters appearing and moving into their final position. At the end, they will glow, and the title Museo Arte will fade in.

2 Choose Window > Animation to display the Animation palette at the bottom left of the image window. Drag the lower right corner of the Animation palette to expand it so that you take advantage of available horizontal space in the work area.

(Optional) You can also move the Animation palette closer to the image window, to keep elements in the work area close together.

3 In the Animation palette, click the Duplicate Selected Frame button. This creates a new frame based on the previous one.

4 In the Layers palette, select the M layer.

5 Select the Move tool (✛) in the toolbox. Drag the *M* to the left side of the image window, holding down the Shift key to keep the movement straight. Press the Left Arrow key on the keyboard to nudge the *M* to the left until it is barely visible.

Be careful not to drag the letter completely out of the image window.

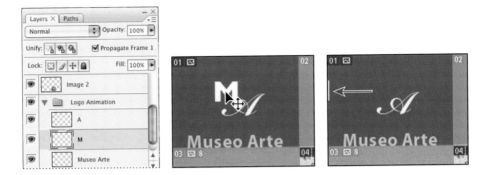

6 In the Layers palette, select the A layer.

7 In the image window, use the Move tool to drag the *A* directly upward—if necessary, hold down the Shift key to constrain the move—until the letter is just out of the frame.

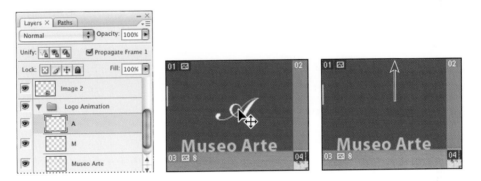

Another way to animate objects is by changing their opacity; over time, they fade away.

8 In the Layers palette, select the Museo Arte layer. Reduce its Opacity to 0%.

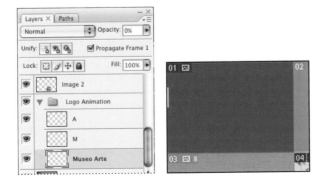

9 In the Layers palette, select the M layer and reduce its opacity to 10%. Then select the A layer and reduce its opacity to 10%.

10 Choose File > Save to save your work so far.

Tweening the position and opacity of layers

Next, you'll add frames that represent transitional image states between the two existing frames. When you change the position, opacity, or effects of any layer between two animation frames, you can instruct Photoshop to *tween*, which automatically creates as many intermediate frames as you specify.

You'll begin by making frame 2 the starting state of the animation.

1 In the Animation palette, drag frame 2 to the left of frame 1. The frames are instantly renamed in sequence.

Now you'll add a tween between these two frames.

2 In the Animation palette, make sure that frame 1 is selected, and then click the Tween button (✺) at the bottom of the palette.

3 In the Tween dialog box, set the following options (if they are not already selected):

• Choose Tween With: Next Frame.

• For Frames to Add, type **5**.

• Under Layers, select All Layers.

• Under Parameters, make sure that all of the options are selected.

4 Click OK to close the dialog box.

5 To test the animation, click the Play button at bottom of Animation palette. This previews the animation; it may be a bit jerky, but it will play fine in your browser.

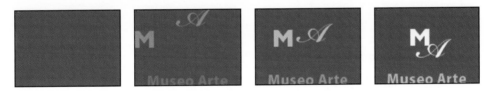

Tweening frames

You use the Tween command to automatically add or modify a series of frames between two existing frames—varying the layer attributes (position, opacity, or effect parameters) evenly between the new frames to create the appearance of movement. For example, if you want to fade out a layer, set the opacity of the layer in the starting frame to 100%, and then set the opacity of the same layer in the ending frame to 0%. When you tween between the two frames, the opacity of the layer is reduced evenly across the new frames.

The term tweening is derived from "in betweening," the term used in traditional animation to describe this process. Tweening significantly reduces the time required to create animation effects such as fading in or fading out, or moving an element across a frame. You can edit tweened frames individually after you create them.

If you select a single frame, you choose whether to tween the frame with the previous frame or the next frame. If you select two contiguous frames, new frames are added between the frames. If you select more than two frames, existing frames between the first and last selected frames are altered by the tweening operation. If you select the first and last frames in an animation, these frames are treated as contiguous, and tweened frames are added after the last frame. (This tweening method is useful when the animation is set to loop multiple times.)

Note: You cannot select discontiguous frames for tweening.

Animating a layer style

When you tweened to create the new frames in the previous procedure, you may have noticed the Effects check box in the Tween dialog box. In this procedure, you will animate a layer effect, or *layer style*. The final result will be a little flash of light that appears and then disappears behind the *M* and *A* letters.

1   In the Animation palette, select frame 7, and then click the Duplicate Selected Frame button to create a new frame with all the same settings as frame 7. Leave frame 8 selected.

2   In the Layers palette, select the M layer. From the Layer Style pop-up menu (*fx*) at the bottom of the palette, choose Outer Glow. In the Layer Style dialog box, set the following options:

• Choose Screen for Blend Mode.

• Set the Opacity to 55. Set the Spread to 0%.

• Set the size to 5.

- For color, click the color swatch and choose a light yellow in the color picker.

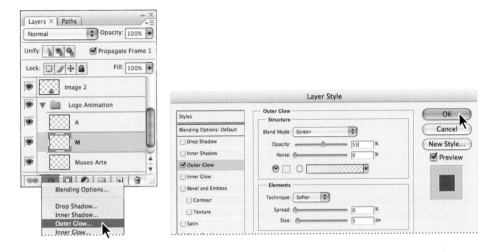

3 Click OK to apply the style to the M layer. Now you'll copy this effect to the A layer.

4 In the Layers palette, press the Alt (Windows) or Option (Mac OS) key, and drag the Effect icon from the M layer to the A layer. This copies the effect to the A layer.

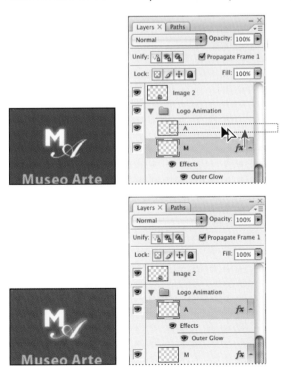

Now you'll tween this copied effect, so that the letters glow at the end of the animation.

5 In the Animation palette, select frame 7. Click the Tween button at the bottom of the palette.

6 In the Tween dialog box, type **2** for Frames To Add. Make sure that Effects is selected under Parameters, and click OK.

7 In the Animation palette, select frame 7, and then click the Duplicate Selected Frame button to create a new frame with all the same settings as frame 7.

8 Drag this new frame 8 to the end of the animation, where it now becomes frame 11.

You'll set this animation to play only once on the website.

9 At the bottom left of the Animation palette, make sure that Once is selected in the pop-up menu.

10 Click the Play button at the bottom of the Animation palette to preview the test movie.

11 Choose File > Save to save your work.

Exporting HTML and images

Like a carpenter who scores a piece of wood before making the final cut, you're ready to make your final slices, define your links, and export your file so that it creates an HTML page that will display all of your slices as one unit.

It's important to keep web graphics as small as possible so that web pages open quickly. Photoshop has built-in tools to help you gauge how small to export each slice without compromising image quality. A good rule of thumb is to use JPEG compression for photographic, continuous-tone images, and GIF compression for broad areas of color—in the case of this lesson's site, all of the areas around the three main art images on the page.

You'll use the Photoshop Save For Web and Devices dialog box to compare settings and compression for different image formats.

1 Choose File > Save For Web And Devices.

2 In the Save For Web And Devices dialog box, select the 2-Up tab at the top.

3 Choose the Slice Select tool ( ) in the dialog box, and select slice 4 from the slices on the left side of the window. Note the file size of the graphic in the lower left of the window.

4 If necessary, use the Hand tool in the dialog box to move the image within the window and adjust your view.

5 From the Preset pop-up menu on the right of the dialog box, choose JPEG Medium. Notice the size of the graphic displayed in the lower left corner of tab.

Now you'll look at a GIF setting for the same slice on the right side of the 2-Up tab.

6 With the Slice Select tool, select the slice 04 (boy portrait). On the right side of the dialog box from the Preset menu, choose GIF 32 No Dither.

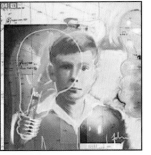

JPEG
11.99K
5 sec @ 28.8 Kbps

GIF
20.49K
8 sec @ 28.8 Kbps

Notice how the color area in the right portrait looks flatter and more posterized, but the size of images are roughly the same.

Based on what you've just learned, you will choose what compression to assign to all of the slices on this page.

7 Select the Optimized tab in the upper left corner of the dialog box.

8 With the Slice Select tool, Shift-click to select the three main art images in the preview. From the Preset menu, choose JPEG Medium.

9 In the Preview window, Shift-click to select all of the remaining slices, and from the Preset menu choose GIF 64 Dithered.

10 Click Save and navigate to the Lesson12/12Start/Museo folder, which contains all the rest of the site and pages that your slices will link to.

11 For format, choose HTML and Images. Use the default settings, and choose All Slices for Slices. Name the file **home.html**, and click Save.

12 In Bridge, click Lessons in the Favorites panel in the upper left corner of the browser window. Double-click the Lesson12 folder in the preview area; double-click the 12Start folder; then double-click the Museo folder.

13 Right-click (Windows) or Control-click (Mac OS) the home.html file, and choose Open With from the context menu. Choose a web browser to open the HTML file.

14 In your web browser, move around the HTML file and try out its features:

• Position your mouse over some of the slices you created. Notice that the pointer turns into a pointing finger to indicate a button.

• Click the portrait of the boy to display a pop-up window with the full image.

• Click the Spanish Masters link and display its pop-up window.

• Click the text links on the left to jump to other pages in the site.

15 When you have finished exploring the file, close your browser.

Optimizing images for the web

Optimizing is the process of selecting format, resolution, and quality settings to make an image efficiently, visually appealing, and useful for web browser pages. Simply put, it's balancing file size against good looks. No single collection of settings can maximize the efficiency of every kind of image file; optimizing requires human judgment and a good eye.

Compression options vary according to the file format used to save the image. JPEG and GIF are the two most common formats. The JPEG format is designed to preserve the broad color range and subtle brightness variations of continuous-tone images such as photographs. It can represent images using millions of colors. The GIF format is effective at compressing solid-color images and images with areas of repetitive color, such as line art, logos, and illustrations with type. It uses a palette of 256 colors to represent the image and supports background transparency.

Photoshop offers a range of controls for compressing image file size while optimizing the on-screen quality. Typically, you optimize images before saving them in an HTML file. You use the Save For Web And Devices dialog box to compare the original image to one or more compressed alternatives, adjusting settings as you compare. For more on optimizing GIF and JPEG images, see Photoshop Help.

1 With a JPEG or GIF file open in Photoshop, choose File > Save For Web And Devices

2 In the Save For Web And Devices dialog box, click the 4-Up tab. The upper left preview shows the original image. Photoshop automatically renders three alternatives—a high–, medium-, and low-quality JPEG preview, or three GIF options.

3 Compare the quality and size differences, and then click any optimized version to experiment with format and quality settings, continuing to judge size compared to quality.

4 When you are satisfied, either click Cancel, or click Save to name and save your file.

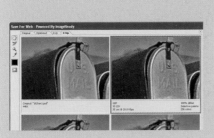

JPEG compression options

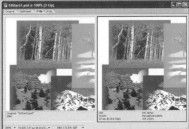

GIF compression options

Adding interactivity

If you've ever wanted to be able to zoom in on an image and magnify spots that interest you, now you can. New in Photoshop CS3, you can create an interactive image with zooming capabilities that can be used with any web browser.

With the Zoomify feature, you can publish high-resolution images on the web that viewers can pan and zoom to see more detail. The basic-size image downloads in the same time as an equivalent size JPEG file. Photoshop exports the JPEG files and HTML file that you can upload to your web

1 In Bridge, double-click the Lesson12 folder in the preview area; double-click the 12Start folder; then double-click the Card.jpg file to open it.

This is a large bitmap image that you'll export to HTML using the Zoomify feature.

Now you'll convert the angel image into a file that will be linked to one of the links that you've just created in the home page.

2 Choose File > Export > Zoomify.

3 In the Zoomify Export dialog box, select the Lesson12/12Start/Museo folder. For Base Name, type **Card**. Set the quality to 12; set the Width to 600 and the Height to 400 for the base image in the viewer's browser. Make sure that the Open In Web Browser option is selected.

4 Click OK to upload the HTML and images to your web browser.

Now you'll check out your work one last time in your browser.

4 In Bridge, double-click the Lesson12 folder in the preview area; double-click the 12Start folder; then double-click the Museo folder.

5 Right-click (Windows) or Control-click (Mac OS) the Card.html file, and choose Open With from the context menu. Choose a web browser to open the HTML file.

6 Use the controls in the Zoomify window to test your zoomify link on the angel image.

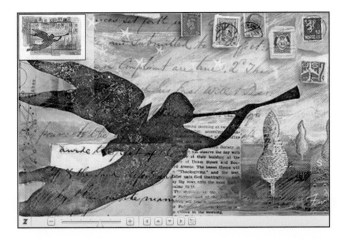

Congratulations! You've learned how to add animation and interactivity to your web page with slices, rollovers, and Zoomify.

⭐ *EXTRA CREDIT: Creating slices for rollovers is an easy way to make buttons more obvious. When creating content for the web, it's always good practice to clearly communicate when users encounter a button. In this lesson, the only clue to buttons is that they change from a pointer to a pointing finger when the user moves the mouse over them. This hint may be too subtle for most people.*

Here's how to make buttons stand out: you create a second state for the navigation slices, to appear when the mouse hovers over each slice. You'll do that here by making layers visible, exporting them to a separate folder, and them dropping them into a file with HTML code already written to make the rollovers work.

1 Return to the 12Working.psd file.

2 In the Layers palette, click the triangle to open the Menu Color Bkgds group and display its layers.

3 Click the Toggle Visibility to the left of the Menu Color Bkgds layers to turn layers cell_1 through cell_5 on and off.

Now notice what happens to the navigation button slices: they become darker gray when selected. This is how the buttons should look when the mouse hovers over them.

4 With the Menu Color Bkgd layers visible, choose File > Save For Web And Devices.

5 In the image window, use the Slice Select tool (✂) to Shift-select the five navigation buttons.

6 In the Save For Web And Devices dialog box, make sure that the GIF file type is selected. Click Save.

7 In the Save Optimized As dialog box, navigate to the Lesson12 folder, and click New Folder. Name the new folder Over States. For format, select Images Only. Leave the default settings, and choose Selected Slices. Click Save.

8 Navigate to the Over States folder you just created, and open one of the image files you just exported.

If you were creating a real web page, you would import these files into an HTML editor such as Adobe® Dreamweaver® CS3. In Dreamweaver, you would program the page so that the images in the Over States folder would swap with the first image slices whenever the mouse hovered over those slices.

We've built a mock-up to show you what a finished version of this web page might look like.

9 In Bridge, double-click the Lesson12 folder in the preview area; double-click the 12End folder; then double-click the site folder to open it.

10 Right-click (Windows) or Control-click (Mac OS) the home.html file, and choose Open With from the context menu. Choose a web browser to open the HTML file.

Review

▶ Review questions

1 What are slices? How do you create them?

2 Describe a rollover and the Over rollover states.

3 Describe a simple way to create an animation.

4 What file formats can you use for animations?

5 What is image optimization and how do you optimize images for the web?

▶ Review answers

1 Slices are rectangular areas of an image that you define for individual web optimization and to which you then can add animated GIFs, URL links, and rollovers. You can create image slices with the Slice tool or by converting layers into slices using the Layer menu.

2 A rollover is a web effect that alters a web page's appearance without switching the user to a different web page—such as a button that changes color when the mouse rolls over it. The Over state indicates the pointer tip is within the defined area, but the user doesn't press the mouse button in any way.

3 A simple way to create an animation is to start with a layered Photoshop file. Use the Duplicate Selected Frame button in the Animation palette to create a new frame, and then use the Layers palette to alter the position, opacity, or effects of selected frames. Add intermediate frames between two frames manually using the Duplicate Selected Frame button, or automatically using the Tween command.

4 Files for animations must be saved in GIF format or as QuickTime movies. You cannot create animations as JPEG or PNG files.

5 Image optimization is the process of choosing a file format, resolution, and quality settings for an image to keep it small, useful, and visually appealing when published to the web. Continuous-tone images are typically optimized in JPEG format; solid-color images or those with repetitive color areas typically are optimized as GIF. To optimize images, choose File > Save For Web And Devices.

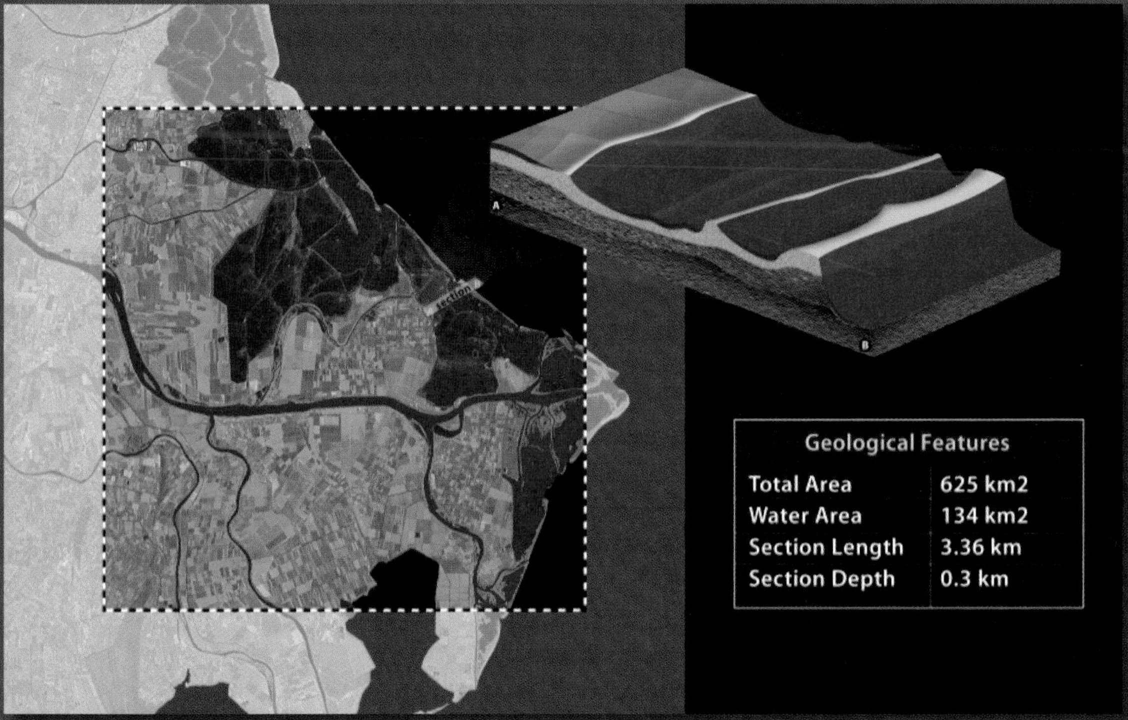
section
A
B
Geological Features
Total Area 625 km2
Water Area 134 km2
Section Length 3.36 km
Section Depth 0.3 km

Creating spiffy infographics is a snap with Photoshop tools and Adobe Bridge organizational muscle—even with very large images. Bridge saves you time with features that organize and rank images so you can see and search for exactly the ones you need. Measurement and image analysis tools in Photoshop Extended give your images additional dimension.

13 | Working with Scientific Images

Lesson overview

In this lesson, you'll learn how to do the following:

- Use Adobe Bridge to add metadata and keywords.
- Search across a collection of files with Adobe Bridge.
- Label, rank, and sort images in Bridge.
- Enhance images for analysis and presentation.
- Create a custom dashed-line border.
- Add notes to images.
- Use the Measurement tool.
- Record measurement data in the Measurement Log palette.
- Export spreadsheet data from the Measurement Log palette.
- Measure in perspective using the Vanishing Point feature.
- Animate a presentation

This lesson will take about 90 minutes to complete. If needed, remove the previous lesson folder from your hard drive, and copy the Lesson13 folder onto it. As you work on this lesson, you'll preserve the start file. However, if you need to restore the start file, copy it from the *Adobe Photoshop CS3 Classroom in a Book* CD.

Getting started

Many professionals use Photoshop for highly technical, precise work. In this lesson, you will assemble an informational graphic on water levels and land masses using graphics provided by the U.S. Geological Survey. You will learn how Bridge is a valuable tool for organizing and identifying images as well as creating a presentation.

1 Start Photoshop and then immediately hold down Ctrl+Alt+Shift (Windows) or Command+Option+Shift (Mac OS) to restore the default preferences. (See "Restoring default preferences" on page 6.)

2 When prompted, click Yes to confirm that you want to reset preferences, and click Close to close the Welcome Screen.

3 Choose File > Browse to open Adobe Bridge.

Your goal in this lesson is to work with very large files, selecting just the area you need to make measurements and comparisons of data. You'll learn that working with very large files in Photoshop is really no different than editing other, smaller images.

This lesson also introduces you to Photoshop Extended, a version of Photoshop CS3 with all the features in the standard edition of Photoshop, plus functions for specialized markets—technical image analysis, film and video work, and three-dimensional design. This lesson shows how to use Photoshop Extended measurement and data analysis tools. If you don't have Photoshop Extended, you can complete this lesson up to "Measuring objects and data" on page 433, and then read through the remaining lesson.

Watch the Measurement QuickTime movie to get a quick overview of the Measurement tool in Photoshop Extended. The movie is located on the Adobe Photoshop CS3 Classroom in a Book *CD in Movies/Measurement.mov. Double-click the movie file to open it; then click the Play button.*

Viewing and editing files in Adobe Bridge

As you've seen in previous Classroom in a Book lessons, Adobe Bridge helps you navigate your image files and folders. Bridge is much more than a navigator. A cross-platform application included with Adobe® Creative Suite® 3 components, Bridge also helps you organize and browse the assets you need to create print, web, video, and audio content. You can start Bridge from any Creative Suite component (except Adobe Acrobat 8), and use it to access both Adobe and non-Adobe assets.

You'll try out some of these management capabilities as you explore and customize the Bridge browser window. You'll also organize map sections for use in your infographics project.

Customizing Adobe Bridge views and workspaces

The panels in Adobe Bridge help you navigate, preview, search, and manage information for your image files and folders. The ideal arrangement and relative sizes of items and areas of Bridge depend on your work style and preferences. Depending on the tasks you're doing, it may be important to see what images are in a file; at other times, viewing information about the file may take priority. You can customize Bridge to increase your efficiency in these different situations.

In this procedure, you'll try out some of the custom views you can use in Adobe Bridge. The following figure shows the default configuration of Adobe Bridge areas, although you won't see these particular thumbnails on-screen yet.

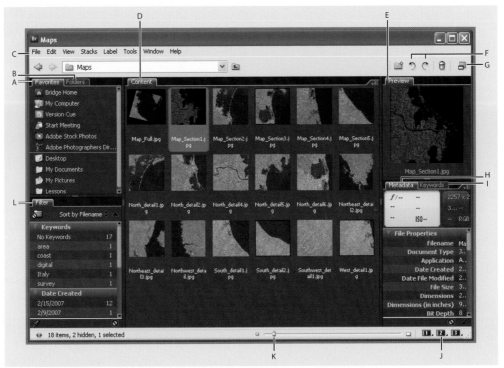

A. Favorites panel *B. Folders panel* *C. Menu bar* *D. Content panel* *E. Thumbnail preview pane* *F. Rotation buttons* *G. Compact mode button* *H. Metadata panel* *I. Keywords panel* *J. View option buttons* *K. Thumbnail slider* *L. Filter panel*

1 In the upper left corner of Bridge browser window, click the Folders tab to bring that panel forward, and navigate to the Lessons/Lesson13/Maps folder that you copied to your hard drive from the *Adobe Photoshop CS3 Classroom in a Book* CD. To navigate, either click the arrows to open nested folders in the Folders panel on the left side of the browser window, or double-click the folder thumbnail icons in the Folders panel.

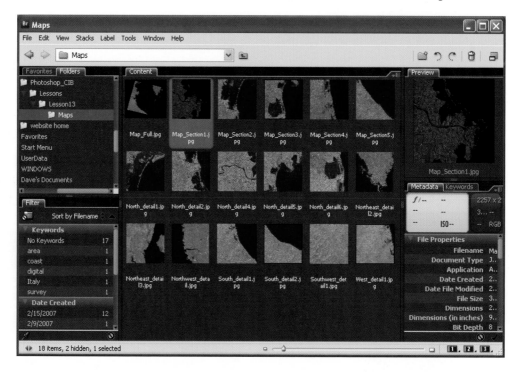

2 In the lower left corner of the Bridge window, click the left show/hide panels button (⏭). This expands the Content panel and hides the left and right series of panels so that only image previews appear.

3 Click the right show/hide panels button (⬤) to redisplay the Bridge window with panels to the left and right of the Content panel.

The Bridge preview pane updates interactively, showing you thumbnail previews of asset files. Adobe Bridge displays previews of image files such as those in PSD, TIFF, and JPEG formats as well as Adobe Illustrator vector files, multipage Adobe PDF files, and Microsoft Office documents.

4 In the Content panel, click the Map_Full.jpg thumbnail to select it.

This is one of a series of aerial photographs taken of the northeastern coast of Italy, near Venice. Other images show section details from this map.

5 On the right side of the browser window, click the Metadata tab if needed to bring that panel forward. At the top of the Metadata section, notice the data about the image and its size.

6 Click the triangle next to File Properties to expand its contents. This panel displays additional information about the image, including the file type, date it was created and modified, dimensions, bit depth, and color mode.

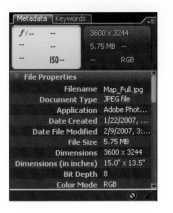

This 3600 x 3244-pixel image is relatively compact in file size (5.75 MB), but physically very large: the image measures 50-inches by 45.1 inches. You'll see how easily you can work with very large images using the precision tools in Photoshop.

7 At the bottom right of the browser window, drag the thumbnail slider to the right to enlarge the thumbnail previews. Enlarging the preview acts as a loupe, to let you zoom in on an image and inspect it more closely.

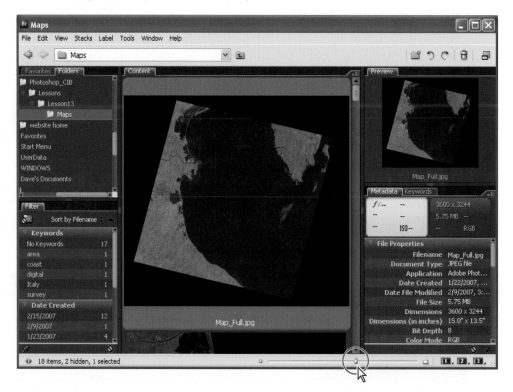

8 Drag to the right to decrease the preview.

9 In the lower right corner of the browser window, click view button 2 to display the images in Horizontal Filmstrip view; then click view button 3 to show them in Metadata Focus view. Click view button 1 to return to the default view.

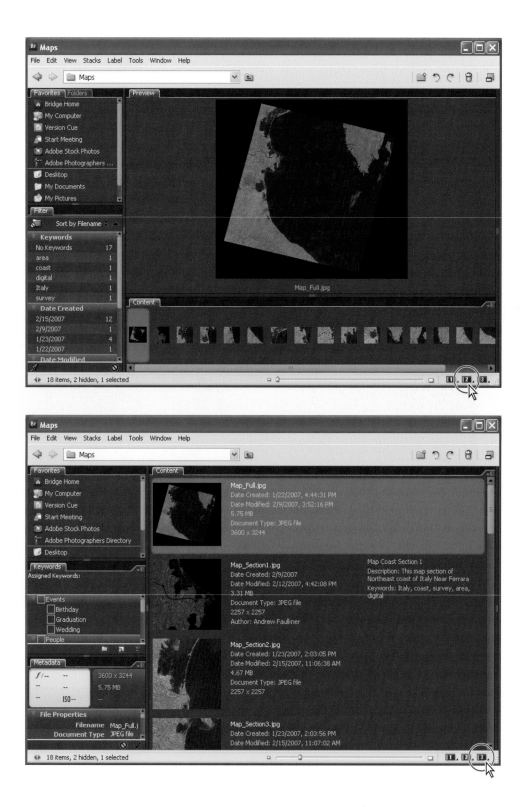

Using Bridge to organize and search your elements

You can quickly see file information in one of several ways: by keywords, by filtered information, or by metadata. Now you will look more closely at the metadata information. Metadata is a set of standardized information about a file, such as author name, resolution, color space, copyright, and keywords applied to it. You can use metadata to streamline your workflow and organize your files.

1 Make sure that you're in the Default (1) view.

2 In the Content panel, click to select the Map_Section1.jpg thumbnail.

3 Drag the right panel's splitter bar to the left, to expand the Preview and Metadata panels.

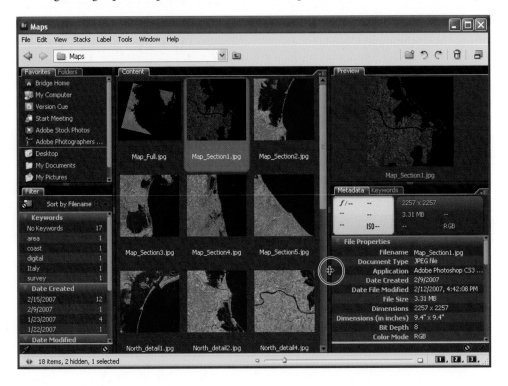

When you work with large amounts of metadata, it helps to enlarge the Metadata panel, even if it reduces or eliminates the Content, Favorites, and Folders panels. This can reduce the amount of scrolling needed to review and edit the information.

4 Scroll down the Metadata panel to the IPTC Core heading.

The information in the Metadata panel is nested under headings that you can expand or collapse by clicking the arrow next to a heading. Three headings relate to images: File Properties, IPTC Core, and Camera Data (EXIF). Additional headings are available for stock photo images. In Bridge, you can directly edit only some of the IPTC metadata.

5 Click the triangle (▶) next to the IPTC Core section to expand its contents so that you can see the items listed under it. You can see that information has been entered about the file creator, including his name and address; the job title; description; and keywords. The pencil icons (✐) on the right indicate items that you can edit.

Now you'll add some metadata of your own to an image.

6 In the Content panel, click the Map_Section3.jpg thumbnail to select it.

7 In the IPTC Core section, click the pencil icon (✐) next to the top Creator field. White fields appear, indicating that you can enter information.

8 For Creator, type your name. Then enter information in the following fields, pressing Tab to advance to the next text box:

- For Job Title, type your professional title.

- For Address, type your address.

- For keyword, type **coast**.

9 Click the Apply button in the lower right corner of the browser window to apply these changes.

You'll search for other images containing the same keyword.

10 To search all images with the keyword "coast," choose Edit > Find. In the Find dialog box, for Source Look In, choose Maps; for Criteria, choose Keywords and Contains from the pop-up menus, and type **coast** in the right text box. Leave the other settings as is, and click Find.

Two images with the keyword coast appear in the Content pane.

11 On the right side of the browser window, click the Keywords tab to bring it forward. Then click an image in the Content panel to display the keywords assigned to it in the Keywords panel.

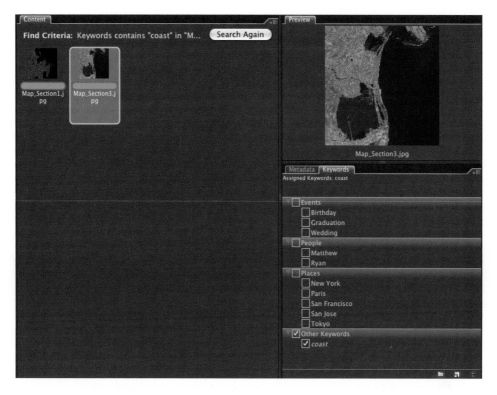

Ranking and stacking images

You can organize images in Bridge with labels, including stars or colors, or by stacking related images.

1 In the Content panel, Shift-click to select both images with the keyword coast.

2 Choose Label > Approved. A green bar appears below the images to indicate their rating. You can also rank images in ascending or descending order using the star labels (1 through 5 stars).

3 At the top left of the Bridge window, click the Go Back button to redisplay all images in the Maps folder.

Now you'll label the top images in the group.

4 In the Content panel, Ctrl-click (Windows) or Command-click (Mac OS) to select the North_Detail5.jpg, South_Detail2.jpg, and West_Detail1.jpg thumbnails.

5 Choose Label > 5 Star to label all of the images with a five stars.

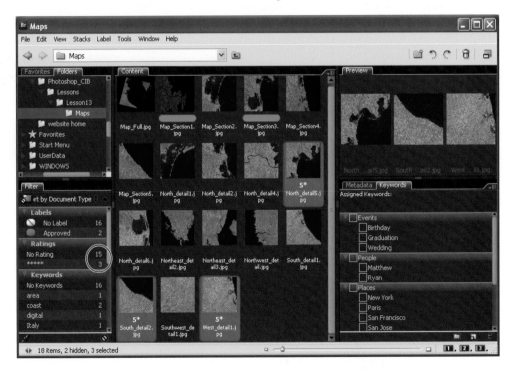

On the left side of the browser window, notice that the Filter panel displays three images with 5-star ratings.

6 Click the 5-star rating under the Filter heading to display just the three ranked images in the Content panel. Once you've ranked images, it's easy to filter your view of the pertinent images for your work.

7 Click the Clear Filter button at the bottom of the Filter panel to redisplay all of the images in the Maps folder, including those marked with the 5-star rating. You can also just click the 5-star rating again to toggle back to the view of all the images.

Rating images helps you sort through a large number of images quickly.

Now you'll group related images into stacks, so that you can view and retrieve them more easily. Stacks are a convenient visual way to group files together.

8 Shift-click to select all five of the North_Detail thumbnails—North_Detail1.jpg through North_Detail6.jpg (there's no North_Detail3.jpg thumbnail). Then choose Stack > Group As Stack or press Ctrl+G (Windows) or Command+G (Mac OS). Click in a blank area of the Content pane to deselect the group you just created.

The number in the upper left indicates the number of files in the stack.

9 Repeat Step 8 for the two Northeast and one Northwest_detail thumbnails, selecting them and pressing Ctrl+G (Windows) or Command+G (Mac OS) to group them together.

10 Repeat Step 8 for the two South_Detail and one Southwest_Detail thumbnails.

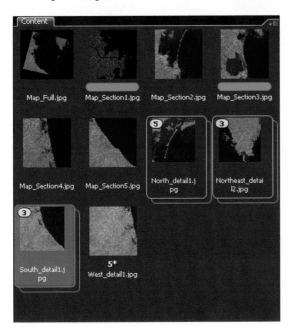

Now you can easily identify the map sections by region, when you need to locate them for your work. To open a stack, you click its number in the upper left; to collapse the stack, click the number again.

Viewing file information

You'll view information about the file you're about to open, to find out what you'll be working with.

1 In the Content panel, click the Map_Section1.jpg thumbnail to select the thumbnail.

Bridge lists myriad information about a selected file in the File Properties panel, which you can display with a single mouse-click.

2 In the Metadata panel on the right side of the Bridge window, click the reveal triangle (▶) next to the File Properties section to display its contents so that you can see the items listed under it.

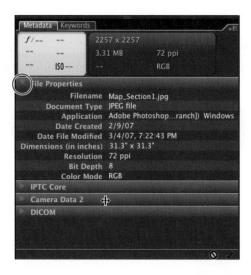

As you review the information about the file, you can see that it is a JPEG image, 31.3-inches square in dimensions, with a 72-ppi resolution, bit depth of 8, and RGB mode. You can display this same information in Photoshop, but in a less concise way.

3 In the Bridge Content panel, double-click the Map_Section1.jpg thumbnail to open the image in Photoshop. Although very large in dimensions—almost 3-feet square—this image appears like any other image on-screen, albeit at 25% to 33% view.

Another way to view file information is using the status bar in Photoshop.

4 In the status bar at the bottom of the image window, click the triangle to display the pop-up menu, and choose Show > Document Dimensions.

5 Try out other status bar Show menu options to display additional file information, including the document profile (untagged RGB), measurement scale (currently set at the default of 1:1 pixels), scratch sizes (193.3M/412.9M—representing the amount of memory currently used by Photoshop to display all open images, and the total amount of RAM available for processing images, respectively), and the current tool.

6 Choose File > Save As. For Format, choose Photoshop, rename the file **13Working.psd**, navigate to the Lesson13 folder, and click Save.

Brightening and boosting color in an image

Before you dive into your measuring project, you'll spruce up the image that you'll work with throughout this exercise—the first map image you looked at in Bridge. This image is a bit dark and lacking in detail. You want to brighten it to bring out more of the details, and boost the color so that it doesn't look so washed out.

1 Choose Image > Adjustments > Levels to open the Levels dialog box.

The histogram shows most of the image's pixels clustered in the shadows and midtones.

2 In the Levels dialog box, make sure that Preview is selected. Then drag the white Input Levels slider to the left, to about the point where the pixels begin clustering, or a value of about 142. We used Input Levels of 0, 1.00, and 142.

3 Click OK to adjust the highlights and spread out the image levels for a fuller gamma and broader range.

But now the image appears very washed out. You'll correct that.

4 Choose Image > Adjustments > Hue/Saturation. Increase the Saturation to +20, and click OK.

5 Choose File > Save to save your work so far.

Creating a map border and work area

To begin creating an infographic from this map segment, you'll select a specific, 25-square kilometer quadrant in the map using a fixed-size selection marquee, and add a border to it.

The map you'll work on has a predetermined scale of 1605 pixels to 25 kilometers. First, you need to set the proper unit of measure, and then you can find the center of the image using rulers.

1 Choose Edit > Preferences > Units And Rulers (Windows) or Photoshop > Preferences > Units And Rulers (Mac OS). Under Units, choose Pixels from the Rulers pop-up menu. Click OK.

You'll add guides to help you measure.

2 In the Navigator/Histogram/Info palette group, click the Info tab to bring the palette forward (or choose Window > Info if it is hidden).

3 Choose View > Rulers to display the rulers. Drag a guide from the top ruler down until the Y axis value in the Info palette reads 326 pixels.

Note: If you position the guide in the wrong spot, press Ctrl (Windows) or Command (Mac OS) and drag the guide out of the image window. Then drag a new guide to the correct location.

The 326-pixel border plus 1605-pixel-square inset equals the size of the 2257-pixel-square image. You can verify this measurement by selecting the image in the Content section of Bridge and reviewing its metadata.

4 Use the same technique as in Step 3 to drag a guide from the left ruler to the right until the X axis in the Info palette reads 326 pixels.

5 Select the Rectangular Marquee tool (▭) in the toolbox. In the tool options bar, choose Fixed size from the Style pop-up menu. Type **1605 px** in both the Width and Height boxes. According to the map's scale, this value is equivalent to 25 kilometers.

6 At the top left corner where the guides intersect, click the Rectangular Marquee tool to set a selection marquee 1605-pixels square. Now your selection area is exactly centered within the image.

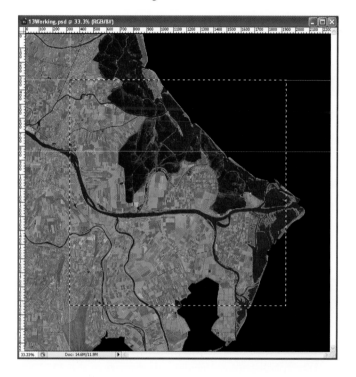

You'll lighten the area around the centered square to bring focus to your work area. First you will invert the selection.

7 Choose Select > Inverse. Then choose Image > Adjustments > Hue/Saturation, or press Ctrl+U (Windows) or Command+U (Mac OS). Increase the Lightness to +31, and click OK.

8 Choose File > Save to save your work.

Making a custom border

You'll add a custom border to the selection to make the image pop a bit.

1 Select > Inverse or press Ctrl+Shift+I (Windows) or Command+Shift+I (Mac OS) to invert the selection again. You want just the inset selected, with a marquee around it.

2 In the Layers palette, click the New Layer button at the bottom of the palette to add a new, empty layer at the top of the palette. Select the layer name and rename it **Border**.

First you'll outline the border, so that you can apply the dashed line to the outline.

3 Choose Edit > Stroke, type **10 px** for stroke, and for Color, choose White. If necessary, click the swatch, and then click the upper left corner of the Color Picker window to choose white; click OK. Select Inside. Click OK.

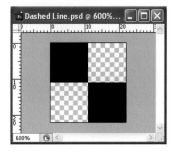

You'll complete the border by applying a dashed line pattern to the white outline.

4 Choose File > Open, navigate to the Lesson13 folder, and open the Dashed Line.psd file.

5 Choose Edit > Define pattern, and in the Pattern Name dialog box, type **Dashed Line**. Click OK.

6 Select the 13Working.psd image to make it active. In its Layers palette, click the icon in the upper right corner and choose Blending Options.

7 In the Blending Options dialog box, select Pattern Overlay from the list on the left to select it and display its options. In the center of the dialog box, to the right of the Pattern proxy, click the down arrow to display the Pattern Picker and the available patterns. Select the Dashed Line pattern you just created; click away from the Pattern Picker to close it. Set the Scale to 220%.

8 Click OK to apply the pattern to the border.

You can use this same technique to add a different colored dashed line. Just vary the Stroke color and the Dashed Line color so that they contrast well. Before you convert the Dashed Line artwork to a pattern, make sure that it is on a transparent background so that the Stroke color will show through. If you adjust the Stroke width, also adjust the Pattern Overlay scale in the Blending Options dialog box, so that the dashed line properly overlays the stroke.

9 If you'd like, zoom in on the line in the image window to examine it more closely by pressing Ctrl+spacebar (Windows) or Command+spacebar (Mac OS) and clicking the image. Zoom back out by pressing Alt+spacebar (Windows) or Option+spacebar (Mac OS) and clicking the image.

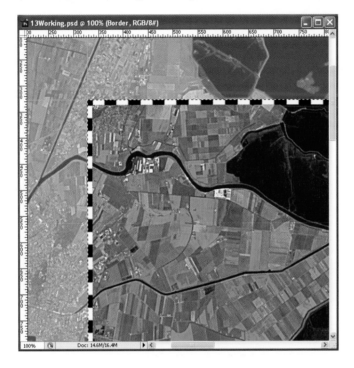

10 Choose File > Save to save your work. Do not deselect.

Measuring objects and data

You may already be familiar with the Ruler tool in Photoshop, which lets you calculate the distance between any two points in the workspace. The Measurement feature in Photoshop Extended is much more sophisticated: it lets you measure any area defined with the Ruler tool or with a selection tool, including irregular areas selected with the lasso, Quick Selection, or Magic Wand tools. You can also compute the height, width, area, and perimeter, or track measurements of one image or multiple images. Measurement data is recorded in the Measurement Log palette.

The Measurement tool is available only in Photoshop Extended, a version of Photoshop CS3 with additional functionality. If you don't have this version of the Photoshop, you can read the next sections to learn about the tool.

Working with the Measurement tool

The first step in working with measurements and the Measurement tool is to set the scale. Setting a measurement scale sets a specified number of pixels in the image equal to a number of scale units, such as inches, millimeters, or microns—or in this case, kilometers. Once you've created a scale, you can measure areas, and receive calculations and log results in the selected scale units.

1 In the Layers palette, select the Background layer.

2 Choose Analysis > Set Measurement Scale > Custom. Many of the features in Photoshop Extended appear in this new Analysis menu.

This map has a scale of 1605 pixels equal to 25 kilometers. You'll use those values now to create a custom scale.

3 In the Measurement Scale dialog box, type **1605** for Pixel Length, **25** for Logical Length, and **Kilometers** for Logical Units.

4 Click OK to set your scaling.

Another way to set the scale is using either the overall dimensions of your image, or a measurement from within your image. You then enter these values in the boxes in the Measurement Scale dialog box. Or, you can select a preset scale from the Presets menu.

You're ready to begin measuring the map. You'll start your measurements with the 25-square kilometer selection, as a control measure against which you can check your work.

5 Make sure that your 1605 px-square selection is still active. If you accidentally deselected the selection, reselect the map inset by clicking with the Rectangular Marquee tool at the top left intersection of the guides.

6 Choose Analysis > Record Measurements. The Measurement Log palette appears at the bottom of the image window.

7 At the bottom of the Measurements Log, use the scroll bar as needed to view the columns of data in this log. Note the Area measurement to the right as 625.00000 and Area Units are kilometers—exactly what they should be. Look through the columns of data to see the information recorded here.

	Label	Date and Time	Document	Source	Scale	Scale Units	Scale Factor	Count	Area
0001	Measurement 1	2/19/2007 6:01:17 PM	13Working.psd	Selection	Custom (1605 pixels ...	kilometers	64.200000	1	625.000000

Now you'll add a note to the file that you or others can refer to later.

8 Select the Notes tool (📝) in the toolbox. In the Notes Tool options bar, type your name or initials as the Author.

9 Click the image to open a new note with your name as the title. Type **1/28/07, preliminary measurements for inland seas project. Area = 625 km2**. Click the note's close box to close it so that it's not distracting.

💡 *To delete a note, select it with the Notes tool, press Delete, and click OK in the confirmation dialog box that appears. To delete all notes, with the Notes tool selected, click Clear All in the Notes Tool options bar, and OK in the confirmation dialog box.*

You can customize the Measurement Log columns, sort data within columns, and export data from the log to a spreadsheet file.

10 Return to the Measurement Log palette. Click the column heading Perimeter and drag it to the right of the Width column; when a black line appears, release the mouse button to insert the column. You can reorder any column heading by clicking its name and dragging it to the right or left.

You can easily reorder the columns so that they display information in the best order for you. Just as easily, you can control which parameters, or data points, are calculated and shown.

11 Choose Analysis > Select Data Points > Custom, and deselect all of the Gray Value options and the Integrated Density option. You won't use these options, so you don't need to record them. Click OK.

You won't do this now, but you can save these settings as presets for future projects. You can even create multiple measurement scale presets. However, only one scale can be used in a document at a time.

12 Alternatively, Ctrl-click (Windows) or Command-click (Mac OS) to select the Circularity, Integrated Density, and four Gray Value columns in the Measurement Log. Click the Trash Can button to remove them. You won't need these data points for this lesson. Click OK in the confirmation dialog box.

		Circularity	Height	Width	Perimeter	Gray Value (Minimum)	Gray Value (Maximum)	Gray Value (Mean)	Gray Value (Median)	Integrated Density	Histogram
0001	221	0.000488	37.676056	37.676056	6046.995305	0.000000	255.000000	76.826400	84.000000	197906728.000000	✓

Animation (Frames) | Measurement Log ×

Record Measurements

13 Choose File > Save to save your work so far.

Measuring irregular shapes

Now you'll calculate the area of an irregular shape, the water inside the 25-km square area, but outside the breakers. As you measure, the Measurement Log tracks this data.

1 Choose Select > Deselect to deselect the inset selection.

2 Select the Magic Wand tool (✎) in the toolbox, under the Quick Selection tool. In the Magic Wand Tool options bar, leave the Tolerance at 32. Deselect Contiguous so that selecting one area will select all similar areas within the Tolerance value.

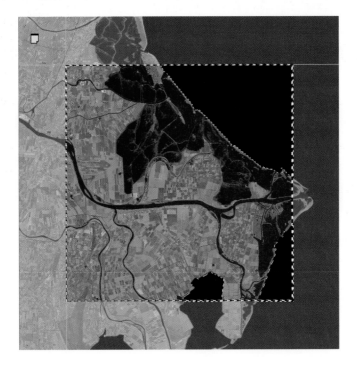

3 Click one of the three black water areas to select all three at once.

4 In the Measurement Log palette, click Record Measurements in the upper left corner. This is an alternative to choosing Analysis > Record Measurements. This command records the area of all three individual selections plus the total of the three selected areas.

5 Look at your results in Measurement Log. The log details each of the three selections for the water area as a line item; the top item, indicated by a Count of 3, totals the three measurements. Our measurement of the total water area was 134.22 (square kilometers).

	Label	Date and Time	Document	Source	Scale	Scale Units	Scale Factor	Count	Area
0001	Measurement 1	2/19/2007 6:01:17 PM	13Working.psd	Selection	Custom (1605 pixels ...	kilometers	64.200000	1	625.000000
0002	Measurement 2	2/19/2007 6:16:32 PM	13Working.psd	Selection	Custom (1605 pixels ...	kilometers	64.200000	8	134.212352
0003	Measurement 2 - Feat...	2/19/2007 6:16:32 PM	13Working.psd	Selection	Custom (1605 pixels ...	kilometers	64.200000		105.153774
0004	Measurement 2 - Feat...	2/19/2007 6:16:32 PM	13Working.psd	Selection	Custom (1605 pixels ...	kilometers	64.200000		0.000243
0005	Measurement 2 - Feat...	2/19/2007 6:16:32 PM	13Working.psd	Selection	Custom (1605 pixels ...	kilometers	64.200000		19.197941
0006	Measurement 2 - Feat...	2/19/2007 6:16:32 PM	13Working.psd	Selection	Custom (1605 pixels ...	kilometers	64.200000		0.000243
0007	Measurement 2 - Feat...	2/19/2007 6:16:32 PM	13Working.psd	Selection	Custom (1605 pixels ...	kilometers	64.200000		0.000243
0008	Measurement 2 - Feat...	2/19/2007 6:16:32 PM	13Working.psd	Selection	Custom (1605 pixels ...	kilometers	64.200000		0.000243
0009	Measurement 2 - Feat...	2/19/2007 6:16:32 PM	13Working.psd	Selection	Custom (1605 pixels ...	kilometers	64.200000		9.859425
0010	Measurement 2 - Feat...	2/19/2007 6:16:32 PM	13Working.psd	Selection	Custom (1605 pixels ...	kilometers	64.200000		0.000243

Your measurements here and in the remaining procedures may vary from those we recorded, depending on the accuracy of your selection.

6 Double-click the note in the image to open it. This automatically selects the Notes tool in the toolbox. With the note selected, type **Water area: 134.22 km2**. Close the note so that it doesn't distract you.

7 Choose Select > Deselect to deselect the selection of the three seas.

8 Choose File > Save to save your work.

Measuring lines

Measuring lines with the Measurement tool in Photoshop Extended is similar to measuring with the Ruler tool in the toolbox.

1   Choose Analysis > Ruler Tool.

2   Position the tool pointer at the end of the river on the left side of the map, just within the selection, and drag a line to the right end of the river at the boundary of the selected area.

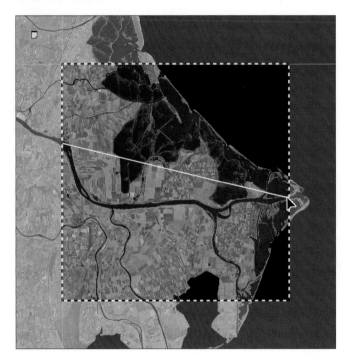

3 In the Measurement Log, click Record Measurements. The distance appears as a Length of about 25 kilometers and an Angle of 13 degrees in the log. This is the length of the river "as the crow flies."

	Scale	Scale Units	Scale Factor	Count	Area	Height	Width	Perimeter	Histogram	Circularity	Length	Angle
0008	Custom (1065 pixels ...	Kilometers	42.600000		0.009919	0.093897	0.187793	0.023474	✓	226.194671		
0009	Custom (1065 pixels ...	Kilometers	42.600000		22.403513	4.741784	6.877934	95.422535	✓	0.030919		
0010	Custom (1065 pixels ...	Kilometers	42.600000		0.001653	0.046948	0.046948	0.000000	✓	1.#INF00		
0011	Custom (1065 pixels ...	Kilometers	42.600000	1							49.095019	-14.481418

Exporting measurements

You can export selected measurements as a CSV (comma separated value) file that can be opened in a spreadsheet application, such as Microsoft® Excel®. You can then use the spreadsheet application to perform further calculations on your data. You'll use the data you've recorded so far later in this lesson.

1 Return to the Measurement Log palette.

2 Shift-click the measurements to select all of the items in the list.

3 Click the icon in the upper right corner of the Measurement Log palette, and choose Export Selected from the palette menu. You can also choose to select only some of the items.

4 In the Save dialog box, rename the file **13_inland_seas**, browse to the Lesson13 folder where you'll save the file, and click Save.

Creating a cross section

Now let's add a little dimension and color. In this part of the lesson, you'll import a three-dimensional graphic that represents a cross-section view of the coastline. Then you'll measure the cross section in two- and three dimensions.

1 Switch to Bridge, navigate to the Lesson13 folder, and double-click Cross-Section.psd to open it in Photoshop.

2 Click the 13Working.psd image to make it active. You'll increase its canvas size to create a black area to its right.

3 Choose Image > Canvas Size. Set the width to 3700 pixels. Click the lower left corner of the proxy so that the additional space will be added on the right. For Canvas Extension Color, choose Black. Click OK.

A black area about ⅓ the width of the image window is added to the right of the image.

4 Click the Cross-Section.psd file to make it active.

You'll reposition the cross section in the upper quadrant of the map, aligning its section letters to the map's section letter.

5 Select the Move Tool ($\blacktriangleright_{\oplus}$) in the toolbox, and drag the illustration onto the 13Working.psd image. Position the illustration as shown in the following figure, so that the gold bar labeled Section overlaps the letters "A" and "B" in the upper left quadrant of the map.

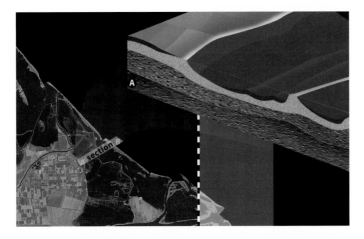

For design aesthetics, the three-dimensional rectangular cross section is rotated relative to its two-dimensional representation, the gold bar.

If you were to fit the 3D cross section into the 2D gold bar of the map like a puzzle piece, you would rotate the cross section towards the top left corner of the map by about 90 degrees, matching the letter "A" on the cross-section to that on the map. (The gold semitransparency swath represents this rotation.)

You'll make several measurements of the cross section, starting with the length of its 2D representation.

6 Choose Analysis > Ruler Tool.

7 Using the Ruler tool, click a corner of the gold bar labeled Section, and drag the length of its side to measure the section's length.

8 In the Measurement Log palette, click Record Measurement at the top of the palette. Note the length: it should register as about 3.36 (kilometers) long, which was our measurement.

Label	Date and Time	Document	Source	Scale	Scale Units	Scale Factor	Count	Length
0002 Ruler 9	2007-02-26T16:25:55-...	13End.psd	Ruler Tool	Custom scale (1605 pi...	kilometers	64.200000	1	3.367729

9 To help you keep track of this measurement, double-click your note, type **Cross section length: 3.36 km**, and then close the note.

You'll use this value in the next part of the lesson.

Measuring in perspective using the Vanishing Point filter

Now you'll take some measurements of the cross section itself, this time in three dimensions. Being able to measure in three dimensions is especially helpful for measuring topographic information from a similar map, an architectural CAD drawing—or any object in space whose dimensions you need to determine.

1 In the Layers palette, make sure that the Cross Section layer is selected.

2 Choose Filter > Vanishing Point. The Vanishing Point dialog box appears, with the Create Plane tool selected.

You'll draw a plane on the front side of the cross section.

3 Using the Create Plane tool (⊞), click the lower left corner of the section to set the first anchor point. Then click the lower right corner, the upper right corner of the section, and then the upper left corner to draw a plane on the side of the cross section.

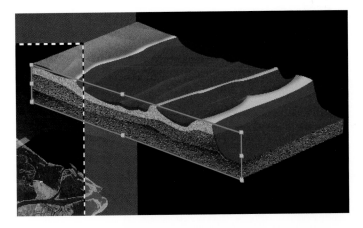

4 In the Vanishing Point dialog box, select the Measure tool in the toolbox on the left.

5 Position the pointer over the left bottom edge of the cross section. Make sure that your pointer is over the grid (a cross with a ruler icon will appear); then click the left bottom edge of the cross section to set the first measuring point. Then, drag to the right bottom edge.

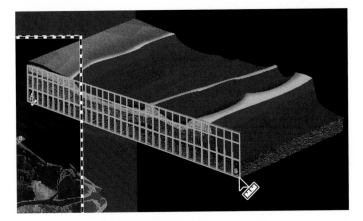

6 In the Length box at the top of the window, enter **3.36**, the length in kilometers of the section. This is the value you ascertained in the previous procedure, when you measured the cross section with the Ruler tool. The value updates in the Vanishing Point window.

Now you'll measure the depth of the section by measuring vertically along the left edge of the cross section.

7 Drag again along the bottom edge of the cross section. A readout appears of the length of the cross section (3.36) and the angle (89.7 degrees).

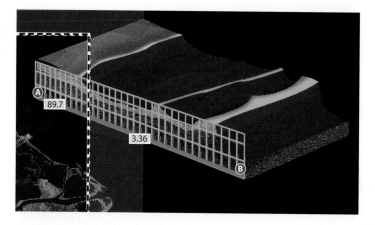

8 Using the Measure tool, click the top left edge, and then drag downward to the bottom left edge. The length and angle of the vertical line appear in the window, based on the length you entered in Step 6. The line shows the depth of the cross section, 0.3 (kilometers) in our measurement.

9 Double-click the note in the image window to open it, and type **Section Depth: 0.3 km**. Then close the note.

10 Click OK in the Vanishing Point dialog box to close it.

With your measurements done, you're ready to add the data to the infographic.

Adding a legend

You'll complete the infographic by creating a legend for it, using the various measurements you've taken.

1 Switch to Bridge. In the Folders panel, navigate to the Lesson13 folder, and double-click the Legend.psd file to open it.

2 In the Layers palette of the Legend.psd file, drag the Legend Group layer into the 13Working.psd image.

3 Using the Move tool (⬈) position the Legend artwork in the lower third of the black background on right.

4 If you have a spreadsheet application, such as Excel, start the application. Browse to the Lesson13/Maps folder, and double-click to open the 13_Inland_Seas.csv file.

5 Select the Type tool (T) in the toolbox.

6 Refer either to the measurements displayed in the spreadsheet file, 13_Inland_Seas that you just opened, or to the values you recorded earlier in your note. In turn, select the "0000" next to each entry, and type the correct information into the legend table:

- For Total Area, enter **625 km2**.

- For Water Area, enter **134 km2**.

- For Section Length, enter **3.36 km**.

- For Section Depth, enter **0.3 km**.

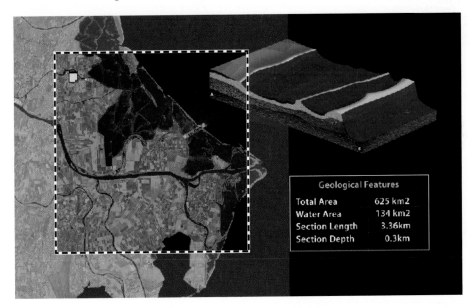

7 Choose File > Save to save your work.

Creating a slide show

Your infographic is complete. After so much measuring and precise design work, it's time to create a slide show to show off your beautiful work to your colleagues.

1 Switch to Bridge, and navigate to the Lesson13/Maps folder. Double-click the Maps folder to display its contents. Shift-click the five Map_Section files to select them.

2 Choose View > Slideshow Options. You'll set up your slide show of the five map sections to dissolve from one image into the next.

3 In the Slideshow Options dialog box, select Scaled To Fit for the When Presenting, Show Slides option; for Transition, choose Dissolve. Leave the other options as is.

4 Click Play to play slide show. To stop the slide show, press the Esc key on your keyboard.

5 When you have finished viewing the slide show, click Done to close the Slideshow Options dialog box.

You can repeat the slide show by choosing View > Slideshow. To flip through the images, simply press the Right Arrow key on your keyboard; or to move backwards through the images, press the Left Arrow key.

6 Choose File > Save to save your work.

Congratulations! You've completed the lesson. Now you're ready to try out your measuring skills on other images in your portfolio.

Review

▶ **Review Questions**

1 What is metadata? How do you add it to a Photoshop file?

2 How do you measure an object in Photoshop Extended with the Measurement tool?

3 What's the difference between the Ruler tool and the Measurement tool?

4 How do you measure in three dimensions?

5 How can you create a slide show of your work?

▶ **Review Answers**

1 Metadata is standardized information about a file, including the author name, resolution, color space, copyright, and keywords applied to a file. You can add metadata in Adobe Bridge, in the IPTC panel.

2 To measure an object in Photoshop Extended, you set a measurement scale (Analysis > Set Measurement Scale); make a selection or use the Ruler tool to measure two points; and then choose Record Measurement either from the Analysis menu or in the Measurement Log.

3 The Ruler tool in Photoshop lets you calculate the distance between any two points in the workspace. The Measurement feature in Photoshop Extended lets you measure any area defined with the Ruler tool or with a selection tool, including irregular areas selected with the lasso, quick select, or magic wand tools. You can also compute the height, width, area, and perimeter; or track measurements of one image or multiple images. Measurement data is recorded in the Measurement Log palette, where you can sort the data or export it to a spreadsheet file.

4 You can measure in three dimensions by applying the Vanishing Point filter, creating a grid, and then using its Measure tool to measure distances along the grid.

5 To create a slide show of your work, you can use Adobe Bridge. You select thumbnails of the images to include in the slide show, choose View > Slideshow Options to set display options, and then press Play to run the show. Once you've set slide show options, simply choose View > Slideshow to play the animation.

To produce consistent color, you define the color space in which to edit and display RGB images, and in which to edit, display, and print CMYK images. This helps ensure a close match between on-screen and printed colors.

14 | Producing and Printing Consistent Color

Lesson overview

In this lesson, you'll learn how to do the following:

- Define RGB, grayscale, and CMYK color spaces for displaying, editing, and printing images.

- Prepare an image for printing on a PostScript CMYK printer.

- Proof an image for printing.

- Create and print a four-color separation.

- Understand how images are prepared for printing on presses.

This lesson will take less than an hour to complete. If needed, remove the previous lesson folder from your hard drive, and copy the Lessons/Lesson14 folder onto it. As you work on this lesson, you'll preserve the start files. If you need to restore the start files, copy them from the *Adobe Photoshop CS3 Classroom in a Book* CD.

This lesson requires that your computer be connected to a PostScript color printer. If it isn't, you can do most, but not all, of the exercises.

Reproducing colors

Colors on a monitor are displayed using combinations of red, green, and blue light (called RGB), while printed colors are typically created using a combination of four ink colors—cyan, magenta, yellow, and black (called CMYK). These four inks are called *process colors* because they are the standard inks used in the four-color printing process.

RGB image with red, green, and blue channels

CMYK image with cyan, magenta, yellow, and black channels

Because the RGB and CMYK color models use different methods to display colors, each reproduces a different *gamut*, or range of colors. For example, RGB uses light to produce color, so its gamut includes neon colors, such as those you'd see in a neon sign.

In contrast, printing inks excel at reproducing certain colors that can lie outside the RGB gamut, such as some pastels and pure black.

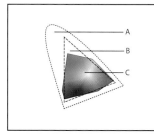

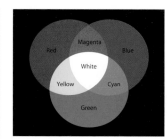

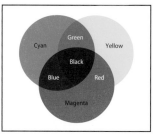

A. Natural color gamut
B. RGB color gamut
C. CMYK color gamut

RGB color model

CMYK color model

But not all RGB and CMYK gamuts are alike. Each monitor and printer model differs, and so each displays a slightly different gamut. For example, one brand of monitor may produce slightly brighter blues than another. The *color space* for a device is defined by the gamut it can reproduce.

RGB model

A large percentage of the visible spectrum can be represented by mixing red, green, and blue (RGB) colored light in various proportions and intensities. Where the colors overlap, they create cyan, magenta, yellow, and white.

Because the RGB colors combine to create white, they are also called additive colors. Adding all colors together creates white—that is, all light is transmitted back to the eye. Additive colors are used for lighting, video, and monitors. Your monitor, for example, creates color by emitting light through red, green, and blue phosphors.

CMYK model

The CMYK model is based on the light-absorbing quality of ink printed on paper. As white light strikes translucent inks, part of the spectrum is absorbed while other parts are reflected back to your eyes.

In theory, pure cyan (C), magenta (M), and yellow (Y) pigments should combine to absorb all color and produce black. For this reason, these colors are called subtractive colors. Because all printing inks contain some impurities, these three inks actually produce a muddy brown and must be combined with black (K) ink to produce a true black. (K is used instead of B to avoid confusion with blue.) Combining these inks to reproduce color is called four-color process printing.

An ICC profile is a description of a device's color space, such as the CMYK color space of a particular printer. In this lesson, you'll choose which RGB and CMYK ICC profiles to use. Once you specify the profiles, Photoshop can embed them into your image files. Photoshop (and any other application that can use ICC profiles) can then interpret the ICC profile in the image file to automatically manage color for that image.

For information on embedding ICC profiles, see Photoshop Help.

Getting started

Unlike other lessons in this book, this lesson does not require that you preview a final image to see what you will be creating. However, you do need to launch Photoshop and restore default preferences.

1 Start Photoshop and then immediately hold down Ctrl+Alt+Shift (Windows) or Command+Option+Shift (Mac OS) to restore the default preferences. (See "Restoring default preferences" on page 6.)

2 When prompted, click Yes to confirm that you want to reset preferences, and Close to close the Welcome Screen.

Note: Make sure that your monitor is calibrated before continuing. If your monitor does not display colors accurately, the color adjustments you make to an image displayed on that monitor may be inaccurate.

Specifying color-management settings

In the first part of this lesson, you'll learn how to set up a color-managed workflow. To help you with this, the Color Settings dialog box in Photoshop contains most of the color-management controls you need.

For instance, by default Photoshop is set up for RGB as part of a web workflow. If you are preparing artwork for print production, however, you would likely change the settings to be more appropriate for images that will be printed on paper rather than displayed on a screen.

You'll begin this lesson by creating customized color settings.

1 Choose Edit > Color Settings to open the Color Settings dialog box.

Note: By default, the Settings menu should show North America General Purpose 2. If it doesn't, the settings must have been changed at some point. Choose it now.

The bottom of the dialog box interactively describes each of the various color-management options, which you'll review now.

2 Move the mouse pointer over each part of the dialog box, including the names of areas (such as Working Spaces) and the options you can choose (such as the different menu options), returning the options to their defaults when you've finished. As you move the mouse, view the information that appears at the bottom of the dialog box.

Now, you'll choose a set of options designed for a print workflow, rather than an online workflow.

3 Choose Settings > North America Prepress 2. The working spaces and color-management policy options change for a prepress workflow. Then, click OK.

Proofing an image

In this part of the lesson, you'll work with a typical file of the kind you might scan in from a printed original. You'll open it and select a proof profile so that you can see a close on-screen representation of what it will look like when printed. This will let you proof the printed image on your screen for printed output.

You'll begin by opening the file.

1 Click the Go To Bridge button (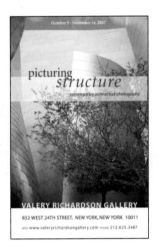) in the tool options bar to open Adobe Bridge, or choose File > Open, to open the 14Start.tif file in the Lessons/Lesson14 folder.

An RGB image of a scanned poster opens.

2 Choose File > Save As, rename the file **14Working**, keep the TIFF format selected, and click Save. Click OK in the TIFF Options dialog box to save a copy of the Start file.

Before soft-proofing—that is, proofing on-screen—or printing this image, you'll set up a proof profile. A proof profile (also called a *proof setup*) defines how the document is going to be printed, and adds those visual properties to the on-screen version for more accurate soft-proofing. Photoshop provides a variety of settings that can help you proof images for different uses, including print and display on the web. For this lesson, you'll create a custom proof setup. You can then save the settings for use on other images that will be output the same way.

3 Choose View > Proof Setup > Custom. The Customize Proof Condition dialog box opens.

4 Make sure that the Preview box is checked.

5 From the Device To Simulate menu, choose a profile that represents a final-output source color profile, such as that for the printer you'll use to print the image. If you don't have a specific printer, the profile Working CMYK - U.S. Web Coated (SWOP) v2 is generally a good choice.

6 Make sure that Preserve Numbers is *not* selected. Leaving this option off simulates how the image will appear if colors are converted from the document space to their nearest equivalents in the proof profile space.

Note: This option is not always available, and it is grayed out and unchecked for the U.S. Web Coated (SWOP) v2 profile.

7 From the Rendering Intent menu, choose a rendering intent for the conversion, such as Relative Colorimetric, which a good choice for preserving color relationships without sacrificing color accuracy.

8 If it's available for the profile you chose, select the Simulate Black Ink check box. Then deselect it and select the Simulate Paper Color check box; checking this option automatically selects the Simulate Black Ink option.

Notice that the image appears to lose contrast. Paper Color simulates the dingy white of real paper, according to the proof profile. Black Ink simulates the dark gray you really get instead of a solid black on many printers, according to the proof profile. Not all profiles support these option.

Normal image

Image with Paper Color and Black Ink options selected

9 Click OK.

To turn the proof settings off and on, choose View > Proof Colors.

Identifying out-of-gamut colors

Most scanned photographs contain RGB colors within the CMYK gamut, and changing the image to CMYK mode (which you'll do later in order to print the file) converts all the colors with relatively little substitution. Images that are created or altered digitally, however, often contain RGB colors that are outside the CMYK gamut—for example, neon-colored logos and lights.

Note: Out-of-gamut colors are identified by an exclamation point next to the color swatch in the Color palette, the Color Picker, and the Info palette.

Before you convert an image from RGB to CMYK, you can preview the CMYK color values while still in RGB mode.

1 Choose View > Gamut Warning to see out-of-gamut colors. Adobe Photoshop builds a color-conversion table and displays a neutral gray in the image window where the colors are out of gamut.

Because the gray can be hard to spot in the image, you'll now convert it to a more visible gamut-warning color.

2 Choose Edit > Preferences > Transparency And Gamut (Windows) or Photoshop > Preferences > Transparency And Gamut (Mac OS). Then click the color sample in the Gamut Warning area at the bottom of the dialog box.

3 Choose a vivid color, such as purple or bright green, and click OK.

4 Click OK again to close the Transparency And Gamut dialog box. The bright, new color you choose appears instead of the neutral gray as the gamut warning color.

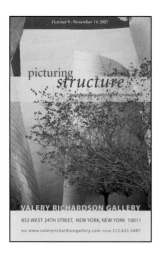

5 Choose View > Gamut Warning to turn off the preview of out-of-gamut colors.

Photoshop will automatically correct these out-of-gamut colors when you save the file in Photoshop EPS format later in this lesson. Photoshop EPS format changes the RGB image to CMYK, adjusting the RGB colors as needed to bring them into the CMYK color gamut.

Adjusting an image and printing a proof

The next step in preparing an image for output is to make any color and tonal adjustments that are necessary. In this exercise, you'll add some tonal and color adjustments to correct an off-color scan of the original poster.

So that you can compare the image before and after making corrections, you'll start by making a copy.

1 Choose Image > Duplicate and click OK to duplicate the image.

2 Arrange the two image windows in your workspace so that you can compare them as you work.

Now you'll adjust the hue and saturation of the image. You can adjust color various ways, including by using the Levels and Curves commands. You'll use the Hue/Saturation command.

3 Select 14Working.tif (the original image).

4 Choose Image > Adjustments > Hue/Saturation. Drag the Hue/Saturation dialog box aside so that you can still see the 14Start.tif image, make sure that the Preview box is checked, and then do following:

• Drag the Hue slider until the colors, especially the tops of the buildings, look more neutral. (We used +15.)

• Drag the Saturation slider until the intensity of the colors looks normal (we used –65).

• Leave the Lightness setting at the default value (0), and click OK.

Note: Before going on to print this image, try toggling the gamut warning back on, and you should see that you have removed most of the out-of-gamut colors from the image.

5 With 14Working.tif still selected, choose File > Print.

6 In the Print dialog box, do the following in the right column of options:

• Choose Color Management from the pop-up menu at the top of the column.

• In the Print area, click the Proof button to select your proof profile.

• For Color Handling, choose Printer Manages Colors from the pop-up menu; then for Proof Setup, choose Working CMYK.

• (Optional) Press Alt (Windows) or Option (Mac OS) to change the Done button to Remember, and click Remember to save these settings for the next time you print.

• Click Print to print the image to a color printer, and compare it with the on-screen version.

Saving the image as a separation

In this exercise, you'll learn how to save the image as a separation so that it can print out on separate cyan, magenta, yellow, and black plates.

1 With 14Working.tif still selected, choose File > Save As.

2 In the Save As dialog box, do the following:

• Choose Format > Photoshop EPS.

• Under Color, select the Use Proof Setup: Working CMYK check box. Don't worry about the save-a-copy warning icon that appears.

Note: These settings cause the image to be automatically converted from RGB to CMYK when it is saved in the Photoshop Encapsulated PostScript (EPS) format.

• Accept the filename 14Working copy.eps, and click Save.

3 Click OK in the EPS Options dialog box that appears.

4 Save and then close the 14Working.tif and 14Working copy.tif files.

5 Choose File > Open, navigate to the Lessons/Lesson14 folder, and select and open the 14Working copy.eps file.

Notice in the image file's title bar that 14Working copy.eps is a CMYK file.

Printing

When you're ready to print your image, use the following guidelines for best results:

*   Print a *color composite*, often called a *color comp*. A color composite is a single print that combines the red, green, and blue channels of an RGB image (or the cyan, magenta, yellow, and black channels of a CMYK image). This indicates what the final printed image will look like.
*   Set the parameters for the halftone screen.
*   Print separations to make sure the image separates correctly.
*   Print to film or plate.

Printing halftone separations

To specify the halftone screen when you print an image, you use the Screen option in the Print dialog box. The results of using a halftone screen appear only in the printed copy; you cannot see the halftone screen on your computer screen.

When you print color separations, you print four grayscale screens, one for each process color. Each screen contains halftone information for the respective channel, including screen frequency, screen angle, and dot shape.

The *screen frequency* controls the density of dots on the screen. Since the dots are arranged in lines on the screen, the common measurement for screen frequency is lines per inch (lpi). The higher the screen frequency, the finer the image produced (depending on the line-screen capability of the printer). Magazines, for example, tend to use fine screens of 133 lpi and higher, because they are usually printed on coated paper and on high-quality presses. Newspapers, which are usually printed on lower-quality paper, tend to use lower screen frequencies, such as 85 lpi.

The *screen angle* used to create halftones of grayscale images is generally 45 degrees. For best results with color separations, select the Auto option in the Halftone Screen dialog box (which is accessible through the Print dialog box, as you'll see in a minute). You can also specify an angle for each of the color screens. Setting the screens at different angles ensures that the dots placed by the four screens blend to look like continuous color and do not produce moiré patterns.

Diamond-shaped dots are the most commonly used in halftone screens. In Photoshop, however, you can also choose round, elliptical, linear, square, and cross-shaped dots.

Note: By default, an image will use the halftone screen settings of the output device or of the software from which you output the image. You usually don't need to specify halftone screen settings unless you want to override the default settings. And you should always consult your prepress partner before specifying halftone screen options.

In this exercise, you'll adjust the halftone screens for the poster image, and then print the color separations.

1 With the 14Working copy.eps image open from the previous exercise, choose File > Print.

2 At the top of the right column of options, choose Output from the pop-up menu.

3 Click the Screen button on the right side of the dialog box.

4 In the Halftone Screen dialog box, do the following:

- Deselect the Use Printer's Default Screen check box.

- Toggle through the Ink menu to see the Frequency, Angle, and Shape information for each color channel.

- For the Cyan ink, choose Shape > Ellipse.

- Toggle through the Magenta, Yellow, and Black Ink menus again, and notice that all of the Shape menus now show Ellipse. We could change other options, but we'll leave them as they are for this exercise.

- Click OK to close the Halftone Screen dialog box.

By default, Photoshop prints a CMYK image as a single document. To print this file as separations, you need to explicitly instruct Photoshop in the Print dialog box.

5 Back in the Print dialog box, do the following:

• Choose Color Management from the pop-up menu at the top of the right column.

• In the Print area, click the Document button.

• In the Options area, choose Color Handling > Separations.

• Click Print.

6 Choose File > Close, and don't save the changes.

This completes your introduction to printing and producing consistent color using Adobe Photoshop. For more information about color management, printing options, and color separations, see Photoshop Help.

Review

▶ **Review questions**

1 What steps should you follow to reproduce color accurately?

2 What is a gamut?

3 What is an ICC profile?

4 What are color separations? How does a CMYK image differ from an RGB image?

5 What steps should you follow when preparing an image for color separations?

▶ **Review answers**

1 Calibrate your monitor, and then use the Color Settings dialog box to specify which color spaces to use. For example, you can specify which RGB color space to use for online images, and which CMYK color space to use for images that will be printed. You can then proof the image, check for out-of-gamut colors, adjust colors as needed, and—for printed images—create color separations.

2 A gamut is the range of colors that can be reproduced by a color model or device. For example, the RGB and CMYK color models have different gamuts, as do any two RGB scanners.

3 An ICC profile is a description of a device's color space, such as the CMYK color space of a particular printer. Applications such as Photoshop can interpret ICC profiles in an image to maintain consistent color across different applications, platforms, and devices.

4 A color separation is created when an image is converted to CMYK mode. The colors in the CMYK image are separated into the four process-color channels: cyan, magenta, yellow, and black. An RGB image, by contrast, has three color channels: red, green, and blue.

5 You prepare an image for print by following the steps for reproducing color accurately, and then converting the image from RGB mode to CMYK mode to build a color separation.

Index

Contributors

Russell Brown is a Senior Creative Director at Adobe Systems, Inc. The Photoshop guru has worked with Adobe Photoshop since its introduction more than 12 years ago. Russell contributed the movie and assets for the CloneSource tutorial in Lesson 10, and the DancingWithType and OpenType tutorials in Lesson 8.
http://www.russellbrown.com

Jay Graham began his career designing and building custom homes. He has been a professional photographer for more than 22 years, with clients in the advertising, architectural, editorial, and travel industries. He contributed the "Pro Photo Workflow" tips in Lesson 7.
http://jaygraham.com

Arne Hurty is an award-winning technical illustrator and designer who composed the scientific illustration for Lesson 13.
http://www.baycreative.com

Tyler Munson lent his design and art direction to Lessons 4, 11, and 14. With his San Francisco design and branding firm, munsonDesign, Tyler has created programs for clients that include Gap, Palm, Oracle, and music producer Paul Oakenfold.
http://www.munsondesign.com

Lee Unkrich has directed major films for Pixar. His photographs appear in Lessons 6 and 10 of this book.

Tune In To
PeachpitTV

Point your browser to www.peachpittv.com where your favorite authors are bringing their best tips and tricks directly to your desktop.

Missed Photoshop World or Macworld Conference & Expo? Insist on learning from the best? PeachpitTV's newest show, *Author Tips*, features your favorite authors demonstrating their top tips, tricks, and tutorials. You won't want to miss new and upcoming episodes starring Matt Kloskowski, Kevin Ames, Dan Margulis, Ben Willmore, Rich Harrington, and Terry White talking about:

- *Truly Automatic Automations with Adobe Photoshop*
- *Customizing Web Galleries in Adobe Photoshop*
- *Understanding Alpha Channels*
- *Understanding LAB Color*
- *LAB Color: Fixing a Color Cast*
- *Integrating Adobe Bridge*
- *Retouching Interiors*
- *Retouching Portraits: Eye Enhancements*

Photoshop, graphics, design, the Web—you name it—PeachpitTV's *Author Tips* covers everything you need to know to be more creative and get the most from your favorite software.

Also available on iTunes

Author Tips podcast